Penn Center

Penn Center

A HISTORY PRESERVED

Orville Vernon Burton *with Wilbur Cross*

FOREWORD BY Emory S. Campbell

The University of Georgia Press

Athens & London

A Sarah Mills Hodge Fund Publication

This publication is made possible, in part, through a grant
from the Hodge Foundation in memory of its founder,
Sarah Mills Hodge, who devoted her life to the relief and education of
African Americans in Savannah, Georgia.

Unless otherwise noted, all photographs are from the Penn School Collection
archived at the UNC–Chapel Hill Wilson Library. Permission granted by
Penn Center, Inc., St. Helena Island, S.C.

Designed by Erin Kirk New
Set in 11 on 16 Garamond Premier Pro
Printed and bound by Thomson-Shore, Inc.
The paper in this book meets the guidelines for
permanence and durability of the Committee on
Production Guidelines for Book Longevity of the
Council on Library Resources.

Most University of Georgia Press titles are
available from popular e-book vendors.

Printed in the United States of America
14   15   16   17   18   C   5   4   3   2   1

Library of Congress Control Number: 2014947884

British Library Cataloging-in-Publication Data available

This book is dedicated to three of the Burton grandchildren:

Charlotte Burton Harleston, June Burton Harleston, and Henry Vernon Harleston.

These are the children of our eldest daughter, Vera Joanna Burton,

and her husband, Paul Harleston, both of whom have

deep South Carolina roots.

More than a century since its founding, Penn Center

still remains at the forefront in the fight for human dignity.

—CONGRESSMAN JOHN LEWIS

CONTENTS

FOREWORD

In 2008, Tuskegee University awarded me the George Washington Carver Public Service Award for my work at Penn Center, formerly Penn School, on St. Helena Island, South Carolina. I had retired as Penn Center's executive director six years earlier. I consider the award my highest honor, not because it recognized my twenty-two-year tenure at Penn Center but because it called my attention to how educational institutions like Penn Center and Tuskegee have been so very effective in linking education to citizenship and community improvement. In my acceptance remarks, I related memories of my boyhood on Hilton Head Island. My older siblings and relatives, who were graduates of the Penn School, would return home to Hilton Head with skills and knowledge that they put to good use in helping make life better. Whether it was blacksmithing, teaching at one-room neighborhood schools, implementing better farming methods, or doing carpentry, we were indebted to the teachings of Penn School. But I also told the audience that Penn School had modeled its school-community program after the Hampton Institute–Tuskegee Institute mission. This book narrates the story that I wish I could have told that evening.

Penn School was organized on St. Helena Island in 1862, less than six months after the Union brought more than fifty ships and about ten thousand troops into the Port Royal Sound and captured the South Carolina sea islands. Gullah people refer to November 7, 1861, as "Big Gun Shoot Day" and relate that everyone wanted to "catch the learning." This book tells the rest of the story in very engaging prose.

This is truly a book for public-history consumers. My two distinguished author friends Orville Vernon Burton and Wilbur "Will" Cross have smoothly presented the more than 150-year history of this renowned institution. They provide a good view of Penn Center in each of ten different eras with ten different leading personalities, from Laura Towne, the founder of Penn School in 1862, to Michael Campi, the executive director of Penn Center from 2013 to 2014. The reader will get a sense of the community of teachers, students, and a wide range of citizens—local, national, and international—that Penn has become over the years.

Among the stories of efforts to heal the effects of long years of chattel slavery and legal segregation in America, perhaps none is more compelling than Penn Center's. That is why I am honored to write this foreword to this important book by two good friends and excellent writers.

It was Will Cross who first approached me about writing a book on this unique institution. I met Will in the mid-1990s when his wife, Sonny, joined the Penn Center Advisory Board, which supported the Board of Trustees in shaping policies and fundraising projects. Will and Sonny had retired to Hilton Head Island a few years earlier after his long career in New York, working at *Life* magazine and authoring more than fifty trade books. Will, who calls himself a Connecticut Yankee, quickly related to me that his grandfather, for whom he is named, served two distinguished terms as governor of that state. Upon his first visit to Penn Center, he was obviously very excited about its history and said that he thought it was one of the most important of the lesser-known monuments to American history. I, who had grown up knowing about Penn Center, had thought that it was common knowledge to most everyone. As an outsider, Wilbur quickly discerned the important aspects of this institution. Fascinated by the historic photograph archive at Penn Center, Will wanted to do a photographic history of Penn Center. Despite our ambitions, the project stalled for several years before regaining its momentum.

The University of Georgia Press introduced Will to Orville Vernon Burton, and they would jointly complete the project. I first met Vernon Burton at an Association for the study of African American Life and History conference in Birmingham, Alabama. I was seated next to him, as we both had book sales booths. I was offering my book, *Gullah Cultural Legacies*, a short guidebook on Gullah culture, and Vernon was selling his then recently published *The Age of Lincoln*. As we talked we soon found that we had both grown up in segregated South Carolina and had left the state for a while, only to return. I had lived in Boston briefly in the 1960s; Vernon—who was born in Ninety Six, known as the birthplace of Benjamin Mays—had taught history at the University of Illinois for many years and was returning home to a teaching position in South Carolina.

Will and Vernon were a good fit. While they both viewed the Penn Center story with a wide lens, their differing approaches to telling the story have resulted in a colorful history of Penn Center. Will brought to the team a penchant for telling the story through photographs, whereas Vernon brought a desire to tell it in writing. The result, I think, is a salient history of one of the most important Historic Landmark Districts in America. I am so very pleased that I was privileged to meet Vernon and Will. We have become good friends, and I cannot think of two people who have become more intimately familiar with the history of Penn Center than them.

From the beginning, this account makes it clear that Penn School was established to transform formerly enslaved Africans into Euro-Americans. Citing the diary of Laura Towne, the school's compassionate founder in 1862, the book vividly shows that although Towne bravely came to help the sea islands' Africans during the early days of the American Civil War, she had no knowledge of their culture. Her misinterpretation of the praise house shout is pointed evidence of her unfamiliarity with African ways, as are disparaging entries in her journal and the school curriculum's failure to recognize the students' African cultural heritage, except for basket making. Apparently cofounder Ellen Murray was not prepared any better. Later, Charlotte Forten, the school's first black teacher, became emotionally attached to the students. For example, at her request, Forten's friend John Greenleaf Whittier wrote a poem that describes the eventful transition from slavery to freedom on St. Helena Island.

Just when we think the school is on a smooth road to success in its early days, we confront stories of the teachers' hardships and adventures. They endured numerous threats from the Confederates and lamented the defeat of the

Fifty-Fourth Massachusetts Black regiment at Fort Wagner under the leadership of Robert Gould Shaw, but they also attended the reading of the Emancipation Proclamation across the river from St. Helena on January 1, 1863, and had dinners with Union generals. The details of this event reinforce our understanding of the movie *Glory* and the reinterment of nineteen remains of this gallant regiment in the Beaufort National Cemetery in 1989. No matter the hardships, Laura Towne and her team were determined to make a difference in the lives of those they came to help.

Perhaps Towne and her team experienced their lowest moments when President Lincoln was assassinated in April 1865 and when Reconstruction officially ended in 1877. This book vividly takes us to a South of starving children during an era that my grandmother famously referred to as "rebel time." Hope was fading fast among Towne and friends, and by the end of the century the old South, excepting legal chattel slavery, had returned. In the face of enforced racial segregation that would last until the civil rights movement in the 1960s, the aging Towne and Murray continued to struggle for financial support until their deaths in the early twentieth century. However, their students had been taught how to "catch the learning," and hope had been born among them and their families.

The new century brought new leadership and an affiliation with the Hampton-Tuskegee mission. Hampton Institute took sponsorship of Penn School, and Horace Burke Frissell, Hampton Institute's president at the time, became chairman of Penn School's board of trustees. With the school's new leaders, Rossa B. Cooley and Grace B. House, providing strategic community service programs for St. Helena and the surrounding islands, there would be much to celebrate during the school's fiftieth anniversary in 1912. Students marched in a parade led by veterans of the First South Carolina Volunteers, a regiment of black soldiers in the Union army. Honored guests included Civil War hero Robert Smalls. The school had adopted a program for teaching agriculture, the trades, and normal education, all of which were geared for improving island communities. Vernon Burton's interest in the first half of the twentieth century is clear as the text takes us into the thinking of southern white society at that time. In some ways Penn School followed the philosophy that Booker T. Washington presented in his 1895 Atlanta Exposition speech: "Cast down your bucket where you are," meaning that "Negroes should accept segregation as a way of life and develop their own community." For example, hoping to ensure that the island would remain separate from mainstream society, Cooley and House opposed construction of the bridge that would eventually connect St. Helena to the Beaufort City area.

The pastoral lifestyle of the island provided a perfect laboratory for academic research. Social science researchers from the University of North Carolina and others came to Penn School to observe general conditions on St. Helena Island and to study the Negro for retentions of African culture. Although their findings indicated general upward mobility, the researchers, all of whom were white, reported no retention of Africanisms in speech, art, spirituality, or other cultural practices. These conclusions largely prevailed until nearly the end of the twentieth century, when Penn Center began to focus on Gullah history and culture.

It may be that chapter three, which details the end of the Penn School era, was the most challenging to write. It pointedly describes how the board eventually decided to close the school. This brought a somewhat bittersweet conclusion to an era that had borne more than its share of social and financial struggles. The chapter carefully explains Ira Reid's objective report recommending the school's closure. One senses that Penn School officials may have based their decision on a desire to position their students for equal public education, as equal rights had begun blowing in the wind about that time. With his outspoken advocacy of equal rights, Penn School's last principal, Howard Kester (1944–48), had offended most islanders, who by that time were content with their self-reliant lifestyle. But beginning in 1950 the political landscape would move toward desegregation in the South.

Near its end, the book brings us face to face with the civil rights movement at the institution newly reorganized as Penn Center. New directors Courtney and Elizabeth Siceloff converted the old Penn School student dormitories and classrooms into a conference center that primarily would serve civil rights workers, including Martin Luther King Jr. In addition to hiring "Black Field Workers" to address local socioeconomic inequities, they initiated conscientious objectors work programs and hosted stateside Peace Corps training that would continue periodically at Penn Center until the last of the twentieth century.

In relating Penn Center's history from the 1950s forward, the book benefits from hours of interviews with primary sources—the people who made the history happen. We hear Tom Barnwell and Joe McDomick, the first field workers hired under the Siceloffs' leadership, recount their interactions at Penn Center with Martin Luther King Jr. and others. We witness King's casual mealtime settings with staff members in the Penn Center dining hall, and we listen in on some of the speeches he made to local community members at the end of every visit to Penn Center. Inspiring events like these are indelibly captured in photographs and thoroughly documented throughout the book.

Finally, we are engrossed in yet another transition at Penn Center when white leadership gives way to black leadership. After the Siceloffs resigned in 1969, John Gadson became the first black person to head the institution in its then 107-year history. Gadson immediately developed a land-loss-prevention education program and a museum devoted to the enduring Gullah culture. His aim was to preserve the culture that had evolved with the able assistance of Penn School.

The irony that Penn Center—with its origins as a place to turn the island's Africans into Euro-Americans—is now a place for preserving and teaching Gullah cultural history is not overlooked. Penn Center Heritage Days has become one of the most popular celebrations of Gullah culture in the sea islands. Not only is Penn Center renowned for being one of the first schools in the South for formerly enslaved Africans, it is also the place where people can learn about the African heritage of African Americans.

This is an extraordinary book. It is the most complete history of Penn Center that has ever been written. Many stories and famous academic accounts have been concerned indirectly with Penn Center over its 150-year history, but this book goes straight to its heart.

It happens often that one crosses paths with others and a new relationship soars. This book exemplifies what can happen when the paths of people with a common interest cross. I am certain that readers of this book will be happy that Burton and Cross crossed paths, and I am very happy that my path crossed theirs.

On behalf of Americans everywhere and particularly African Americans, I say thank you to Vernon Burton and Will Cross for an outstanding book at a most important time.

EMORY S. CAMPBELL
Penn Center Executive Director Emeritus

ACKNOWLEDGMENTS

I am indebted to many who helped with this project. The former University of Georgia Press director Nicole Mitchell, now director of the University of Washington Press, was enthusiastic about a book on Penn Center. Nancy Grayson, now retired from the University of Georgia Press, sought me out and encouraged this manuscript from the beginning. Others at the Press have continued Grayson's supportive endeavors, especially director Lisa Bayer; her assistant, Sydney Dupre; and John Joerschke; thanks also to Kip Keller, a freelance copy editor, for his help with the book. Each of them has been a pleasure to work with. Wilbur Cross began writing a manuscript about Penn School, and his work was very useful in providing an outline. He is not a fan of footnotes, and I appreciate that he has tolerated my notes in the new manuscript.

Scholars do not work in isolation, but are part of a community of knowledge, and I have benefited from the work of other historians who have written about Penn Center. Other authors who wrote about Penn School include Edith McBride Dabbs, Margaret Hegstrom, Michael Wolfe, and Elizabeth Jacoway, who wrote an especially careful scholarly study of Penn. Reading parts of this manuscript and providing feedback were Peter Eisenstadt, Edda L. Fields-Black, Clarence Lang, Daniel Littlefield, James M. McPherson, Russell Motter, Lewis Reece, Lawrence Rowland, Julius Scott, and Stephen Wise. Alex Moore of the University of South Carolina Press helped in locating books, manuscripts, and sources. My students at Coastal Carolina University and at Clemson University in my courses on the civil rights movement gave me feedback on this project; special thanks go to Martin Maloney and Jack Tine for valuable comments and suggestions. For chapter 4, I am grateful for the input of activists in the civil rights movement. Many who had attended events at Penn Center shared their memories, and I am especially grateful to those who provided comments and suggested revisions of my drafts: Jack Bass, Millicent Brown, Dan Carter, Connie Curry, David Dennis, Harvey Gantt, Mary Gaston, Charles Joyner, Charles McDew, Hayes Mizell, William Saunders, Cleveland Sellers, John Siceloff, Selden Smith, and Bob Zellner. Researcher Beatrice Burton was an immense help in putting all the information together and compiling the index. I appreciate the research assistance of Ryan Conway, Collin Eichhorn, Adrienne Margolies, and Elizabeth Vogt, and the mapping and demographic skills of Jonathan Hepworth. The Reverend Marvin Lare made available unpublished oral history interviews, and Mark R. Schultz found related materials that he and Adrienne Petty shared while doing research on black farmers.

I appreciate very much the photographs and the photographers who made them possible. David Duffin and Bob Fitch took marvelous photographs of Martin Luther King Jr. at Penn Center. The photographer of the civil rights movement in South Carolina, Cecil Williams, of Orangeburg, was extremely generous in sharing his photographs. I urge readers who are interested to check out the galleries and books of photographs of these two amazing artists. In addition, the photograph collection of the Penn School Papers at the Southern Historical Collection is a treasure trove beyond compare.

A librarian is a historian's best friend, and a number of librarians provided great assistance. First, I am grateful to the staff at the Clemson University Library, especially Priscilla Munson, Anne McMahan Grant, and Pam Draper, along with all those who helped with the huge amount of interlibrary loan orders. The Clemson historian Jerome V. Reel guided my wife, Georganne, and me in the archives of Clemson University. Michael Kohl, director of Special Collections, and his staff at Clemson University were a great help in seeking out information on Penn Center in Clemson's collections. I worked closely with Mathew Thomas Turi, Holly A. Smith, and other librarians at the Southern Historical Collection at the Louis Round Wilson Special Collections Library at the University of North Carolina at Chapel Hill, where copies of the Penn Center Papers are housed. I also appreciate the help received from the staff at the Avery Center

Archives of the College of Charleston. The instructor-archivist Avery L. Daniels of the South Carolina State Historical Collection and Archives generously made copies of materials and sent them to me. In addition, Henry G. Fulmer, director of the South Caroliniana Library, was, as usual, brilliant in his help, as was Herb Hartsook, director of South Carolina Political Collections at the University of South Carolina. Both went out of their way to help me find materials often buried in collections one would not assume were associated with Penn school.

I have been especially blessed by the people and staff at Penn Center: Thomas C. Barnwell, J. Herman Blake, Emory Campbell, Michael Campi, Walter Mack, Joe McDomick, Victoria Smalls, John Siceloff, Mary Siceloff, and others. Meeting the people and learning the remarkable history of Penn Center has been a true joy.

Finally, this project would not have come together without the assistance of Georganne R. W. B. Burton. Her editorial ability and her diligence in meeting deadlines were essential, and my gratitude to her is enormous. Any errors, of course, are my responsibility, and all who have so generously helped on this book should be held blameless.

Penn Center

Map of
St HELENA SOUND
AND THE
COAST
BETWEEN
CHARLESTON AND SAVANNA
COMPILED FROM THE
U.S. COAST SURVEY.

Published by A. WILLIAMS & Cº, Bos
1861.

6C

Introduction

Penn Center on St. Helena Island, near Beaufort, South Carolina, was born of the abolitionist spirit in 1862. That spirit took firm root during Reconstruction and continued into the twentieth century. Even when the rest of the nation accepted segregation and turned its back on African American rights, Penn Center continued as a place where blacks and whites could interact with and learn from one another. That abolitionist spirit shows the link between Reconstruction and the civil rights movement. The last African Americans elected to local offices during South Carolina's "long Reconstruction" were in St. Helena and Beaufort in the early twentieth century, and the first African American elected to local office in South Carolina as part of the civil rights movement was a Penn Center employee, Leroy Browne, of St. Helena, who was elected in 1960. That abolitionist spirit continues today at Penn Center as it encourages the preservation of culture and black land ownership.

Penn School furthered African American education when doing so was controversial. It maintained close ties to Africa when anything other than a European focus was controversial. It supported civil rights when that was controversial, and it always stood for the inclusion of all peoples, black and white, rich and poor, in the body politic, an idea that remains controversial to this day.

This brief history of Penn School and Penn Center reveals the need for new studies. History tells the stories of people, their relationships to one another and to the land. Penn Center is a cultural treasure because of its rich history, natural beauty, and advocacy for social change. This book is for those who want to discover or rediscover something about this wonderful place. We hope this brief account of Penn School and Penn Center in the context of American history will inspire others to investigate the story further. More needs to be written about this remarkable place.[1] This book only just introduces people such as Laura Towne, Rossa Cooley, Leroy Browne, Joseph McDomick, Thomas Barnwell, Courtney Siceloff, Emory Campbell, and others who themselves deserve full-length biographies. Much more can and should be said about Penn Center and its people. Just as a good story moves us to ask what happened before and what happened next, this brief history should encourage others to seek more information about Penn Center's past and future. As the local activist Bill Saunders declared, "There was a lot went on at Penn in a short time that I don't think anybody has captured."[2]

For the original habitants of the sea islands off the coasts of Georgia and South Carolina, life was centered on water. Tides, marshes, rivers, and creeks provided fish, oysters, and turtles. Transportation was by water. And while storms could be cruel and terrifying, the water offered amazing beauty.

Spanish explorers arrived from the south in the 1500s. Lucas Vásquez de Ayllón, a sugar planter on Hispaniola, arranged and, with the help of authorities in Spain, financed expeditions to the north, exploring the coast of Florida and beyond.[3] In an advance expedition for Ayllón, Pedro Quexos explored the coast and came upon a large body of water on May 22, 1525. He named it La Punta de Santa Elena.[4] Ayllón began his journey in the summer of 1526. He made landfall and established the colony of San Miguel de Gualdape in 1526.[5] This colony included the first enslaved Africans in what would become the United States, and in a prelude to other slave rebellions, some of the enslaved men at Gauldape set fire to buildings in the compound.[6] In 1562, Jean Ribault established a French outpost on Parris Island, predating Jamestown (1607) and Plymouth Colony (1620).[7] According to the historian Paul Hoffman, "the Cape (or Point) of St. Elena became an important place in North American geography and a focus for imperial conflict."[8]

English settlers became interested in the late 1600s when William Hilton from Barbados explored the area and found it suitable for agriculture. English,

Spanish, and Scottish invaders fought and skirmished with each other and with the native Indians. By the end of the Yamasee War of 1715, English planters from Barbados with their enslaved workforce dominated the economy on the South Carolina sea islands.[9] Indigo was the cash crop of choice from the 1740s through the 1780s, when England refused to purchase it from the upstart United States.[10] On the sea islands, rice was not a good crop because it needed fresh rather than salt water. The islands had plenty of marsh mud, however, which was perfect for Sea Island cotton. More luxurious, soft, supple, and expensive than the standard short-staple cotton, and also more difficult to grow, Sea Island cotton was craved by the wealthy in Europe. Cultivated by the enslaved population, it brought riches galore to the white planters. A 1935 encyclopedia, written during a time of southern white nostalgia for slavery and romanticized race relations, quoted a female slaveholder's statement in 1791 that cotton profits had been "mostly expended in the purchase of Negroes, and nothing is so much coveted as the pleasure of possessing many slaves."[11]

One of the sea islands was St. Helena Island. By water, St. Helena was thirty-five nautical miles from Savannah, Georgia, to the south, and fifty from Charleston, South Carolina, to the north. To the west were Lady's Island and then Beaufort, South Carolina. The black population on St. Helena Island became the majority during the time of the indigo trade in the mid-1700s, and African Americans have retained that status to this day. Long after 1808, when the Constitution banned U.S. participation in the international slave trade, waterways provided smugglers an avenue for bringing slaves into South Carolina.

Many of the enslaved were taken from Africa, and the link between Africa and the Gullah people of the sea islands remains strong. African drums were an important communication tool in 1739 during a large slave revolt nearby when enslaved people used drums to send information from plantation to plantation along the Stono River between Charleston and St. Helena. After the Stono Rebellion was put down, drums were forbidden in the enslaved communities.[12] Yet Africanisms continued to dominate St. Helena Island. The white population was sparse, and the absence of a bridge to the mainland fostered isolation and community.

Penn School began in 1862, in the midst of civil war, after the U.S. Navy moved into the area. The white landowners fled, and the newly freed people immediately wanted land ownership and education.[13] The African American congregation at the Brick Church offered space for a school. Located near the plantation of Frogmore, later the crossroads town of Frogmore, Penn Center was often later referred to as "Frogmore" in newspaper accounts. During the war, the school was never far from military skirmishes as Confederates worked to retake the area. Nevertheless, Laura Towne, Ellen Murray, and their financial supporters worked to answer the people's call for education.

Penn School (and then Penn Center) survived other conflicts in American history. For example, the "rehearsal for Reconstruction" took place there.[14] And yet labor issues during Reconstruction were not the same on St. Helena as elsewhere; one reason was that on St. Helena the freedpeople bought land. Reconstruction ended when white elites fraudulently and violently took over the government in South Carolina and across the South. As elsewhere, the African Americans on St. Helena lost much of their political power. And yet for the most part, the people were left alone. No sharecropping system developed, although some residents rented land. During the nadir of race relations in the United States, when segregation became solidified, the people of St. Helena did not feel the discrimination as blatantly as others, because so few whites interfered with them. There were no lynchings on the island.[15]

Female missionaries began the school. Laura Towne and Ellen Murray lived and worked on St. Helena Island for the remainder of their lives—roughly the first forty years of Penn School's existence. They taught according to the system that they had been taught, the New England model of education, in which students in elementary schools learn reading, writing, arithmetic, history, geography, and music. In the early 1900s, two other northern white women, Rossa Cooley and Grace House, directed the school. At a time when many opposed any education for African Americans, the school persevered. Cooley and House revised Penn School's educational goals, and for the next forty years it followed the Hampton or Tuskegee idea of industrial education, adhering to Booker T. Washington's philosophy rather than that of W. E. B. Du Bois and the "talented tenth." Under their leadership, Penn School gave up "some of the 'higher' studies like algebra and Latin." Despite this change in educational mission,

Cooley, the white principal, admired the people of St. Helena: "My belief is that religion is the gift of the Negro to our American life." Their spirituals, for example, echoed "the history of a people who have come through the valley of the shadow."[16]

Two world wars and the Great Depression brought change throughout the United States, and electricity and bridges altered the cultural isolation of the sea islands. Finding itself in dire financial straits, Penn School turned over its educational functions to the public schools on the island, which were unfortunately of poorer quality than what Penn had offered. In 1948, Penn School was redefined as Penn Community Services.

Without the school as its focus, the Penn Center Board of Trustees slowly changed its membership, and southern liberals took over from northerners who had met in New York, Philadelphia, or Boston. These progressive southern whites were less paternalistic than their northern counterparts and showed themselves willing to work with the African American community to establish racial equality. While this stance was of a piece with Penn's abolitionist tradition, other actions by the southern white leaders at Penn Center marked a break with long-established precedents. White northerners had wanted to help African Americans by teaching them to be "civilized," that is, to be more Euro-American. The new board members instead wanted to listen to and learn from the African American community. They came to understand the Christian commitment and theological worldview of southern African Americans before Martin Luther King Jr. brought it to the attention of the world. These southern whites looked to African Americans to save the South from the sins of segregation and disfranchisement.

From its founding, Penn Center had been a source of civil rights activism. Abolitionists who were part of a biracial movement started the school, and the abolitionist legacy remained over the years. Penn School's role in education and community service solidified during Reconstruction, and by the 1950s, Penn Center demonstrated the link between Reconstruction and the modern civil rights movement. While historians debate "the long civil rights movement," none question the long freedom struggle.[17] Penn Center was fertile soil for the cultivation of a new southern society, and geographic isolation was no barrier to the ideas of revolutionary change needed to challenge segregation. Penn Center started subtly at first, by facilitating interracial groups, and then grew bolder by setting up citizenship schools. These schools were linked with Penn's earlier abolitionist heritage and drew upon its industrial school model of education, that is, their function was to better lives. At the same time, their purpose was political activism. Some might see activism as contradictory to the industrial model, which stressed agricultural and homemaking skills over racial justice. And yet Penn always embodied diverse traditions.

Penn Center became a fixture in the movement when the South Carolina Council on Human Relations (SCCHA) hosted integrated "stay-ins" there. As Penn Center became increasingly involved in the civil rights movement, Martin Luther King Jr. found solace at the center, where he held staff retreats and planned strategy. According to a South Carolinian archivist, King's visits to Penn "represent yet another example of the institution's central—and continuing—significance to black history and culture not only in South Carolina but throughout the United States."[18] In 1968, when Penn Center hosted a meeting of African American activists to discuss education, Stokely Carmichael of SNCC was scheduled to speak, but he had to cancel because of death threats. His remarks, read by his press secretary, included greetings: "It's good to be here today with all my beautiful brothers and sisters at Frogmore—you know I feel especially close to all of you, since a few weeks ago I spent a most soulful Christmas on St. Johns Island and was really at home with some of the most together black folks I've ever come across."[19] Penn Center was a meeting place for CORE, the SCLC, SNCC, the NAACP, and others; it welcomed a broad range of ideas and approaches, all of which fostered racial justice.

Progressives still gather at Penn Center. In October 2013 the SC Progressive Network gathered for a retreat, meeting "in the same hall where Joan Baez once sang to Dr. Martin Luther King Jr." The network was founded at Penn Center in 1996, and organizers felt that grassroots activists met there "in the true spirit of the place."[20]

The civil rights movement changed America, but poverty, unemployment, and unequal schools continued to take their toll on minority populations. With the end of official Jim Crow, the fight for racial and social justice moved to court-rooms and away from sit-ins and demonstrations. Poverty and subtler forms of discrimination were harder to fight against than legal discrimination. Penn Center, however, kept up its efforts in community organizing. Developments of the late twentieth century brought to the forefront conflicts over questions of the environment and of land ownership. For example, the diminished availability of sweetgrass has a bearing on residents' cultural heritage of basket making. Moreover, as land on the sea islands became a commodity for speculation and a target for developers of resorts, the people of St. Helena felt the impact. No longer is there free access to any beach areas. The state park on the coast instituted an admission fee, and Fripp Island, between St. Helena and the Atlantic Ocean, became a gated community. In the midst of this resort-building frenzy, Penn Community Services was instrumental in helping the people of St. Helena keep their land. This struggle continues today, and Penn Center works diligently on matters related to land preservation.

Just as important, Penn Center now focuses on preserving the unique Gullah culture of the sea islands. This new mission again highlights the creative tension of the school's history. In the early twentieth century, during Penn School's Hampton-Tuskegee period, white leaders stressed the need to move beyond "backward" sea island cultural practices. The school was to transform the people, to inculcate Eurocentric values. Now Penn Center cherishes the Gullah heritage and works to preserve it. Moreover, since the Gullah culture is international, Penn Center furthers globalism and continues to reinforce the close connections with Africa that Penn has fostered throughout its history.

Today Penn Center is a nonprofit organization working on land-use education and cultural preservation. It is an African American cultural center and the major research center for Gullah culture. Its mission is "to promote and preserve the history and culture of the Sea Islands." Penn Center serves "as a local, national and international resource center" and acts "as a catalyst for the development of programs for self-sufficiency."[21] The center was instrumental in helping Congress establish the Gullah Geechee Cultural Heritage Corridor in 2006.[22] Many are coming to appreciate that the culture of St. Helena and the sea islands is an integral part of southern heritage.

Honoring the past is often done with memorials, but the memorials to South Carolina history on the statehouse grounds in Columbia are introduced by the flying of the Confederate flag in front of the capitol. The statues of significant South Carolinians that adorn the grounds honor people who supported slavery and segregation and opposed integration. Penn Center presents a different cast of characters, black and white, persons who cut against the grain and fought for interracial democracy. Their faith in the ideals of the United States and in God enabled them to fight for justice, and they should be considered an alternative group of heroes for South Carolina and the nation. Their story needs to be told. Not even realizing the wonderful compliment he was paying, Hugh Gibson, a reporter for the *Charleston News and Courier*, wrote in 1964, "It was difficult to realize that American history was written at Penn Center under the old oaks festooned with Spanish moss."[23]

CHAPTER ONE

Penn School Begins amidst War

On November 7, 1861, less than seven months after the Confederates fired on the U.S. flag in Charleston Harbor at Fort Sumter, the sound of guns resonated over Port Royal Sound in South Carolina. Southern plantation owners in the Carolina sea islands were surprised by the ease of the Union victory. The owners, rich beyond measure, were unwavering defenders of the slaveholding way of life. The area near Port Royal included the four parishes of Beaufort District, home to 939 property owners with 883,048 acres of improved land. Twenty percent of these landowners held the vast majority of the area's 32,530 slaves.[1] St. Helena Island, one of the largest of the sea islands, was home to fifty-five plantations in 1860. On those plantations, enslaved workers grew every bit of the luxurious Sea Island cotton that was in worldwide demand.[2]

All the plantation owners' riches, all their proslavery and secessionist feelings, could not prevent the advance of Union captain Samuel Du Pont as he sailed his fleet into the waters around the sea islands of South Carolina. The flotilla of sixty-four ships, "the largest fleet ever assembled to date under the American flag," carried some twelve thousand troops under the command of General Thomas W. Sherman.[3] Artillery in the two Confederate forts defending the Port Royal area, Fort Beauregard and Fort Walker, hit Union ships, but the shots were fired high and hit more spars than hulls.[4] The St. Helena Mounted Volunteer Riflemen gathered to defend their homes on the island, but they saw quickly that the battle was lost almost before it had begun. They returned to their homes and prepared their families for a journey inland.[5]

When the Union forces captured Port Royal, they acquired one of the largest natural harbors on the Atlantic coast, which became an important asset in creating the naval blockade along the southern coastline. They also captured cotton plantations, the sale of whose cotton would help the United States finance the war. They also brought freedom to enslaved workers on the sea islands, and though perhaps unaware of the full implications of that act, they thereby began a rehearsal for what would become known as Reconstruction.[6]

Sherman reported in the official records, "Every white inhabitant has left the islands."[7] The white owners abandoned their plantations, their stores of cotton, and much of their personal property. Throughout the sea islands, plantation owners tried force, persuasion, and threats to convince their enslaved workers to accompany them to the interior, but many refused. Some owners then resorted to murder.[8] Very few acted with the compassion of Captain John Fripp of St. Helena Island. The owner of Coffin Point (a 2,000-acre plantation), a Union sympathizer, and a man known for treating his workers relatively kindly (though, like other white slave owners, he had a whipping post close to his house), Fripp advised his slaves to hide until the Confederate soldiers had left and then to work the land for food, not cotton.[9] Many enslaved workers knew what was coming and tried to remain behind; about ten thousand were successful.[10]

During the first few days after the whites fled, African Americans performed spontaneous acts of self-liberation. Many broke open storehouses and helped themselves to the food they had planted, cultivated, and harvested, and the animals they had bred and raised. They crossed masters' thresholds and destroyed pianos and fine china. They donned fine clothes, appropriated plush furniture, drank expensive liquor, slept in soft beds, and called it all their own. They danced and feasted. Many of them gave up work, while others went out to the fields and began to mark off the boundaries of acreage they claimed for themselves, a long-held, impossible dream come true. In a prelude to what would happen over the next four years of the war, African Americans who found themselves suddenly unmastered committed deliberate acts of unambiguous self-government. By the decisions of everyday life—when to eat and sleep and work, how to speak, when to sing and pray and love and hate—African Americans made themselves free. They expected freedom to include land ownership and the opportunity for education (denied them since 1740 by the South Carolina Slave Code). As the

Union army took control of the South Carolina sea islands in late 1861, however, an essential question remained unanswered: what was their legal status?

No such question existed in the mind of Beaufort native Robert Smalls, who was enslaved in Charleston. The Union victory at Port Royal signaled a new hope, and he worked out a plan of freedom for himself and his family. On May 13, 1862, in the wee hours of the morning, federal ships off the coast of Charleston noticed a Confederate transport steamer heading their way. Preparing to shoot, they held their fire when they saw the white flag of surrender. As the vessel came alongside, Smalls, the pilot on board, saluted and announced, "I am delivering this war materiel, including these cannon, and I think Uncle Abraham Lincoln can put them to good use."[11] Smalls, who had rented himself out as a deckhand to the captain of the *Planter*, stole the boat and organized the escape with his wife and children and others seeking freedom. In the dark of night, Smalls stood boldly on the prow in the white captain's own stance, sailing the vessel past Confederate lookouts and giving the correct signals for passage. Smalls delivered to the federal fleet the boat, cannons, and guns as well as a naval codebook and information on the location of rebel troops. According to the *Charleston Daily Courier*, "Our community was intensely agitated Tuesday morning by the intelligence that the steamer *Planter*, for the last twelve months or more employed both in the State and Confederate service, had been taken possession of by her colored crew, steamed up and boldly run out to the blockades."[12] Information that Smalls supplied to the U.S. fleet led to the Union seizure of Stono Inlet and River, an important base for future operations. In a report to the Thirty-Seventh Congress, President Lincoln quoted the secretary of the navy as crediting the success of the operation on "information derived chiefly from the contraband pilot, Robert Smalls, who had escaped from Charleston."[13]

Even before Smalls's military and public relations success, conditions at Port Royal received close attention from the U.S. government. On December 20, 1861, U.S. secretary of the treasury Salmon Chase, needing money for the war effort, saw the financial benefit of maximizing profits from the abandoned cotton plantations. He assigned Treasury Department employee William H. Reynolds to supervise the collection of abandoned cotton and to prevent the workers, no longer enslaved, from destroying property and cotton gins. In addition, the fiercely antislavery Chase appointed his friend Edward L. Pierce, an outspoken antislavery attorney from Milton, Massachusetts, to oversee the conditions of the blacks left behind by their fleeing masters. In a note dated February 15, 1862, President Abraham Lincoln wrote to Secretary Chase: "I shall be obliged if the Sec of the Treasury will, in his discretion, give Mr. Pierce such instructions in regard to Port Royal contrabands, as may seem judicious."[14] Chase appointed Pierce "special Government agent, with duties relating both to negroes and cotton."[15] Pierce devised a plan for the education, welfare, and employment of the former slaves. The "Port Royal Experiment" included the planting and harvesting of cotton by former slaves, supposedly as paid laborers.[16]

A week after Pierce arrived at Port Royal, the Reverend Mansfield French journeyed to the area at the request of the American Missionary Association.[17] This association, responding to the wishes of the African American freedmen, appealed to teachers and doctors to come help, and many northern abolitionists responded to the appeal. On March 2, 1862, a group of fifty-three missionaries from New York and Boston left New York City, bound for Port Royal. Some cynics called them "Gideonites," laughing at their plans and goodness. But the assemblage took delight in being named after the biblical Gideon's select group, which God used to defeat a much larger army. Months later a remark to some of the men that they should be called "knights" elicited a reply: "Yes, we are Gideonites."[18] When the Gideonites left for Port Royal on the steamship *Atlantic*, some went without salary; others were paid between $25 and $50 a month by the missionary association and other sources.[19]

Philadelphia was not to be outdone. Under the leadership of the prominent abolitionist James Miller McKim (1810–1874),[20] the Port Royal Relief Committee voted to send money and, more important in the long run, Laura Matilda Towne. Towne, born in Pittsburgh on May 3, 1825, was reared and educated in Boston. She took advanced classes as a homeopathic physician at the Female Medical College of Pennsylvania. She moved in socially progressive circles. She was recognized in the community for teaching underprivileged children in "charity" schools and for doing some "doctoring."[21] As a member of the First

Unitarian Church of Philadelphia, she followed her natural inclinations—and the teachings of her abolitionist pastor, the Reverend William Henry Furness (1802–1896)—and became thoroughly antislavery.[22] In April 1862, Towne was appointed by the Port Royal Relief Committee of Philadelphia to distribute provisions and to teach the former slaves the "habits of self-support" and to "elevate their moral and social condition."[23]

Towne and some twenty others, mostly of her own age and with similar high hopes, boarded the *Oriental*, a steam-and-sail vessel so old that it was of no practical use to the federal navy and had been all but scrapped. Towne described briefly some of the passengers; next to her own name she wrote one word: "abolitionist."[24] The volunteers knew full well that in South Carolina they might be sitting on a powder keg. About four thousand Union troops were stationed in the Beaufort and Port Royal area, and rumors persisted that Confederate soldiers might at any moment decide to attack.

While residing in picturesque Beaufort, Towne noticed the brilliant flowers, waving palms, and stately oaks adorned with Spanish moss. During her first walk down the road into town, however, she saw the effects of the ongoing war. She was pained by the desolation and somewhat unnerved by the ill manners of the Union troops, some of whom galloped past recklessly on horseback and others who lounged idly on street corners in dirty uniforms and stared at the women in an unfriendly manner.[25]

On another walk, Towne encountered a language strange to her ear, children using, as she described it, a "mode of speaking . . . not very intelligible."[26] They spoke Gullah, a creolized form of English.[27] Towne mostly had kind words to say about the children. Schools were a high priority for the Sea Island people; as soon as they had the opportunity to learn, they requested teachers. Towne visited two local schools taught by northern missionaries and observed the children learning their letters and one-syllable words. Although the children seemed happy enough in school, Towne noticed the lack of a system in their education, and she noted the students' poor concentration.[28]

When Towne visited African Americans on farms and plantations in the countryside, she found them hard at work: planting, caring for livestock, and taking care of all the farm chores. At the time, Towne thought the people had little sense of economics, since they tended to give far more attention to growing the foodstuffs that would keep them from starvation than they gave to cotton, which would give them cash.[29] Although the federal government preferred that they grow cotton, many African Americans were aware that their newfound freedom included the freedom to starve. (There would be a time in the future when the government discouraged the planting of cotton and encouraged planting more food.)

Towne decided to work with a school on the Oaks Plantation on nearby St. Helena Island. St. Helena's population was largely African American. Whites preferred to stay off the sea islands, plagued as they were by insects and malaria.[30] Towne found that the best transportation on the island was the marsh tacky. *Tacky* means "horse" in Gullah.[31] Almost everyone had one of these small, sturdy, sure-footed, and smart horses, useful in swamps and marshes.

While learning the ways of the people, Towne decided that religion would probably be her strongest ally. Most of the people were "ardent and settled Baptists," with just "a little sprinkling of Methodists."[32] Soon after her arrival, Towne was invited to a "praise house," and she noted that there were singing, praying, and reading from a tattered old Bible. More unusual for a northern white woman, she attended a "shout," which she described as "a savage, heathenish dance" that seemed to embody "the remains of some old idol worship."[33] In one of the larger cabins, lit only by burning logs in a small fireplace, the participants sang a clamorous chorus. Three leaders in front of the group clapped and gesticulated, and then led the group in a movement around the room in a circle. They shuffled and occasionally turned one way and another. They bent their knees in a kind of curtsy and stamped their feet with such vigor that the whole floor vibrated.[34] While her first impression was negative, Towne came to admire the religious fervor and basic integrity of the Sea Islanders, and had kind words to say about "Maum Katie," a bright and influential "spiritual mother."[35]

Towne appreciated the religious leaders as cultured and forward-looking people, though few had any formal training as ministers. She described one black minister, Mr. James T. Lynch, as a "very eloquent and ambitious" man who would surely "make his mark in the world." With good humor, Towne wrote that he was horrified to find "that [she] was a Unitarian," and that "he expected better things" of her. She liked that he was "wonderfully liberal" and paid him the compliment of surmising that "by reason of his eloquence and genius, he will one day perhaps be a Unitarian himself."[36] Most of the people relied on God and hymns and prayer meetings to cope with their harsh living conditions, and most of the African American ministers preached hope and salvation. In some of the Sunday worship services in Beaufort and outlying villages, Sunday schools included reading lessons, and the people appreciated and respected teachers. At one of the worship services on St. Helena, an elder prayed for blessings for "the little white sisters who came to give learning to the children."[37]

Towne soon realized that some older women had the respect of the community.[38] African American women were often considered leaders in the family. Whites, on the other hand, sometimes held women in less esteem. Edward Pierce, hesitant about working with female Gideonites, had been persuaded by the Reverend French to allow them to help. When Pierce saw the effective work of the women, he declared that they were "the best part of this work of civilization."[39] Towne felt vindicated by his change of heart: "This is quite a triumph, after having been rejected as useless."[40]

Towne's first business was medical and educational, and she was happy to receive in a batch of much-delayed letters from her family and friends in Pennsylvania the welcome news that her good friend and associate Ellen Murray was soon to join her as a teacher.[41] Murray, who was born in Canada and educated in Europe, was fluent in English, German, and French.[42] Towne relied upon her friendship: "I shall want Ellen's help. We shall be strong together—I shall be weak apart."[43] The two women took up residence at Oaks Plantation, and Murray taught her first class on June 18, 1862: "Ellen had her first adult school to-day, in the back room—nine scholars. I assisted."[44]

As classes grew larger, Oaks Plantation became too small. That fall the Brick Church on St. Helena offered its building. The Brick Church had been built by enslaved workers in 1855 for white plantation owners, and when whites fled the area in 1861, former slaves made the church their own. School buildings were in demand, and churches often filled the need.

Classes in the Brick Church began on September 22, 1862, as Towne noted: "Ellen & I began our school in the Baptist church with forty-one scholars."[45] The school grew quickly, and in later years she wrote, "We opened the Penn School in September, 1862, in the Brick Church, with about eighty scholars, some of whom we had already taught in a room on the Oaks Plantation."[46] Towne began teaching a class of her own. Women pupils greatly outnumbered the men, who needed to work in the fields and catch fish or game for their families. Towne worried that the students "had no idea of sitting still, of giving attention, of ceasing to talk aloud." With no experience of school, they had little idea of how to conduct themselves in class: "They lay down and went to sleep, they scuffled and struck each other. They got up by the dozen, made their curtsies and walked off to the neighboring fields for blackberries, coming back to their seats with a curtsy when they were ready." And there was the language barrier: "They evidently did not understand me, and I could not understand them."[47] In October, Towne recorded in her diary, "I have 62 in my class, the school numbers 110."[48]

Other than the missionaries, many whites across the South did not support education for the freedmen. The teachers were told that "the field hands of these islands were too low to learn anything, that it was a waste of time to educate or civilize them, that few of them could count their fingers correctly, their language was an unintelligible jargon, and it was impossible to teach them arithmetic."[49] The students who attended school showed just how wrong those people were.

The growing school benefited in many ways from the arrival in late October 1862 of Charlotte Forten. Born in Philadelphia into an influential and affluent black family, staunch abolitionists all, Forten was tutored at home because her father refused to send her to the inferior segregated schools in Philadelphia. Racial conditions were better in Salem, Massachusetts, and Forten attended the Salem Normal School there. After graduation, she began her teaching career in the town.[50] Forten volunteered for a teaching assignment on the sea islands of South Carolina because she wanted to be part of the new educational movement. Volunteering so close to Confederate lines was dangerous for an African American woman. If captured, Forten ran the risk of being sold into slavery.

After arriving at Port Royal, Forten and the others had to sign a paper "wherein we declared ourselves loyal to the Government, and wherein, also, were set forth fearful penalties, should we ever be found guilty of treason."[51] On the last leg of the journey, the rowboat ride from Hilton Head to St. Helena, she was delighted by the African American boatmen singing "Roll, Jordan, Roll"; she found it "so sweet and strange and solemn."[52]

When Forten observed the teaching at Penn School, she "noticed with pleasure" the enthusiasm of the students, "how bright, how eager to learn many of them seem."[53] Forten thought that they were more enthusiastic about learning than the students in New England and that "coming to school is a constant delight and recreation to them."[54] On November 5, however, Forten's first day of teaching, she confided to her diary, "It was *not* a very pleasant one." She taught the very young, "too young even for the alphabet," and they were "restless." She planned to write home and ask her family to send her picture books and toys.[55] Forten enjoyed sewing with Venus, an elderly woman on St. Helena, who told her that it was a wonderful year: "Nobody to whip me nor drive me, and plenty to eat. Nebber had such a happy year in my life before."[56] In her teaching, Forten always included heroes, such as John Brown and "the noble" Toussaint-Louverture: "It is well that they sh'ld know what one of their own color c'ld do for his race. I long to inspire them with courage and ambition (of a noble sort,) and high purpose."[57] Forten came to love teaching and instituted night classes for adults unable to attend day school.[58] Pupils loved Forten also. Elizabeth Smalls, daughter of Robert Smalls, attended Penn School and declared to her father, "Miss Forten knows everything."[59]

When Forten joined the staff at Penn School, Laura Towne remarked, "We like Miss Forten very much indeed."[60] Towne respected Forten, describing her as "quiet, gentle, sweet, & very intelligent, cultured highly indeed."[61] And Forten reciprocated the compliment: "[Towne] is housekeeper, physician, everything, here. The most indispensable person on the place, and the people are devoted to her . . . I like her energy and decision of character."[62] Forten had kind words for Ellen Murray too: "I like Miss Murray so much. She is one of the most whole-souled warm-hearted women I ever met. I felt drawn to her from the first."[63] Towne worried somewhat about the feelings of the St. Helena residents toward this educated African American woman: "The people on our place are inclined to question a good deal about 'dat brown gal,' as they call Miss Forten."[64] Towne had to persuade one of the servants to clean Forten's room. The people did come around and show Forten respect; her ability to play the piano helped.[65]

All the teachers welcomed letters from home, and in the fall of 1862 Forten was delighted to receive a package that contained a copy of the *Liberator*, William Lloyd Garrison's abolitionist newspaper, which was forbidden in the Confederacy. She wrote about the significance of reading a paper that advocated human rights "here in the rebellious little Palmetto State," and she rejoiced that a part of South Carolina was "for the first time, a place worth living in."[66]

As part of Thanksgiving celebrations that fall in 1862, a large crowd assembled in the Brick Church.[67] After a prayer and sermon, General Rufus Saxton spoke. Saxton (1824–1908) played many roles in the Port Royal Experiment, including quartermaster in charge of food and supplies, military governor, and military leader in charge of recruiting black troops. His camp for the new recruits suffered from discrimination by the supply officer; about 3,000 tents, available in the warehouse on Hilton Head, were denied to the abolitionist Saxton and the black soldiers.[68] Saxton urged the young men present at the church to enlist in the army as part of a regiment forming under the command of Thomas Wentworth Higginson.[69] Higginson (1823–1911), appointed to lead the first African American unit in the Union army, was a Unitarian minister and an abolitionist. Another speaker at the celebration was Mrs. Frances D. Gage (1808–1884), an abolitionist and a women's rights advocate from Ohio. She appealed to mothers to allow their sons "to fight for liberty." Although Forten thought that "it must have been something very novel and strange to them to hear a woman speak in public," it probably was not so strange to the people of St. Helena.[70]

Aside from holidays, life was hard, and sometimes the northern-born teachers got homesick. When Forten began to feel sorry for herself, she wrote in her diary, "Let me not forget again that I came not here for friendly sympathy or for anything else but to work, and to work hard. Let me do that faithfully and well."[71] By December 15, 1862, attendance at Penn had grown to 147 students. Of Forten's 58 pupils, most were "tiny A.B.C. people." Weather affected attendance. Some days were "too cold for [her] 'babies' to venture out." Attendance varied widely. On December 18, the school had almost 100 students; on December 19, 127.[72]

December 25 was a special day at the school, with much singing and the giving of presents. The poet John Greenleaf Whittier, a staunch abolitionist from Massachusetts, wrote a song for the occasion, the "St. Helena Hymn," at the request of his "dear friend" Charlotte Forten.[73] The song begins: "Oh, none in all the world before / Were ever glad as we! / We're free on Carolina's shore; / We're all at home and free." When Whittier sent the song to Forten, he wrote an accompanying letter expressing "surprise and pleasure" at having heard from her: "Most sincerely, dear friend, do I rejoice at the good providence of God which has permitted thee to act so directly for the poor yet deeply interesting people of the Sea Islands . . . I send herewith a little song for your Christmas festival. I was too ill to write anything else, but I could not resist the desire to comply with thy request."[74] Whittier had described Forten to Theodore Dwight Weld (the abolitionist author of *Slavery As It Is* [1839]) as "a young lady of exquisite refinement, quiet culture and ladylike and engaging manners, and personal appearance."[75] It was Whittier who had suggested to Forten that she apply to teach former slaves in Union-held territory. Forten noted in her journal on August 9, 1862: "[Whittier] advised me to apply to the Port-Royal Co. in Boston. He is very desirous that I sh'ld go. I shall certainly take his advice."[76]

A time of very special celebration came one week later, on January 1, 1863: Emancipation Day, described by Forten as "the most glorious day this nation has yet seen, *I* think."[77] The Emancipation Proclamation took effect on that day, and the event was celebrated at Camp Saxton in Port Royal, the site of the regiment of the First South Carolina Volunteers, made up of African Americans who had made their escape from slavery. Amid much festivity, William Henry Brisbane (1806–1878) read the president's proclamation, "which was warmly cheered."[78] Brisbane had been a South Carolina planter, Baptist minister, and writer of proslavery tracts. In analyzing his own arguments, he became uneasy about being a slaveholder, so he sold his slaves and moved to Ohio in 1837. There he became an avid abolitionist. He returned to the South, purchased back all the people he had sold, and gave them their freedom, all except one man, whom he could not locate. Brisbane continued to feel remorse over that one slave until they found each other one day in Beaufort and Brisbane learned that the man had freed himself.[79]

Many approved the choice of Brisbane to read the Emancipation Proclamation. Higginson thought it was "infinitely appropriate, a South Carolinian addressing South Carolinians—he was reared on this very soil, and emancipated his own slaves here, years ago." Higginson described the celebration at length, noticing the presence of Charlotte Forten, the "pretty little Quadroon" who was in the South "as a teacher." He also approved of a spontaneous outburst of song when the crowd began singing "My Country 'tis of Thee." That song included the phrase, "Land where my fathers died," and the African American community well knew that their ancestors, brought from Africa, had made this land a home for them. Now home meant the "Sweet land of Liberty." Higginson wrote that this was "the first day they had ever had a country, the first flag they had ever seen which promised anything to their people."[80] Other important people at the festivities were the black soldiers Prince Rivers and Robert Sutton, each of whom "made very good speeches indeed, and were loudly cheered."[81] Another person in attendance was Dr. Seth Rogers. Rogers had treated Forten's respiratory disorder in 1860 in Massachusetts, and she was so happy to see "the face of a friend from the North, and *such* a friend."[82]

At the end of the ceremony, the regiment sang "John Brown." The children at Penn School also loved singing "John Brown," and Forten "felt to the full the significance of that song being sung here in SC by little negro children, by those whom he—the glorious old man—died to save." Forten appreciated that Towne had taught the children about Brown.[83]

At Penn School, teachers worked seven days a week, teaching Sunday school as well as regular classes. In addition, Towne, the only person in the area with training as a doctor, continued her medical work. She treated ulcers, injuries, respiratory ailments, measles, mumps, snake and insect bites, and an assortment of other ailments. She delivered babies and cared for the ones with colic and infant-related maladies. She reported in one letter that she regularly got up at six, ate a hasty breakfast, and then saw three or four patients. By nine o'clock, she was on her way to one or two of five outlying plantations to see other patients. "The roads are horrible," she wrote, "and the horses ditto, so I have a weary time getting around." One of her antidotes for the dreariness and monotony of the drive was to read aloud to everyone on the wagon. They "hurried" home by two o'clock in order to "snatch a lunch" and begin their classes. They then spent two hours with the children before going on to the adults. Murray and Forten bore the brunt of the classes, and Towne alternated between teaching and doctoring.[84]

The Penn School curriculum was rigorous and no-nonsense, modeled after those in New England and Philadelphia. The teachers, all northerners, taught as they had been taught. In this Penn was typical; subjects in post–Civil War black schools were similar to those taught in northern white schools. Students in elementary schools learned reading, spelling, writing, grammar, diction, history, geography, arithmetic, and music.[85]

After work was dinnertime, and the teachers found the people generous with what they had. Sometimes the meals were better than they had expected. "We have nice melons and figs," Towne reported, "pretty good corn, tomatoes now and then, bread rarely, hominy, cornbread, and rice waffles . . . We have fish nearly every day . . . and now and then turtle soup."[86] Meat of any kind was a scarcity; livestock was rarely raised for that purpose on the island, and the northern women did not like the game the islanders caught—mainly squirrels and possums. Occasionally there was not enough food to "satisfy hunger." At times like those, when hunger was added to other pressures, Towne could find herself "sick, tired, & cross."[87]

Making up for troublesomeness was the delightful beauty of St. Helena. "I wish you could see the wild flowers," Towne wrote to her friends up north, "the hedges of Adam's needle, with heads of white bells a foot or two through and four feet high; the purple pease with blossoms that look like dog-tooth violets— just the size—climbing up the cotton plant with its yellow flower, and making whole fields purple and gold; the passion flowers in the grass; the swinging palmetto sprays and the crape myrtle in full bloom."[88] She also wrote about the midges, fleas, and mosquitoes that were so pervasive at certain times of the year that she had to sit in her room at night under netting. This was a major problem for Towne, who used the evening to write her correspondence. Twice she set the netting on fire while writing by candlelight.[89]

Even in the best of times, no one could forget that a war was raging and that Penn School was very close to enemy lines. Safety was always a concern; on September 26, 1862, Towne worried about "Secesh spies" at Port Royal. She wrote, "It is said there is every probability of an attack."[90] Penn School felt the threat of skirmishes on St. Helena and farther out, where Confederate army units were engaged in intermittent rearguard harassments. "We hear the guns all day and night," Towne wrote to her northern friends in July 1863.[91] Towne worked with a small detachment of freedmen who had been ordered to train in the event that southern pickets invaded the area in search of supplies and equipment. For this purpose, the army gave the group an assortment of muskets and pistols. Their drills proved useful against a foray by Confederate insurgents. "Three boats of rebels attempted to land on these islands last night, two at the village and one at Edding's Point," Towne wrote in her diary in late October 1862. "The negroes with their guns were on picket; they gave the alarm, fired, and drove the rebels off."[92] All on St. Helena were apprehensive when, on November 28, 1862, the island became "wrapped all day in the smoke of battle," and the people heard "the roll of cannon." Some twenty miles away, at the mouth of the Savannah River, was Fort Pulaski, which the Union had captured in April 1862. Rumors proliferated that the fort was being attacked and that it would fall back into the hands of the enemy. Fortunately, the rumors were wrong; calm returned a few days later, and the Penn School students continued their studies.[93]

In July 1863 a major battle occurred at Fort Wagner on Morris Island near Charleston, about fifty miles by sea from Penn School. African Americans' determination to fight and die for freedom was made abundantly clear when the Fifty-Fourth Massachusetts, the Union's preeminent African American unit, attacked Fort Wagner in the first real test of its fighting prowess. Forced to advance along a narrow front because of the fort's proximity to the ocean, the Fifty-Fourth suffered heavy casualties before even reaching the fort. Prolonged hand-to-hand fighting was fierce. The soldiers managed to reach the parapet of the fort, maintaining their position for an hour before being pushed back.[94] Forten wrote about the death of Colonel Robert Gould Shaw, commander of the unit and the son of prominent white abolitionist parents: "It makes me sad, sad at heart . . . It seems very, very hard that the best and the noblest must be the earliest called away."[95] After the battle, Confederate troops buried the Fifty-Fourth Massachusetts's dead in one long ditch and disposed of Shaw in the same mass grave, reputedly saying, "We have buried him with his niggers!" They assumed that a burial with black soldiers would bring shame, but Shaw's father disagreed. Reflecting a growing idealism among many white northerners, he declared, "I can imagine no holier place than that in which he is, among his brave and devoted followers, nor wish him better company."[96] The attack on Fort Wagner provided concrete evidence to President Lincoln and the nation that African American soldiers were brave fighters and an important asset to the Union.[97] Their courage and discipline demonstrated very clearly what white southerners had always dreaded most: given the opportunity, African Americans would not hesitate to shed their own blood—and that of their oppressors—in a war to overthrow slavery.

Confronted with such heavy casualties, the St. Helena community responded immediately. The teachers at Penn School hastened to Beaufort to help nurse those who had been transported there by the hundreds. Forten wrote, "My hospital life began to-day."[98] In addition to nursing help, the island offered provisions; the field hospital was inundated with food donations from African American farmers, including melons, sweet potatoes, and chickens.[99]

School resumed, but the health of Charlotte Forten, which was never good, became of grave concern as the physical and emotional stress of life at Penn took its toll. She suffered from "respiratory ailments," such as those that had caused her mother's death.[100] She got some relief from "the intense heat" when a "good breeze generally" came in during the evening. Except for that breeze, Forten wrote, "I think we c'ld not live through the heat. We spend our evenings on the piazza, sitting up quite late generally in fear of the fleas, which torture us so that bed, to me at least, is almost unendurable—sleep almost impossible."[101] Because she could not bear the heat of the day, Forten had already stopped traveling to school and instead held classes at a carriage house where they lived, about half a mile from Penn at Frogmore Plantation.[102] Although Forten loved teaching and loved assisting the school in its early development, the deterioration of her health forced her to resign in July 1863. She noted: "My strength has failed rapidly of late. Have become so weak that I fear I sh'ld be an easy prey to the fever which prevails here, a little later in this season."[103] Forten traveled north on a furlough for her health, leaving on July 31, 1863. She returned to St. Helena on October 16, 1863, teaching for eight months at other places around the island and helping at Penn School when Ellen Murray was very ill with malaria. Forten's influence at Penn extended well beyond her time there. As an educated African American woman, she was a role model for the students, and her work helped put the school on the path to success.[104]

January 1864 was a low point for Laura Towne. "We have no milk, and at times no wood," she wrote in her diary, explaining that there was not a single man at the school who was well enough to bring in supplies, and that even the boys and girls were too sick to attend classes. She felt poorly herself: "It is a tight time. I am nearly ill too."[105] And yet the people of Penn School remained undaunted, and health and good cheer returned.

In March 1864, Towne worried about losing the Brick Church as the location of the school, noting that some in the church wanted "to turn us out."[106] In fact the church, their school for the past year and a half, was not suitable for their growing student body: "We cannot make the school convenient for writing, blackboards, etc. We have the noise of three large schools in one room, and it is trying to voice and strength, and not conducive to good order."[107] Fortuitously, Towne received an alternative offer. General Saxton wrote to her and asked whether there was a need for schoolhouses, and Towne eagerly and gratefully accepted the offer. They finished the spring term and began the fall term at the Brick Church. Towne reported that the school had "a full number of scholars, one hundred and ninety-four last Friday," who were "generally good, and eager to come back, pretty quiet and inclined to study."[108] But she was looking forward to relocating: "We hope soon to get into our new building."[109]

The new school was ready in January 1865. A gift from the Freedman's Aid Society of Pennsylvania, the three-room frame building arrived in already-built sections.[110] This building, one of the first prefabricated structures in American history, was put into service as the first real schoolhouse in the South designed for the instruction of former slaves.[111] Towne and Murray gave the school its name: Penn School, in honor of William Penn (1644–1718), "that great lover of liberty."[112]

The school was located on fifty acres of land across from the Brick Church, land sold to Penn School by Hastings Gantt, a freedman, entrepreneur, and local civic leader on St. Helena.[113] Towne declared, "How we do enjoy our new school-house. It is so delightful to have quiet, and the desks are wonderfully convenient."[114]

One of the concerns at the new Penn School was how to tell the students that it was time to come to school; no one had clocks. Towne asked her family to donate a school bell. Some Penn students had to travel from five to six miles away, but Towne figured that "no bell could be heard so far," so requested and received one that could be heard from three miles away.[115] The bell was inscribed "Proclaim Liberty," like the Liberty Bell in Philadelphia.[116]

While education at Penn was progressing, war continued. General William Tecumseh Sherman's March to the Sea brought him to Savannah in January 1865, and in February he began his trek northward. According to Sherman, "the whole army" was "burning with an insatiable desire to wreak vengeance upon South Carolina."[117] One South Carolinian general, Wade Hampton, did not want Sherman to dally in the state. Hampton wrote, "Do not attempt to delay Sherman's march by destroying bridges, or any other means. For God's sake let him get out of the country as quickly as possible."[118] Sherman's march had already freed many former slaves in Georgia and South Carolina. Thousands of African Americans followed his army.

This new freedom meant an ongoing stream of refugees arriving at St. Helena, where the people shared their already-scant resources. Towne wrote in January 1865, "It is astonishing with what open hearted charity the people here—themselves refuges from Edisto two years ago—have received these new comers right into their houses."[119] The teachers at Penn School were overwhelmed by the number of African American refugees who lacked housing, food, and clothing. In one of many such entries, Towne noted, "Pierce Butler's slaves have just arrived among this lot. We have no clothes to give these poor shivering creatures, and I never felt so helpless."[120] Pierce Mease Butler had been one of the richest men in America, with large plantations on Butler and St. Simons Islands, off the coast of Georgia, but his enslaved workers never fared well. His treatment of slaves was a major reason that his wife, the notable British actress Fanny Kemble, sued for divorce in 1849 and became an ardent abolitionist.[121] When Butler needed cash in March 1859, he sold 436 of his slaves at an auction outside Savannah, about fifty miles south of Beaufort. National newspapers reported that it was the largest single slave auction in U.S. history.[122]

Hungry and homeless wartime refugees were not the only problem on St. Helena. There was a shortage of workers to harvest the corn and cotton crops, which were needed for food and income. Fewer men were available to help in fields, and those who were working were in danger of impressment. In one instance, a platoon of U.S. soldiers arrived, spread out through the school's fields and buildings, seized about twenty men, and marched them off to Fort Pulaski to serve as laborers, often unpaid ones.[123] The problem continued throughout the war. In 1864, Edwin M. Stanton, the Union secretary of war, visited the sea islands and verified what the people of St. Helena already knew, namely, that freedmen were being kidnapped and even shot by recruiting officers of the Union army.[124]

On April 9, 1865, Confederate general Robert E. Lee surrendered to Ulysses S. Grant at Appomattox Court House in Virginia, but Confederates under General Joseph E. Johnston did not surrender until April 26 in North Carolina.[125] Before the official end of war, before any joy could be complete, the nation suffered devastating news. The people on St. Helena, who had been jubilant five months earlier when President Abraham Lincoln won reelection, were shocked and overwhelmed. When Robert Smalls heard the news of Lincoln's assassination, the former slave exclaimed, "Lord have mercy on us all."[126] On April 29, 1865, Towne recorded the peoples' reaction to the news: "It was a frightful blow at first. The people have refused to believe he was dead. Last Sunday the black minister of Frogmore said that if they knew the President were dead they would mourn for him, but they could not think that was the truth, and they would wait and see."[127]

They also had to wait and see what the new president, Andrew Johnson, would do about Reconstruction. Problems and poverty did not end with victory in April 1865. But Penn School persevered.

CHAPTER TWO

Penn School from
Reconstruction to 1901

Under Lincoln's leadership, Congress endorsed the Thirteenth Amendment
to the Constitution: "Neither slavery nor involuntary servitude . . . shall exist
within the United States." Lincoln was adamant about the need for such an
amendment because he did not want the proponents of slavery to take freedom away on the constitutional basis that emancipation was no longer needed
as a war measure. State ratification followed, and on December 6, 1865, eight
months after Lincoln's death, the Thirteenth Amendment became part of the
U.S. Constitution.

As emancipation and freedom began to affect education and land ownership, groups differed in how the new status of former slaves should be handled.
Penn School, as it had been during the war itself, was again in the midst of conflict, this time over the meaning of Reconstruction.[1] Members of the American
Missionary Association continued to volunteer as teachers, some willingly serving in dangerous locales in the former Confederacy to bring "the glorious liberty of the gospel" by doing God's work in structuring a new order on moral
principles.[2] But the freedpeople had their own agenda. Thousands of African
Americans began to record marriages long since consummated, or to pay taxes,
or to set their marks on labor contracts, or simply to call the sheriff in time of
trouble, asserting their right to live in peace among their fellows under the protection of the Constitution. They were not chattels or dependents, interlopers
or charity seekers; they claimed rights, endured responsibilities, and enjoyed
freedoms guaranteed by the power "of the people." Throughout the nation,
Reconstruction involved a daily working out, by whites and blacks, men and
women, rich and poor, of how they ought to treat one another in changed times.

In the former Confederacy, African Americans strode toward a liberty defined by property ownership and legal rights. As elsewhere, the people of St. Helena Island wanted sanctity of family, education for their children, the end of corporal punishment, and the payment of reasonable wages. Most southern white people were of the mind that African Americans must not receive the abundant freedom that whites enjoyed, and they contested every step. The freedpeople knew that one of the few resources available to them was the right to vote. A letter to President Johnson from the "Office Superintendent of Freedmen" in Port Royal, South Carolina, on June 20, 1865, referred to the attitude of southern elite whites and "the disposition they have to trample upon the *rights* of the Negro," and the superintendent asked the president, "I pray you Sir to give the Loyal inhabitants of this State the protection of the ballot, as their only security against those whose hands are still red with the life blood of the Nation, in their attempts to destroy it."[3]

On June 29, 1865, a letter to "His Excellency Andrew Johnson" from a group of "South Carolina Black Citizens" argued that they "be granted the Inestimable and protective rights of the Elective franchise, which privilege we regard as the only means by which our class of the population . . . will have the power of protecting ourselves and our interest against oppression and unjust legislation." They reminded Johnson that "Born and Raised in this country, we claim it as our native land, and regard the United States Government as our common parent, intitled to our fealty love and affection, and we glory in the name of American Citizens." They also suggested the names of four "very competent Gentlemen," all abolitionists, whom Johnson might consider appointing as provisional governor of South Carolina: General John C. Frémont of South Carolina, William H. Brisbane of South Carolina, Brevet Major General Saxton, and General B. F. Butler of Massachusetts.[4] Johnson was not sympathetic to these appeals. As Towne wrote the following spring, "We have been so shocked and disgusted with Johnson's speech."[5]

In additional to meaningful voting rights, an essential ingredient of freedom was education. African Americans knew the value of reading the Bible and labor contracts. They knew that reading would help them participate in the new political system and hoped that education would allow the next generation to progress. Nearly all freed African Americans agreed with Robert Smalls's sentiment that educational opportunity was part and parcel of a determination "never to be made slaves again."[6] As part of this educational imperative, Penn continued to flourish. Towne wrote in the spring of 1865, "Our school does splendidly, though I say it." These students, who had not seen a school before Penn, made astonishing progress. "The children have read through a history of the United States and an easy physiology, and they know all the parts of speech, and can make sentences, being told to use a predicate, verb, and adverb, for instance. Ellen's class is writing compositions." In preparation for the end of the school term, students worked on "dialogues, exercises in mathematics, in grammar, geography, spelling, reading, etc., etc."[7]

Further good news included advances in secondary education; as Towne noted: "Our school is the high school already, and we mean to make it more so."[8] By 1867, secondary education at Penn School had become the best on the island, and the most qualified elementary students applied to Penn for high school education. Murray selected the most promising secondary school students from "an endless list of applicants for admission" from the island's other schools.[9] In December 1868, Penn began its "Normal practice," that is, teacher preparation and training.[10] Coursework included U.S. history, civics, geography, physiology, grammar, spelling, and writing.[11] Two years later Towne wrote, "The state has called upon us for several teachers, in a very complimentary letter."[12] Teacher training continued to be an important function of Penn School. In 1894 a visitor commented: "We listen to recitations on the theory and practice of teaching, and household hygiene. Some examples in cube root, partnership and discount are rapidly and easily worked, and we inspect beautifully written books, filled with simple bookkeeping."[13]

The good news in education went along with good news on land matters. In addition to an education, freedpeople wanted to own land. Whatever managers of plantations might have thought, few former slaves confused wage labor with freedom. Real freedom, as republican ideology understood it and religious expectation framed it, required autonomy, and in an agricultural economy that meant living off one's own land. For centuries, enslaved workers had been told they did not belong; owning land proved they did. Moreover, for almost 250 years enslaved people had tilled the soil of their masters and watched them become rich and powerful thereby. After the war, the federal government owned land that the fleeing Confederates had not paid the taxes on, and the government wanted money for that land. The freedpeople thought they were the most deserving, but they were not the only ones interested in purchasing land—so were white farmers and speculators. Towne had earlier worried about speculators. On February 1, 1863, she wrote, "General Saxton is much opposed to the sale of the land to speculators." Towne and others worried that land sales during the war would proceed so quickly that the freedmen would be excluded. She suggested to Saxton that the army stop the sales: "General Saxton caught at the idea. He went to Hilton Head yesterday and the sales are stopped as a military necessity."[14] She wrote later that month, "Hurrah! Jubilee! Lands are to be set apart for the people so that they cannot be oppressed, or driven to work for speculators, or ejected from their homesteads."[15]

The people of St. Helena benefited from Abraham Lincoln's earlier suggestion that William Brisbane be appointed one of the tax commissioners there.[16] As mentioned in the last chapter, Brisbane was a South Carolina planter who, uneasy about slavery, became an abolitionist and freed his slaves. As a tax commissioner, he expected the former slaves to be treated fairly. Brisbane was complicated, however; his view of fair play meant that he opposed selling the land to the former slaves for less than its market value.[17] Nevertheless, under his leadership much property of former Confederates was sold to former slaves. Many whites then referred to him as "the most hated man in the Beaufort District."[18]

In June 1865, the diarist Mary Boykin Chesnut gave an account of a friend who visited her former plantation in Beaufort. Chesnut recorded her friend's reaction: "Our Negroes are living in great comfort. They were delighted to see me, and treated me with overflowing affection. They waited on me as before, gave me beautiful breakfasts and splendid dinners; but they firmly and respectfully informed me: 'We own this land now. Put it out of your head that it will ever be yours again.'"[19]

It was soon clear, however, that the new president, Andrew Johnson, was no friend of the former slaves. Johnson opened a virtual pardon mill in the White House, restoring land and power to local Confederate leaders with startling eagerness. The people of St. Helena had to wonder what the future would hold. Towne wrote on September 1, 1865, that "Secesh" (secessionists) are "coming back thick. . . . They are crawlingly civil as yet, but will soon feel their oats."[20] At first the freedpeople of St. Helena were wary of the former owners. Towne reported, "The people receive the rebels better than we expected, but the reason is that they believe Johnson is going to put them in their old masters power again, and they feel that they must conciliate or be crushed. They no longer pray for the President—*our* President, as they used to call Lincoln—in the church. They keep an ominous silence and are very sad and troubled."[21] More whites were returning to the town of Beaufort, across the river. According to Towne, "On the mainland it is so dangerous for a negro to go about, especially with the United States Uniform on, that orders are out that no more will be allowed to go to recover their families and bring them here as they have been doing."[22]

Like others throughout the nation, Towne found that whites' racial bias persisted, even in the absence of supporting evidence. "It is not true that the negro soldiers do not behave well," she wrote. "These stories about them are manufactured for a purpose."[23] Other racial prejudice smeared the freedpeople as unable or disinclined to work. And yet when roads on St. Helena needed repair, the voluntary laborers were African Americans, who "turn out *very* well"; on the other hand, "the white proprietors . . . refuse to help, though they use the roads most."[24] When working the land for white owners or managers, African Americans had a problem: they were tired of working for no money.[25] Military agents who handled the governmental enforcement of work contracts were very often not interested in fairness.[26] Towne described a pattern that fit northern agents in much of the former Confederacy: "They are often more pro-slavery than the rebels themselves, and only care to make the blacks work—being quite unconcerned about making the employers pay. Doing justice seems to mean, to them, seeing that the blacks don't break a contract and compelling them to submit cheerfully if the whites do."[27] Two years later, Towne was still complaining about lazy white planters who wanted their land to lie idle so they could collect government money: "It is not the colored people that this plan is to aid, but the planters—a thriftless, greedy set of Southerners, and some Northerners who have been unfortunate here."[28]

But land ownership was not without its problems. Hastings Gantt, the freedman who sold land to Penn School in 1864, faced two difficulties with his new landholdings. First, the cotton crop was not selling at a good price, "not more than fifty cents a pound, ginned." Moreover, he had bought a large tract of land as part of a cooperative venture, but some of his partners died and others withdrew from the deal. Towne wrote, "I think this is the hardest winter he has known."[29]

The freedpeople who purchased land had to wonder about the security of its title. President Johnson was steadily returning confiscated land to former rebels, but land that the government owned because of nonpayment of taxes was in a different category than confiscated land. As Towne explained in January 1868, the land on St. Helena had not been confiscated: "It was sold for taxes, and has been resold too often to be in danger of return. The old owner can and will claim indemnity, but that cannot affect title deeds to the land."[30] African American landowners worked together against lawsuits instigated by former rebels for the return of property.[31] When one such case developed, Towne was hopeful of the outcome because juries were chosen from the people: "As the jury is composed mostly of colored men who own land held by this same title, *this* court will probably settle the case as we should wish, but then it will undoubtedly be carried up by the usual steps to the Supreme Court."[32]

Political power determined much about life during Reconstruction. The people on St. Helena wanted education and a fair livelihood, but they knew that many whites would not support those aims. On May 12, 1867, at a mass meeting of Republican citizens, all the speakers were men, and all but one were African American. Towne wrote that the white men did not attend because they were "going to have a *white* party, they say." Her report included a conversation between a black man, who said he wanted no white men on their platform, and the majority of others, who disclaimed all such feelings:

"What difference does skin make, my brethren. *I* would stand side by side a *white* man if he acted right. We mustn't be prejudiced against their color."

"If dere skins *is* white, dey may have principle."

"Come, my friends, we must n't judge a man according to his color, but according to his acts."[33]

The one white man was John Hunn, an early arrival to the Port Royal Experiment, a Quaker who had come to St. Helena Island to open a store. Hunn was an abolitionist from the slaveholding state of Delaware; in 1848, Hunn had been fined heavily in Delaware for his work in helping fugitive slaves escape.[34]

The sea islands offered education to the freedpeople after the war in other schools besides Penn. Mather School, for example, had a good reputation. By 1867, however, many public schools included white teachers who whipped the children and made them say "massa" and "missus."[35] Other supposedly free public schools became pay schools, and Towne feared that "the best and brightest will be cut off, many of them, from school privileges."[36] One of Towne's priorities was funding, not only for Penn but also for the public schools on St. Helena. In January 1868, she expressed her worries: "I am now trying to get the people to support the schools, and they are taking the matter up with a will, but whether it will be a well-controlled and enlightened will remains to be seen. . . . But now it seems that with good will enough, they can do little, for want of money, of which they have none, as they were not paid in money this year, and in previous years had put all their savings into land, house, horses, etc."[37] She also asked about funding from the Philadelphia Relief Association: "Tell me something about the prospects of the Pennsylvania Branch supporting school another year. Does n't it look dark? Is interest dying out?" In 1868 she hoped at the very minimum to receive "some clothing for my 'mudderless.'"[38]

In 1868, St. Helena Island, along with all of South Carolina, planned for the drafting of a new state constitution. Elections were open to all men, and African American men for the first time were eligible to vote and to run to be delegates. Towne's assessment of the elected delegates, "half black, half white . . . a wise body," was that it wrote "an excellent constitution."[39] One of the delegates was the war hero Robert Smalls. Besides his valiant sail to freedom on May 13, 1862,

Smalls piloted the *Planter* in more than twelve engagements, skirmishes, or expeditions against the Confederates during the Civil War.[40] In 1868, as a delegate to the state constitutional convention, Smalls introduced and won support for a provision for compulsory education for all children between the ages of seven and fourteen, the schools "to be opened without charge to all classes of the people." Describing himself as "deeply interested in the common school system," Smalls bought and donated the land for a school in Beaufort to which freedmen came "at all hours . . . expecting to catch a lesson."[41]

Public education was a double-edged sword. Public funding for Penn School would have been useful; as Towne wrote, "Our school exists on charity, and charity that is weary." And yet if money came from the State of South Carolina, so would certain regulations: "If turned over to the state, no Northern colored person has a chance of being appointed teacher of a state school. There are too many here who want the places and the school trustees are not men capable of appointing by qualification."[42] The Towne family supported Penn School financially, and Laura Towne often worked without pay. Penn remained in the financial hands of the Philadelphia Relief Association, weary as it was, and had the good fortune to become a school sponsored by the Benezet Society of Germantown, Philadelphia. A fierce abolitionist who believed that blacks and whites were equal, Anthony Benezet (1713–1784) organized night schools for enslaved children. While not a wealthy man, he left a small endowment after his death to help support schools for African Americans.[43] In July 1871, Towne and the staff at Penn received the news that "the Penn. F. R. A. [Pennsylvania Freedmen's Relief Association] exists no longer." Funds from the Benezet Society remained, but Towne declared that the school would last only one more year. Although her future was uncertain, Towne insisted, "I shall not give up teaching; I could n't live without it now."[44]

Private charitable giving kept the school alive for longer than a year. In early 1873, Towne wrote, "School prospers finely. The work is more and more interesting and refreshing." With some money sent from her family, she enthusiastically reported on improvements: "The new roof is on my school-room and the whole force of teachers is in active play."[45] The trustee for the Benezet Fund was Francis

R. Cope (1821–1909), a wealthy Quaker in Philadelphia who would in the future act as financial agent for the Penn School.[46] Trustees managed the funds, and Towne could draw upon them when needed.[47]

Funding was never lavish, and Penn watched all expenses. Towne wrote in 1874 about salvaging textbooks:

> For three weeks now, all day, and for a long time in the evening too, I have been mending school-books. . . . Sometimes I put nearly a hundred patches in one book, so you may know the labor. I use thin paper and paste over the print. These books have been put away as worn out, but now that the fund is so nearly exhausted, we cannot afford new books, and must have some, so I have undertaken a heavy, tiresome job. It will take me another week of incessant labor all day long to finish, and then I shall have secured them to twenty dollars' worth of—before—worthless books. I like to do it, fortunately. There is a satisfaction in turning out a neat, nicely bound, and patched book from a horrid old pair of covers and many ragged leaves. In some cases I put two half-worn books together, rejecting bad parts, and so make one as good as new.[48]

Winter terms at Penn began in October and ended in July (public schools in the area ended the term in May). Penn teachers loved the excitement students felt at gaining an education. In 1875 Towne wrote, "The school-children are almost wild with excitement over our approaching exhibition. Don't you think it promises well for the people that at evening parties and merry-makings the chief entertainment is the rehearsal of school lessons by the youngsters? That darling school is such a joy and pride!"[49]

While the school continued its mission of teaching, the staff there also found itself in the sad situation of having to dole out charity. Just as the people had provided for the teachers during the war, now the teachers tried to help those in need. In the spring of 1876, Towne wrote, "For the first time in my experience down here, I have had people come to the back porch, and say (pitifully ashamed, too), 'Miss Towne, I hungry.' Real nice people, who never asked a thing before! I take only the very old, and motherless, except in some cases where there are very large families. The *allowance* is the same as in slavery times—a peck of grits a week."[50] The sad truth was that the economy was in shambles. As cotton production worldwide increased, prices plummeted more than 80 percent. People were short of tools, fertilizer, and draft animals. Old seed was a problem, as were the dreaded "army worms" that ate the crops. In July 1876, Towne reported on dire conditions: "The people are actually starving here and there, but the neighbors share what they have—and sometimes it is one's turn to be flush, sometimes another's." Towne expected the situation to improve because of a new business on the sea islands: phosphate mining. Phosphate, called the rock, was used as fertilizer. Phosphate mining provided the African American men in St. Helena with almost three thousand decent-paying jobs. Towne took note of this development: "Nearly all the men are now at the rock, so some money is coming back to the island."[51] Phosphate mining posed significant health hazards. Working conditions were strenuous and often involved diving from boats to collect the phosphate nodules. Phosphate also put out low levels of radioactivity. The industry was short-lived, and the long-term economic situation at St. Helena was not much improved.[52]

Politics were likewise mixed, and as the African American community knew, economic rights depend on political rights. In South Carolina and throughout the former Confederacy, the political aftermath of the Civil War included the extension of voting rights to African Americans. In 1867 in South Carolina, 80,832 African Americans and 46,929 whites were registered to vote.[53] A coalition of African Americans and their white Republican allies formed an interracial democracy, and African Americans in South Carolina won election as lieutenant governor, secretary of state, and state treasurer. They controlled a majority of seats in the lower house for six years.[54] Elected to the South Carolina House of Representatives from the Beaufort District was the freedman who sold land to Penn School when it moved from the Brick Church in 1864: Hastings Gantt.[55] Gantt was a leading organizer of the local Republican Party coalition of freedmen and some supportive whites. The group worked to diversify the economy and support public education.[56] In July 1876, Towne reported, "Another of our great days passed this week—the annual school district meeting. I read my report. It was duly approved and all my suggestions carried out, the three-mill tax voted, school-books provided for, and all smooth for next year."[57]

That interracial democracy did not last long. White Democrats in South Carolina, a minority in the state, were not content to win elections fairly. They ushered in a reign of terror, and no action, no matter how heinous, went untried in the effort to eliminate African American voting power. One effective tactic was to murder those who voted or held office. Seven state legislators were murdered between 1868 and 1876.[58] According to a white witness at one of the murders, "The struggle in which we were engaged meant more than life or death. It involved everything we held dear, Anglo-Saxon civilization included."[59] This witness was Benjamin Ryan Tillman, a future South Carolina governor and U.S. senator.

In the elections of November 1876, both political parties courted the African American vote. Towne reported the speech of a black man talking about the political speeches: "He said, 'Dey says dem *will do* dis and dat. I ain't ax no man what him *will do*—I ax him what him *hab done*.'" Towne was confident that the Republicans would prevail: "Pretty hard on the Democrats, that, and it tells well for the Republicans so far as the negro is concerned above all."[60]

With a profound faith in America as a democratic republic, Towne vastly underestimated the fraudulent and violent efforts of elite whites to undermine elections: "On Tuesday there will be excitement all over the country except here, where all goes one way, and after that some peace, I hope, even if there is bitter disappointment among the good. But I don't believe it possible that the Democrats will succeed. It will be ever so long before we, in this out-of-the-way place, find out what is the true state of the election, and who is over us at Columbia [capital of South Carolina] and at Washington. Meanwhile, our school goes on happily, and we are not too much disturbed in our minds by anything out of it."[61]

Towne's complacency was unwarranted. In the national election of 1876, the Electoral College chose the Republican Rutherford B. Hayes over the Democrat Samuel Tilden, but the deal making that gave Hayes the presidency included the end of political Reconstruction, meaning that the nation was no longer willing to enforce voting rights, or any civil rights, for African Americans.[62] In the decade after Appomattox, all but a few of the brightest and most hopeful spirits who had guided and propelled the antislavery movement from the 1830s onward had died. Many of their political successors averted their eyes and turned their backs on the freedmen. In all of American history there is perhaps no spectacle of abandoned ideals more wrongheaded or depressing. Acquiescing in widespread northern self-interest, apathy toward the problems of others, and racial prejudice, Congress did little to prevent white southern elites' return to political power. The nation willingly left southern politics to white southerners, who claimed that they were better suited to handle their institutions of state and local government.

In April 1877, Towne was still angry about the presidential election and its potential effect on the African American population: "I have been in raging indignation at Hayes. I hope we have not another Buchanan in the President's chair, but I fear we have. He is too easy and ready to think well of everybody. He won't believe in rebellion till he sees it again, I suppose. Nobody seems to remember that the South is only half-civilized, and that the negroes are nearly as well informed and a great deal more loyal than the whites."[63] When Towne wrote to "My dear R.," she told of the indignities faced by South Carolina state representative Hastings Gantt and other Republicans who won election in 1876. They were forced to "ask pardon for having been republicans." She remonstrated, "You can hear plainly what Wendell Phillips calls the 'crack of the slave-whip' now." According to Towne, "The political leaders want to get rid of the northerner, want the negroes landless—and want yankee school-ma'ams out of the reach of the growing population."[64]

And indeed, as in the state as a whole, local whites, even in the heavily black area of the sea islands, soon controlled all local political boards. Where blacks held a majority, where they were able to elect school board members of their choosing, the system was changed to one of appointment rather than election. By June 1877, the people on St. Helena were "forbidden to raise any money for school purposes,—that is, to levy the usual three-mill, or *any* school tax." Without any local financial support for the few public schools on St. Helena, teachers were left without jobs. Towne was clear about the result: "There is no prospect of any schools worth calling so, after this, and there will be an almost total retirement of all Northern teachers."[65] Penn, not publicly funded, continued.

St. Helena did not accept the new status quo easily. Although residents were unable to "vote to levy any school tax, because the Democratic legislature had forbidden it," they held a mass meeting "of the most influential men among the blacks of the island"; the local store owner, J. R. Macdonald, and Towne were there "representing the whites."[66] The group passed a resolution "to the effect that St. Helena might be excepted from the operation of the new law which forbids district taxes, because the people here are the taxpayers, there being on the island five thousand blacks and not fifty whites, twelve hundred and eighty black children of age to attend school, and only seven white children, and because the few white people here are as anxious for schools as the blacks, and as willing to pay the tax voted at these meetings." Towne was optimistic because the resolution, which would "be published in the newspapers, . . . will show not only the injustice done in forbidding people's providing for the public schools adequately,—and as handsomely as they please,—but also that the St. Helena folk are awake to their rights."[67] According to Towne, the *Ledger, Commonwealth, Nation,* and *Charleston Journal of Commerce* published her resolutions; she reported, "All praise the action of St. Helena."[68] But the white elite at Beaufort took little notice, and St. Helena's resolution was ignored.

The political situation was permeated by "the brimstone smell of the social and political atmosphere." Towne realized that whites were determined to revive "old slavery." A new rule established a poll tax; for nonpayment of that tax, "a man can be put into the penitentiary, and sold out of it as a slave for the time of his sentence." A man charged with stealing a hog, "not convicted nor taken in the act, but only charged with it," could be severely whipped in order to save the expense of a trial. "If that doesn't look like slavery times, what could?" Towne asked in August 1877.[69]

All understood the importance of the vote. In a speech entitled "An Honest Ballot Is the Safeguard of the Republic," delivered in the U.S. House of Representatives in 1877, Congressman Robert Smalls, of Beaufort, told how slavery had taught white masters "to ignore and trample the rights of those they could not control."[70] The right to vote brought protection against such trampling. The right to vote meant political power and elected officials responsive to the needs of constituents. No vote meant no political power.

Before local elections near Beaufort in November 1878, whites turned to methods that had worked in Upcountry South Carolina two years earlier. In 1876, white supremacists in "red shirts" had been extremely successful in disrupting elections in Edgefield, South Carolina. In Beaufort, white men in red shirts deliberately set about to disrupt political meetings, "hitting and abusing the people."[71] Towne wrote, "Political times are simply frightful. Men are shot at, hounded down, trapped, and held till certain meetings are over, and intimidated in every possible way. It gets worse and worse as election approaches."[72] According to Towne, the local paper, the *Beaufort Tribune*, reported, "In order to prevent our county falling into such hands (Republican), *any* measure that will accomplish the end will be justify-able, *however wicked* they might be in other communities."[73] Local elections in the fall of 1878 showed a Republican majority on St. Helena Island: "The result on this island was nine hundred and eighteen votes, only nine of them Democratic and only one of the nine a colored man's vote."[74] The city of Beaufort, where most white residents were not native southerners, continued to elect a town council that included African American and white men until 1913.

White Democrats tried to eliminate Robert Smalls from politics, charging him with corruption. Smalls remained in the U.S. Congress as a representative from Beaufort, but a gerrymandered district meant that he was no longer the county commissioner. Instead, whites elected a local Democratic commissioner, "who used to be so cruel and burn the people with pine tar dropped blazing on their backs."[75] Towne was outraged at the charges made against Smalls, and Smalls continued to respect Towne and her work. He invited a member of the British Parliament to have lunch with her while the international guest was on tour in 1878.[76]

In the 1890s, two assaults hammered the St. Helena community. One came from Mother Nature, the other from the politics of racial hatred. A hurricane in 1893 almost annihilated the community of St. Helena. Some refer to this hurricane as "perhaps the most remarkable storm in South Carolina's hurricane history."[77] Homes, cotton, food crops, and roads were flooded, trees uprooted, and Penn School buildings damaged or destroyed. Clara Barton, first president of the Red Cross, visited the island, but did little to help. As had been done before and has been done since, "The people buried their dead and salvaged what was left."[78] After the hurricane, migration off the sea islands intensified.

The community was unable to salvage its voting or citizenship rights as African American disfranchisement took hold throughout the Deep South. In 1896, only 5,500 African Americans were registered to vote in South Carolina; though a majority in the state, they comprised a mere 10 percent of all registered voters.[79] Nevertheless, whites demanded a new constitution that would eliminate all African American voting. Robert Smalls, a delegate to that constitutional convention, pleaded, to no avail, for a constitution that was "fair, honest and just."[80] Instead, Benjamin Ryan Tillman, a U.S. senator from South Carolina and virulent white supremacist, got his way: "We have done our level best. We have scratched our heads to find out how we could eliminate every last one of them. We stuffed ballot boxes. We shot them. We are not ashamed of it."[81]

The outward effects of reform may have decreased, but the inner spirit of the freedmen and freedwomen continued to thrive. Political equality and economic opportunity were taken away, but hard-earned educations and knowledge of the experience of freedom could not be. African Americans and white allies in the Republican Party had created an interracial democracy, and that experience gave the community hope for the future even in bitter times. St. Helena had an additional benefit. Unlike their counterparts in other areas of the American South, the households on St. Helena managed to keep their land. At the end of 1878, 75 percent of the land in Beaufort County was owned by African Americans.[82]

In spite of many disappointments in the years following Reconstruction, the African American community remained optimistic and hopeful and continued to put its faith in education. Apart from the corrupt political system run by the white elite, Towne found much to be grateful for at Penn School: "Our school is a delight. It rained one day last week, but through the pelting showers came nearly every blessed child. Some of them walk six miles and back, besides doing their task of cotton-picking. Their steady eagerness to learn is just something amazing. To be deprived of a lesson is a severe punishment. 'I got no reading to-day,' or no writing, or no sums, is cause for bitter tears. This race is going to rise. It is biding its time."[83] In 1884, Towne wrote about a train ride to Beaufort from a visit north to see family. The conductor, "that old plague," told her that "the whole race of niggers ought to be swept away." Towne stoutly contradicted him: "I told him my business was with that race and that they would never be swept away."[84]

The turn of the century was a milestone for the school that had been founded four decades earlier by Laura Towne. At the age of seventy-five and in failing health, Towne decided the best way to keep Penn School active in the future was to pass on the leadership role. In 1900, her niece Helen Jenks, well connected in philanthropic circles, contacted Hollis Burke Frissell, the white principal of the Hampton Institute in Virginia, to ask whether Hampton would consider sponsoring Penn School. Frissell traveled to St. Helena to meet with Towne.[85] Before she died on St. Helena Island on February 22, 1901, Towne was assured that Penn School would continue under the auspices of Hampton and of Frissell. Frissell took a strong leadership role in the development of Penn and its programs from the time of his first involvement in 1901 until his death in 1917.

Under the patronage of the Hampton Normal and Agricultural Institute, Penn School adopted the Hampton program.[86] Hampton was a postsecondary school for African Americans who wanted to become teachers. It was founded in 1868 by Samuel C. Armstrong (1839–1893), the son of missionaries in Hawaii.[87] In the Civil War, Armstrong was a Union officer commanding the Eighth Regiment of U.S. Colored Troops, who fought gallantly at Petersburg. At that time he became vitally interested in education after discovering that his soldiers, former slaves, had had little opportunity for learning. Armstrong thought that people who had been held in slavery were in need of "moral uplift." Calling for practical, "industrial education," he firmly believed in education for African Americans; at the same time, he believed that education should prepare them to accept a subservient role. Not all white missionaries agreed with that sentiment. Missionaries often differed on whether nonwhite people were equal to whites, even as most agreed that all people deserved an education of some sort. Armstrong thoroughly disapproved of a liberal, classical education for African Americans, and he opposed their having voting rights for at least generations to come.[88] Hollis Frissell succeeded Armstrong as principal at Hampton in 1893 and continued to promote the Hampton ideal. While he knew that for some African American educators "there is a perhaps natural feeling among them against this form of instruction," nevertheless he and other Hampton trustees "felt strongly that it is important to stir up the colored people to an interest in industrial education."[89] Penn School offered the opportunity for Frissell to further the Hampton idea.

By the end of the nineteenth century, most of the South was heading toward Jim Crow segregation. In *Plessy v. Ferguson* (1896), the U.S. Supreme Court ruled that states were within their rights to limit freedom and outlaw integration. The infamous dictum "separate but equal" came to mean that southern states would enforce "separate" but never enforce "equal." Penn School had African American students, African American teachers, white principals, and white funders. But its history made a difference: visitors were never segregated, and its personnel never tolerated blatantly racist remarks.

Nationwide, education was changing its emphasis as America became an increasingly industrialized nation, and a new faith in science and technological expertise replaced religious idealism. Some educators looked to the methods of John Dewey (1859–1952), believing that education must involve students as active learners rather than as passive recipients of knowledge doled out by the teacher. Education should be meaningful to students as human beings and as informed citizens. Many entered this debate, including the African American community. African American educators had the additional burden of having to place educational needs in the broader context of an increasingly rigid and entrenched system of racial segregation.

Among many leaders in this debate were Booker T. Washington and W. E. B. Du Bois. Washington, a graduate of Hampton, founded the Tuskegee Normal and Industrial Institute in 1881 in Tuskegee, Alabama, on the principle of industrial education, which became known as the Hampton-Tuskegee idea. For Washington, the political and social course was clear. If African Americans were required to live, for the most part, in the South, if they were expected to remain tethered to the soil, cultivating cotton and tobacco, then they needed to develop themselves as artisans and scientific farmers, growing bigger and better crops than neighboring whites, cooperating and supporting one another, accumulating property, and building strong institutions. Washington thought that a stronger economic base was needed. Racial justice, he advised publicly (even as he quietly funded efforts to promote it), would have to wait. Education was the means to a better life economically.

The countrified Booker Washington had a brilliant aristocratic antagonist in Du Bois, a graduate of Fisk University and the first African American to earn a PhD from Harvard. Du Bois, born in Massachusetts in 1868, after slavery, after civil war, and after passage of the Fourteenth Amendment, viewed the notions of Washington with imperious contempt. Raised to regard himself as equal to all, Du Bois demanded higher education with strong academics for capable African Americans. Du Bois believed that elite African Americans, "the Talented Tenth," were the equal of any white and deserved a comparable education, including college. Du Bois believed these educated elites would become the civil rights leaders of their communities.

The Hampton Institute rejected the ideas of Du Bois. Its goal was industrial education. That did not refer to learning to work in a factory, but to being industrious in practical endeavors. At Penn School, it meant learning about farming and homemaking, about health, about finances and debt avoidance. Penn School would no longer teach by rote memorization, but by emphasizing essential principles. It would no longer teach courses to prepare students for higher learning, but would concentrate on teaching agricultural techniques and trades. To the educational historian James Anderson, it is ironic that the "ideological and programmatic challenge to the ex-slaves' conception of universal schooling and social progress was conceived and nurtured by a Yankee, Samuel Chapman Armstrong, and a former slave, Booker T. Washington."[90] The new view, indeed, came to be seen as refuting the idea that education should foster freedom.

By the end of the 1890s, most of the fifty or so programs launched as part of the Port Royal Experiment had been disbanded. Penn School, however, survived. Its role changed as it moved into the next century, but that Penn School persevered, and even expanded and flourished, was nothing short of astonishing.

CHAPTER THREE

Penn Normal, Industrial, and Agricultural School

When Laura Towne arranged for the future of Penn under the leadership of the Hampton Institute and Hollis Burke Frissell, she also petitioned the state for a charter for the school, and South Carolina chartered Penn School in 1901. Thus began a new phase of education on St. Helena Island and a new name for Penn School: the Penn Normal, Industrial, and Agricultural School.

As Penn School moved into the twentieth century, it sought expertise and corporate financial backing. As a first step, Frissell created a board of trustees. He appointed northern men and women, all religious, public-minded Republicans and progressive philanthropists—and all white. Among them were Francis R. Cope Jr., whose family had been instrumental earlier in raising funds to assist Penn; George Foster Peabody, a noted philanthropist; Henry Wilder Foote, a Unitarian minister from Boston; L. Hollingsworth Wood, a Quaker and leader in the National Urban League; Isabella Curtis, the school's publicist in Massachusetts; and Harold Evans, its banker in Philadelphia. Alfred Collins Maule, another member of the board, wrote with patronizing condescension in his fund-raising letter that Penn School would "raise a pathetically ignorant people to intelligent service for others and for their country."[1]

The new board moved in the Hampton-Tuskegee direction with its choices of several new employees, all African American, all graduates of Hampton. P. W. Dawkins, the vice president of Kittrell College in North Carolina and president of the High Point chapter of the Armstrong League Association for graduates of Hampton and Tuskegee, became the superintendent of industries at Penn School in the fall of 1901.[2] A practical man, he published a pamphlet entitled *St. Helena Island Don'ts*, which read like an excerpt from Benjamin Franklin's writings: "Don't let merchants and agents talk you into buying what you don't need . . . don't make debts you cannot pay . . . don't keep your children out of school."[3] His wife, Emma Dawkins, joined the staff to teach sewing and cooking. She also instituted a new concept: the community class, for the women on St. Helena. Also hired were Mr. and Mrs. Stephens, both from Hampton, he to teach carpentry and she to teach nursing.[4] P. W. Dawkins set to work immediately to organize the farmers on St. Helena into a farmers' conference, modeled after Booker T. Washington's Tuskegee Conference. Several items in the new constitution of the St. Helena farmers' conference reflect the mission of the new Penn School. Penn would strive to rectify the structure of a system that worked against the farmers: "To abolish and do away with the mortgage system just as rapidly as possible." Penn would discourage debt and encourage self-sufficiency in the food supply: "To raise our food supplies, such as corn, potatoes, syrup, peas, hogs, chickens, etc., at home rather than go into debt for them at the store." And Penn would promote moral living: "To stop throwing our time and money away on Saturday by standing around towns, drinking and disgracing ourselves in many other ways."[5] And the new farmers' conference would not allow any political discussions.[6] This was a sharp turn away from the abolitionist, egalitarian legacy of Towne and the other founders of Penn School.

To further the new mission of the school, the board of trustees wanted new leadership. Ellen Murray and her assistant, Alice Lathrop, were not interested in the Hampton-Tuskegee mission. P. W. Dawkins was a strong candidate. He had won over many of the farmers on St. Helena; one of them wrote to Francis Cope: "We Hail Bro P. W. Dawkins as our Booker T. Washington of St. Helena and intend to stay by him as the tick stay on the cow back."[7] Some on the Penn School Board of Trustees, Robert Jenks and Francis Cope, agreed.[8] Frissell, however, did not think an African American was capable of handling such responsibility. According to Jenks, Frissell felt "that Mr. Dawkins was not competent to meet the difficulties of the situation" and that in fact no "negro could make a success out of the plan which we proposed."[9] In a letter dated two days later, Jenks had more to say about Frissell's opinion on this issue: "He believes that we can accomplish very much more by keeping the School under white control." Jenks knew he was touching on a sensitive matter when he wrote, "Dr. Frissell said confidentially that even at Tuskegee under Mr. Washington himself the defects of negro control are very apparent. This remark you will not repeat to any one."[10] Frissell prevailed, and Dawkins chose to return to Kittrell College, where he served as president.

Although careful to recognize the role that Ellen Murray had played at Penn, and would continue to play until her death, Frissell chose as successors to her and Towne two northern white women who would lead Penn over the next four decades. He found at Hampton two effective teachers, Rossa Belle Cooley (1873–1949) and Frances Butler. Butler died of malaria within three weeks of her arrival at St. Helena; Grace Bigelow House, another teacher from Hampton, became Cooley's associate at Penn for the next forty years.[11]

Cooley, who had graduated from Vassar College in 1893, moved to St. Helena Island in 1904, and Grace House arrived a year later.[12] Until Murray's death in 1908, both served as teachers rather than as principal and assistant principal. Cooley and House formed a lasting friendship and partnership similar in many ways to that of Laura Towne and Ellen Murray. Cooley and House were dedicated and remarkable women. Cooley was dynamic, self-assured, and seemingly indefatigable. Paul U. Kellogg, editor of *Survey* magazine, described her as "the outstanding interpreter both of the school and of the islanders." He likewise praised her sense of mission: "She reveals Penn's impact on the island life not as a gesture of paternalism but as an overture of leadership to release nascent forces for self-development and group initiative."[13]

Grace Bigelow House (1877–1965), the daughter of a missionary, was born in the Ottoman Empire (in present-day Bulgaria). She began her formal education at the Mission School for Girls in Constantinople and completed her degree at Columbia University's Teachers College in New York.[14] While she did not overlap with John Dewey's tenure at Columbia, she shared the Teachers College mission of progressive, practical education.[15] After graduation, House worked at Hampton. She was sweet, poetic, and idealistic, known for her spirituality and religious writings. Though shy, she was able to give presentations when Cooley was not available.[16]

When Cooley first visited Penn School, she was taken aback by the lamentably inadequate facilities: "spaces painted black served as blackboards; a few old maps; a globe in Miss Murray's room; rough desks made to seat two but often holding four; some book cupboards; and that was all."[17] Books and teaching materials were scarce or nonexistent, and classrooms had very little in the way of writing materials, notebooks, or paper. Even more distressing to her, lessons were unrelated to the life and future of the pupils. They learned by rote, even the youngest ones reeling off historical facts, such as the names of American presidents, historic dates, and places where battles were fought, without associating them to their lives in any way. Attending one class in geography, during which the teacher explained that the pupils were learning all about South Carolina, where they lived, Cooley observed that they were being told the meaning of symbols on maps, but not about how they related to places in their own lives. Her assessment was that much of the learning process—covering people, places, and things—was aimed at providing answers to examination questions.[18] Having taught at the Hampton Institute, where the aim was to teach students how to succeed in the real world, she could see a formidable challenge ahead for her in the meagerly resourced classrooms of Penn School.

Both Cooley and House brought to the school their unswerving faith, zeal, and dedication to service. With a strong belief in emphasizing life skills and moral living, they outlined a plan of action. The first step was "to get out into the community" to ascertain the conditions and needs of the people.[19] They made plans to improve school-community relationships and to extend their activities to the entire island. They threw themselves into the challenge. Although neither woman had ridden a horse, they boldly mounted school horses for a ride around the area.[20]

Cooley and House brought the progressive approach to Penn. Students began to spend a considerable amount of time outside the classroom, doing fieldwork related to the subject at hand. For example, students in a mathematics class were told to close their books and follow their teacher out into a nearby field. There, they used mathematical formulas to mark off measurements from one place to another and then used geometry to subdivide the field.

In like manner, classes in nature and the sciences ventured into field and for-est or along the coast to make scientific observations in the world. Although Penn School had from its earliest years provided classes in carpentry, metalwork-ing, and crafts, the emphasis was more on maintaining the buildings, grounds, and facilities than on teaching a vocation. Under Cooley and House, however, Penn saw a proliferation of courses in such subjects as wheelwrighting, harness making, cobbling, mechanics, teaching, and other callings that could become careers. Change was hard for some used to the older ways; some teachers were dismayed when one of the smaller buildings, which had been used as a print shop, was changed. Cooley wrote, "But I can understand how hard it must have been for the older teachers when we urged that printing be given up entirely, as it was a trade that failed to fit into the farmer's life; and we needed that little house for the carpenters. So it became our first Industrial building."[21]

To cement relationships between school and community, Cooley and House established a visitation program, not only themselves calling on parents but also requiring all teachers to visit the homes of their students at least twice a year. Towne and Murray had enjoyed pleasant relationships with local families, but much more informally. The new program was established on the principle that teachers who took an interest in families in their homes were greatly strengthened in their ability to cement a bond with the sons and daughters in the classroom. Cooley and House visited teachers in the island's public schools and churches, eventually establishing a teacher's institute that brought in guest speakers from Hampton and other institutions of higher learning. House and Cooley thus pro-moted Penn's objectives and influence to groups with no direct interest in the school itself. In a further effort to reach out to the community of St. Helena, the two educators opened the doors of the Penn campus to townspeople for educa-tional events and made sure that their students had plenty of opportunities to work on repair projects with residents of the island.

Another Cooley-House change was the addition of buildings where a lim-ited number of older students could live and board on campus. Food for the students was local—rice, yams, potatoes, and fish—and the cook of the day was usually a female student in training. For the most part, the dining facilities and kitchens were simple, but Penn School added another dimension to the living-learning curriculum: teaching good manners and proper housekeeping, sometimes with the idea that the students would be domestic workers in white households. Eleanor Barnwell, a former student, remembered that the teachers' dining room "was very formal because some of the students, in particular the girls, would go North and do domestic work in the summer": "It was so formal that before dessert you always brought in the finger bowl and you would have to go out and maybe pick rose petals to drop in the center of the finger bowl in the water."[22] Within two years of Cooley's arrival, Penn had nineteen boarders and a "Boarding Department" headed by an African American staff member named Rosetta Mason, whose main duty was to see that her charges formed habits of industry, orderliness, punctuality, and cleanliness.[23]

In 1908, Cooley hired as secretary Elizabeth Bampfield, who as a youngster had been a student of Charlotte Forten at the Brick Church. This daughter of Robert Smalls had taken her deceased husband's job as postmaster of Beaufort in 1899, but South Carolina politics in 1908 would not allow an African American to hold the post.[24] Penn School was always proud to hire its own students, knowing they were well educated.

P. W. Dawkins, who had instituted agricultural education at Penn, was replaced by Joshua Blanton, another Hampton graduate. From his start in 1906, Blanton was well liked on St. Helena, and he married another favorite at Penn School, a teacher named Linnie Lumpkins, also educated at Hampton. The Blantons moved into a house on the Penn campus and held a house blessing, one of the religious traditions of the St. Helena community.[25] Joshua Blanton was later promoted to superintendent at Penn, and he also served as governmental farm demonstration agent for Beaufort County from 1907 to 1912.[26] The philosophy at Penn School was new to St. Helena: life in the community was based on farming, and so education must be based on farming. Cooley wrote, "Farming did not connect very well with the ideas on education held on St. Helena Island at the time of our coming." At one point she took her students outside "so they might trace the differences in root systems in the soil as well as on the painted blackboards." As a result, "corn roots and cotton roots became interesting when only cube roots had held sway for over forty years."[27] The new school farm did not reach the entire community, so teachers encouraged students to cultivate their own "home acres." Working in conjunction with Clemson University, the white land grant college founded in 1889, students learned the proper diversification of crops and new farming techniques. They kept careful records in order to show the difference between old and new methods; Cooley noted, "We thank Clemson, South Carolina's State Agricultural College, for this idea."[28] The home acres demonstrated the benefits of the new ways of farming by producing much better yields. Cooley wrote, "These home acres have become our best classrooms."[29]

The school continued to develop. Cooley spearheaded fund-raising drives, and Penn constructed several new units, including the Cope Industrial Building. Penn School was also instrumental in the creation of the Cooperative Society, which brought together merchants and the people. One of the projects of this new society was to dig ditches. At first reluctant because of the association of ditch digging with slavery, the members eventually took on the task with a will, even paying an extra tax to enable the excavation of more ditches. They cleared and dug twenty-eight miles of ditches; malaria went down, and crop production went up.[30]

Health concerns were always rife on the island. Local scourges included malaria and typhoid. Rural living meant accidents, snakebites, and other ailments. As Towne had done, Cooley used her medical training when she arrived. The island rejoiced in 1906 at the arrival of Dr. York Bailey, a Penn School graduate who had earned his medical degree at Howard University and who, like other devoted Penn School graduates, came back to St. Helena to work in the community.[31] The economy was not based on cash, so during his early years of practice on the island, Bailey was paid "with corn, peas, chickens, ducks or turkeys, which he sold in Beaufort."[32] For many years, Bailey "was the mainstay of the health program" at Penn School.[33] In 1908, Penn employed its own practical nurse to help and to teach first-aid classes.

One of the programs at Penn School that made a large improvement in the lives of the islanders, including a drastic reduction in infant mortality, was the midwife program. Cooley pointed out that this benefit was not one brought in by whites, but had been traditional on the island: "It must not be supposed that better health has been brought to the community solely by 'foreigners,' as all strangers are called on the Island. . . . There has always been that group of women who have been the obstetrical nurses."[34] As society became more complicated and regulated, these women were required to modernize their procedures.[35] The issuance of birth certificates had been haphazard throughout rural America, and when South Carolina passed regulations in 1915 that births had to be recorded systematically and that midwives had to be duly certified, Penn School was at the forefront. The women, now in uniforms, were proud of their accomplishments. As Cooley put it: "The 'midders' work, now recognized by the state, had become a profession."[36] Filling roles beyond obstretrical, these women were actively involved in public health campaigns such as a "Clean-up Week."[37]

In 1912, Penn School celebrated its fiftieth anniversary. The occasion attracted many visitors of note. In a tribute to the full citizenship rights enjoyed by African Americans after the war, a remembrance that lingered with the St. Helena population even if not with northern whites, guests included some of the country's most famous, albeit aging abolitionists: William Channing Gannett, Harriet Ware, Helen Philbrick, Ray Stannard Baker (a prominent editor and journalist), and Robert Smalls.[38] A key event was the parade of veterans of the First South Carolina Volunteers, the first regiment of black soldiers to serve in the U.S. Army, followed by hundreds of Penn School students and alumni and the singing of John Greenleaf Whittier's "St. Helena Hymn," followed by "My Country 'tis of Thee," both songs meaningful to the history of Penn School.[39]

Penn School continued to thrive. During the 1920s the school buildings were in good condition and able to accommodate both residential and day students. The carpentry department, working with the domestic science department, opened Penn facilities for islanders' use, and the staff and more advanced pupils helped islanders improve their own houses and living quarters. Penn held regular demonstrations of carpentry and construction, often using its own buildings as examples of home design. A pupil in the fifth grade wrote that as part of his weekly assignment to improve his own home, he applied wallpaper, oiled floors, cleaned the stable, made a shelter for the horse cart, laid a flagstone path, and constructed a woodpile and kindling bin.[40] Students and instructors in the farming and earth science departments often worked in agricultural extension, tackling specific assignments to improve gardens, lawns, shrubbery, and fruit-bearing trees.

In 1922, the people of Penn decided to enter the house of one of their teachers in the national "Better Homes Program." Given the stiff competition from 960 other communities, white and black, the endeavor was an immense undertaking. Demonstrating community organization and local democracy at work, the people of St. Helena formed committees to organize the house's surroundings, equipment, furnishing, decorating, and budget, as well as the reception of visitors and a program of events. At the end of the judging, the school received a letter from the secretary of commerce, Herbert Hoover, to announce that Penn had won third prize.[41] Two years later, one of the island houses nearby, in poor condition, was used by the students as a class demonstration project. They replaced shingles, reconstructed the chimney bricks, removed and replaced rotten siding, added a tabby walk (made of oyster shells, sand, and limestone), straightened the porch posts and railings, and gave the exterior a new coat of paint and whitewash. Again, they entered their work in the competition, but this time the contest was limited. After the first year, at the insistence of white southerners, the "Better Homes" competition became segregated. Quite likely, this was because St. Helena's entry had finished ahead of white houses. Nevertheless, the people of St. Helena won a prize in the segregated competition.

On a later trip to Washington, D.C., Grace House called on then first lady, Lou Henry Hoover, and told her about Penn School and the Better Homes Program. Mrs. Hoover asked House to send the school her regards, and in response the community declared her to be "First Lady of the Island, and First Lady of the Church too!" When these sentiments were sent on to Mrs. Hoover, she wrote to Penn School, thanking it for conferring such "titles" upon her.[42] St. Helena was never able to exhibit houses that were up to the standard of middle-class white urban homes: indoor plumbing was rare, let alone a real bathtub; cooking was not on an electric range; electricity did not come to St. Helena until after World

War II. Nevertheless, the prizes fostered community pride on St. Helena and encouraged home improvements and new construction.[43]

Building was booming on campus as well. The centerpiece was construction of the Frissell Memorial Community Building in 1925. The building held a library that "the students loved and used," meetings rooms for small groups, and a large central room for chapel services and community sings.[44] According to Cooley, "Surely there could not be a more beautiful memorial to Hollis Burke Frissell, made possible by the gifts of his friends of both races."[45]

By the end of the 1920s, Cooley and House could see steady growth on campus. Penn School offered five different subject areas for the female students: housekeeping, which included cleaning, cooking, canning and preserving; home management, with courses in furnishing, nutrition, and household accounting; gardening; sewing and millinery; and library science, which required service in the school library. On the high school level, Penn offered practical teaching with opportunities for students in twelfth grade to instruct small classes at some of the public schools on St. Helena. For the male students, there were twelve subject curricula to pursue: farm fields and orchards, forestry and timbering operations, dairy organization and maintenance, livestock selection and care, gardening, roads and grounds, native island basketry, blacksmithing and wheelwrighting, carpentry, cobbling, harness making and upholstery, and machine operation and repairing.[46] The making of sweetgrass baskets continued an African heritage, and as in Africa, basket making was a masculine domain.

Penn School taught these subjects as skills, not mundane labor. Blacksmithing, for example, went beyond simply the making and application of horseshoes; many of the students learned how to forge works of iron that were more closely related to the field of the fine arts. Carpentry was also carried far beyond working with lumber and nails, resulting in fine cabinetry and the laying of quality hardwood floors.

Remembering his school days, Robert Middleton, who graduated from Penn School in 1945, said that many of the classes, as well as vespers, were coeducational. But only boys were taught trades, and only girls learned laundry, cooking, and canning. His typical day was as follows:

7:00 am breakfast: eggs, grits, sometimes fish

Work in shops until 9:00

9:00 am until 4:00: classes with a break for dinner at noon:
    cornbread and beans

4:00 until 5:00: work in shops

5:00 pm: get ready for dinner

6:00 dinner: maybe chicken and greens from garden

7:00 pm: vespers

8:00–10:00 pm: study hall

10:00 pm: taps[47]

Although St. Helena Island was a remote sea island, and although island transportation was by horse and carriage over bumpy dirt roads that were very dusty in the dry seasons and quagmires of mud after heavy rains, the school attracted many visitors. They came to enjoy the beautiful and charming locale, a place to be refreshed, to be close to nature and find peace of mind.[48] Most visitors were interested in educational reform for blacks. Some thought of Penn as a laboratory for the study of racial relationships; others saw it as a community center. Missionaries and scholars from Africa were particularly attracted to Penn. Nicholas George Julius Ballanta, a native of Sierra Leone, visited Penn in 1926 when he was studying "Negro music" in Africa and the United States. He received funding for his study from George Foster Peabody, honorary president of the Penn School board. Ballanta traced the roots of black American music to Africa. In the three weeks he spent at Penn School, Ballanta recorded 103 spirituals.[49]

Cooley and House, who were good at public relations, initiated programs to attract learned authorities to St. Helena; educators, sociologists, authors, editors, artists, ministers, and diplomats came. Many of the visitors, upon returning to their hometowns and institutions, spread the word about this unique school in the sea islands.

One visitor wrote to Cooley, "The work you are doing was indeed a revelation to me. . . . I cannot help feeling what deep personal satisfaction you two must feel in knowing that your life and work means so much in the lives of those people who need what you are striving to give them."[50] Another wrote, "It was like going to a foreign country, into a new language, a new economic life, a new mental attitude and a new folk-lore." He recommended to Cooley and House: "Transcribe all you can of this civilization in which you live—its religion, its superstitions, its folk-lore, its economic life such as methods of work and of living, everything in fact. There are few people so situated as you are in the midst of the older negro life unchanged in many ways by the habits of the city."[51] A particularly influential visitor was Thomas Jesse Jones, director of the Phelps-Stokes Fund and a former teacher at the Hampton Institute. Like many well-intentioned whites during this period, Jones continued to believe in white supremacy; he supported industrial, not academic, education for African Americans.[52] His interest in industrial education led to his work *Negro Education* (1917), subtitled *A Study of the Private and Higher Schools for Colored People in the United States.*[53] Jones was interested in Penn School's programs of health, agriculture, vocational trades, and spirituality for African Americans, and he went on to spread the school's message and techniques across Africa.[54]

Another influential visitor was Mabel Carney, a professor at Teachers College, Columbia University. Carney was interested in rural education and the connections between St. Helena and Africa. She wrote to Grace House, "Everywhere I go up the length and breadth of the whole continent of Africa, *everyone* knows of you and Miss Cooley and Penn School."[55] At Teachers College, Carney taught the courses Negro Education and Race Relations and The Education of Negroes in the United States. As Carney began working with African American leaders such as Mary McLeod Bethune, E. Franklin Frazier, and W. E. B. Du Bois, she began to see the connection between the typical educational model for African Americans and the maintenance of segregation and subservience.[56] Well pleased with Penn School and its approach to education, Carney used Penn as a training school for her students at Columbia. Two such students, however, Africans who came to the United States in the 1930s with support from the Phelps-Stokes Fund to study at industrial schools in the South, found the program of study at Penn School and at Tuskegee Institute too rudimentary.[57]

Carney was also a leader of the country life movement.[58] She wanted rural life to be more fulfilling to farming communities, a goal that fit well with the program of Penn School.[59] That goal coincided with another: keeping people on the farm and out of the city. Among the problems of rural living—reduced soil fertility, the need to conserve natural resources, flooding—Carney found the "most serious" crisis to be "the silent but startling migration of the rural population to towns and cities."[60] Many whites living in northern cities did not want African American neighbors. Other whites, more well meaning, felt that city life was less fulfilling and more sinful than country living.[61] According to Cooley, for example, syphilis was not an island problem until interaction with the city increased: "All the cases discovered were traced to city life, and this added fuel to our fire of enthusiasm to conserve the rural life on the Island and build it up so that it should offer a future for our boys and girls."[62] At one of Penn's first Farmers' Fairs, Cooley asked Moses Dudley, a Penn School graduate, to survey a number of plantations and report on the young people who had left the island. His account was brief and to the point: "I might say one third are still in the North; one third come back damaged; one third come back in their coffins, no good to anybody."[63] Referring back to the days of Laura Towne, Cooley remarked that when young people preferred to stay on St. Helena and work on the land, "there we feel that the old Penn School bell has proclaimed a new liberty."[64] Nevertheless, like the country life movement, Penn School was falling out of step with a country growing more urbanized and industrialized.

People left St. Helena for many different reasons. Late in the summer of 1911, another hurricane caused extensive damage: "A great storm in 1911 destroyed homes and crops and grim poverty had to be endured until the new crop."[65] Damage to the Penn campus was heavy, but insignificant compared with that suffered by the homes and businesses of people on the island, especially along its shores, where many small fishing boats, wharves, and fisheries were either wiped out or damaged beyond practical repair. The Red Cross came to offer some relief, but the merchants in Beaufort decided that St. Helena did not need help: "To call for the Red Cross help will advertise to the outside world that we are a people who are either improvident or who are not of sufficient stamina to meet adversity."[66] Penn School organized relief work, and the people of St. Helena reached out to help those worse off. Nevertheless, the needs were almost overwhelming.

The tendency of Beaufort whites to denigrate the islanders escalated during World War I. During the war, the draft board in Beaufort did not exempt Penn teachers, failing to value the importance of Penn School teachers to the community and even to the war effort through the production of food. Several residents were arrested for draft evasion simply because mail service on the island was haphazard and they did not receive notices to report. Nevertheless, patriotism abounded. Soldiers from the island included fifty-five former students and fourteen Penn graduates and teachers. The men who served in World War I wrote home about how much they appreciated their education at Penn and what a difference it made in their lives.[67]

Most devastating for the St. Helena community was the boll weevil. Cooley wrote, "The first boll weevil year, 1919, will long be remembered. When the people woke up to find they had lost three-fourth of their crop."[68] The loss of cotton, the most important crop on St. Helena, would have destroyed the economy, but financial problems were partly alleviated by help from the St. Helena Cooperative Society, which Penn School established in 1912 to arrange loans for those in need. The determined Cooley used the opportunity presented by the boll weevil to encourage local farmers to improve their farming techniques. To qualify for a loan, borrowers had to agree to the following: rotation of the major commercial crops; the planting of corn, peas, and potatoes for home and family use; and properly measured rows. The Cooperative Society also selected and sold at a discount appropriate kinds of fertilizers to discourage monoculture farming and prevent a recurrence of the cotton tragedy. Nevertheless, some people whose families had lived on St. Helena as far back as could be remembered left the island.

The declining population and the departure of many of the school's graduates who had been counted on to strengthen the community were a blow. The continuation of Penn School in such difficult circumstances owed much to Cooley. Her description of some of her daily activities showed a hectic schedule:

Between nursing visits and calls, there was the inspection of the new dormitory we were building; a discussion perhaps with the white contractor (today our buildings are altogether the work of Negro builders) as to the right place to put the thimble in the chimney; then a visit to the barn and a chance to learn more about mules and horses and boys; then class-room questions; then accounts—and how I hated the week that brought them around, for when they did balance they showed a debit and the need of my stopping the much more interesting work I was doing to get to work on "appealing" letters.[69]

In addition to attending to her numerous teaching and administrative duties, Cooley was a natural in the field of public relations, devoting much of her time to obtaining greater public recognition of the school and its many achievements. She made a special effort to let the public know more about the talents of the students, for example, by organizing trips to other parts of the state by the glee club or by submitting the paintings of her students to art competitions. She studied southern newspapers and periodicals, becoming acquainted with their editors and ensuring that they received news releases relating to school functions and programs. Starting in 1923, she wrote a series of articles for *Survey Graphic*, whose editor, Paul Kellogg, wrote the introduction to her book *School Acres: An Adventure in Rural Education*. Another notable achievement was a series she wrote for David Mebane, editor of the *New Republic*, which was later published by the magazine as a book, *Homes of the Freed*. In her books, Cooley addressed an audience of whites and, she hoped, white contributors. She answered critics who were opposed to any education for African Americans. She described the educational philosophies and methods that she and House were following at Penn School, and the progress the students were making.

The success of Penn School depended upon collaboration. It worked with state programs to develop scientific farming methods, the credit cooperative for local farmers, county teacher-training programs, improved child-care facilities, and outreach programs in such diverse activities as medicine, religion, and culture. The school continued its collaboration with Clemson's extension services on agricultural endeavors and on the creation of the St. Helena Credit Union.[70] On teacher accreditation, Penn School worked with South Carolina State at Orangeburg, the black land grant college founded in 1896.[71]

An early collaboration was with the YWCA and YMCA, two organizations that, unusually for the time, advocated equality in race relations (although the "Y" itself at that time was still segregated in most places). Penn School sponsored discussion groups for whites and blacks, rare in South Carolina or anywhere else in the southern United States. They invited St. Helena residents to come to campus to hear lectures such as those of Willis D. Weatherford, director of the YMCA and a racial moderate. Both Cooley and House offered their services and courses of instruction to the YMCA when it began sponsoring conferences for college students at Montreat, North Carolina. These began with discussions of international and domestic affairs, but in 1910 broke new ground by offering a seminar on African American problems and relationships. At that time, more than one-third of the white student delegates at the conference enrolled in the seminar and engaged in discussions of racial problems with real interest and no hesitancy about expressing opinions or listening to those who differed. As a result, Cooley and House signed up as teachers at Montreat each summer, focusing on such courses as Racial Work in Rural Communities and Negro Advancement. They also spoke at other seminars throughout the South, hosting open discussions about the problems of education in African American communities and often bringing Penn students with them, which integrated the seminars.

In the late 1920s, the University of North Carolina began a relationship with Penn that continues to be strong. In 1926, Thomas Jackson Woofter and his team from the University of North Carolina Social Research Council and the Institute for Research in the Social Sciences went to Penn School for an extended period to study African Americans and their social development. The team wanted to record observations before completion of a bridge that would give St. Helena direct access to the mainland by way of Lady's Island in 1927—an eventuality all suspected would end the isolation of the St. Helena residents. Woofter, a white sociologist, knew about Penn School because of his work with the Commission for Interracial Cooperation.[72] This commission, founded in 1918 by liberal white southerners along with some black moderates such as Robert Moton, president of Tuskegee after Booker Washington (and half brother of Penn School's Joshua Blanton), worked on alleviating the worst aspects of segregation, such as lynching and white mob violence, but it did not advocate the end of segregation itself.[73] Woofter's group of researchers thought that their study would have "practical applications" in "light of the present widespread desire to improve race relations."[74] Woofter appreciated the homogeneity of the population, its isolation from mainstream commerce and travel, and the relative absence of racial friction. Also important to Woofter was the fact of black land ownership. Woofter credited Penn School with many of the accomplishments on St. Helena; in health matters, for example, the team reported that conditions on St. Helena, and particularly at Penn School, were far superior to those found anywhere else in the rural South. They credited the school with promoting health from the beginning, when Laura Towne used her health education to improve conditions on the island. The Woofter group's health report, and subsequent findings, played an important role in public health policies throughout the region. Their analysis of health was "a contradiction to the theory that the Negro in America is naturally a sickly individual."[75]

Woofter's report reflected the prevailing attitude among white liberal scholars in the late 1920s, during the nadir in American race relations: they wanted what was best for African Americans, but what was best was to be determined by knowledgeable whites. Alluding to the Port Royal Experiment begun in 1862, when the people enslaved on St. Helena broke away from bondage, Woofter concluded, "Thus the experiment on St. Helena throws light upon the question as to what can be accomplished with a group of pure-blooded, isolated Negroes, when they are given the stimulus of intelligent paternalism."[76] A major problem with the report is that all members of Woofter's final team were white. He disregarded the advice of the renowned African American scholar Carter G. Woodson to include African Americans among the lead researchers. Before the study, Woofter asked Woodson to provide some historical perspective, but Woodson declined.[77] Although they were not listed as part of the study team, Woofter also talked with two prominent black scholars at Tuskegee, J. L. Whiting, a psychologist, and G. Lake Imes, a scholar of the African American church. The study team may have employed black enumerators to gather data on island residents, but it is difficult to gauge the extent of this cooperation. None of these scholars or researchers are acknowledged in the work.[78] The lack of diversity is apparent throughout the book; there is a listing in the table of contents headed "World-wide significance in dealing with backward races."[79]

Scholarly interest did not necessarily mean monetary support, and providing help to outside scholars could be a drain on the school's finances. Funding Penn had always been problematic. In the beginning, under Towne and Murray, funding came from northern missionary societies and relief agencies, and often from the Towne family itself. During Reconstruction, charitable giving was largely taken up by foundations. An early philanthropic foundation was the Peabody Education Fund, established in 1867 by George Peabody of Massachusetts, who was moved by the poverty of the postwar South.[80] Although Peabody designated the foundation's proceeds to go to education and to "be distributed among the entire population, without other distinction than their needs and the opportunities of usefulness to them," most of the money went to schools for poor southern whites.[81] The Peabody Board of Trustees was composed of white men, half of them from the North and half from the South, and although they tried to avoid politics, they opposed integrated schools when Congress debated the Civil Rights Act of 1875.[82] By 1900, many southern state governments, as well as many southern white individuals, were opposed to education for African Americans, and certainly were not interested in funding such endeavors. South Carolina governor Cole Blease declared in 1911: "I am opposed to white peoples' taxes being used to educate Negroes . . . In my opinion, when the people of this country began to try to educate the Negro they made a serious and grave mistake, and I fear the worst result is yet to come."[83]

Cooley knew how to get the most out of funding agencies. At first, she worked closely with Frissell, who was known to the boards of such philanthropies as the Slate Fund and the Phelps-Stokes Fund. She got to know men like Julius Rosenwald, the Sears, Roebuck magnate who was a supporter of schools for African Americans. She visited with Wallace Buttrick, president of the General Education Board of the Rockefeller Foundation: "In his high office, overlooking the harbor of New York, we talked it over with that educator of delightful humor and earnestness, full of the desire to help the whole world but able to see the needs of a small island community off the coast of South Carolina."[84] Fund-raising often involved convincing white people to open their pocketbooks, and that meant not challenging their prejudiced notions of race. Over and above all, Penn School attracted financial support because of its emphasis on the need for inculcating Christian principles and promoting character development.

A small but enthusiastic group of contributors was made up of former students who established Penn School Clubs. These students, who had moved to the North, wanted to get together with friends and also to contribute financial aid to the school. In 1928–29 the Penn Club in New York City had about forty members. Meeting monthly at the New York Urban League Building, they donated $150 a year to Penn School.[85]

The Great Depression imposed tremendous financial hardships on Penn. In 1930, enrollment dropped to 262 from 600.[86] In 1931, the school had to cut back on its year-round schedule, discontinue some of the industrial classes, and reduce staff salaries by 5 percent; two years later they were cut by 25 percent. Cooley and House wrote to the board of trustees, Clemson College, and several New Deal government agencies to request funding. Replies brought sympathetic responses but very little in the way of financing. The economic situation on St. Helena Island was desperate; the general store from the 1870s, Macdonald-Wilkins & Keyserling Co., had to close its doors, as did the oyster factory.[87]

Cooley's books were part of the fund-raising efforts. She was in line with white culture during the nadir of U.S. race relations. She did not advocate voting rights; she accepted Jim Crow. Without realizing that southerners were both black and white, Cooley thought that those who lived in the South and those "who may claim Southern friends" could not fail "to sense the reason for the separation between the two races."[88] Nevertheless, Cooley and House advocated basic human dignity for all. Even during the era of segregation and Jim Crow, Penn School was integrated. The principals insisted that all teachers be introduced as *Mr.* or *Miss* and treated like ladies and gentlemen, and they would allow no disparagement of African Americans. The leadership was often patronizing, but it was never segregated or blatantly racist. A cooperative working environment of mutual respect held out hope for race relations at a dark time.

The dedication of Penn School to the education of African Americans was met with degrees of acceptance or rejection. It was more than a matter of good people who favored education versus bad people who did not.[89] How much education was to be afforded African Americans, what kind of education it was to be, who would make decisions regarding it—such questions were answered in many different ways in the white and African American communities. William Mills of the Clemson Agricultural Extension Service supported Penn School for several reasons: "all of us together owe it to the Negro to help him to the best in Education"; "as a Southerner, I realize that the White and Negro Races are inextricably bound together in the South"; and "because of its singularly varied program of community work, Penn School is pioneering a trail in which other schools in other lands are following."[90]

But too many white southerners thought that education for African Americans was a waste of time and money. According to 1930 census records, schools in South Carolina differed markedly in the opportunities offered to African American children and white children. On average, the school term lasted 170 days for white children, but only 115 days for black children, almost three months less. State expenditures were $52.15 per white child and $7.97 per African American child. South Carolina had 46,623 white students and 84,173 African American students enrolled in first grade. The state's refusal to build high schools for African Americans had a precipitous effect: 8,030 whites and 766 blacks enrolled in the eleventh grade.[91]

While many whites across the nation refused to note the lack of democracy and the second-class status forced upon its black citizens, they did notice the growth of fascism in Europe. With the surprise attack on Pearl Harbor on December 7, 1941, the nation was fully committed to winning World War II. The Penn community pitched in with enthusiasm. Nearly two hundred men from St. Helena went to war. Among the many islanders who enlisted was Vashti Tonkins, the English teacher and the leader of the Penn School Girl Scout troop, the first such troop for African American girls south of Baltimore. Tonkins became an officer in the Women's Army Corps.[92]

Since Cooley and House were nearing retirement age, the board of trustees began looking for replacements. Board member Ethel Paine Moors put forward the names of Howard and Alice Kester. The Reverend Howard Kester, born in Virginia, came highly recommended. Influenced by the theologian Reinhold

Niebuhr, Kester believed that the church should be at the forefront in battling the evils of racism and oppression. He was a Presbyterian and Congregational minister, an early organizer of the integrated Southern Tenant Farmers Union, a socialist, a leader in the Fellowship of Southern Churchmen, and an active member of many NAACP efforts, including those to stop lynching. Letters of support came from a number of religious leaders, black and white.[93] Benjamin E. Mays, the president of Morehouse College, thought highly of Kester because of their work together in moving the YMCA toward integration. Kester was fired from his job at the YMCA at Vanderbilt in 1926 because of his work for racial equality.[94] Commonly known as "Buck," Kester pursued a life mission of promoting racial justice within a Christian context.[95] The rest of nation, like the South, was slow to accept calls for equality, but forward-thinking men and women kept pushing. The Hampton Institute was also changing; some faculty members as early as the 1920s had called for racial justice. An African American professor of English, J. Saunders Redding, vociferously challenged segregation.

The Penn School Board of Trustees offered the positions of principal and assistant principal to Howard and Alice Kester on July 8, 1943, and they began their tenure in January 1944. (After Cooley left the school, she lamented, "This retiring business isn't so easy as I always thought it was.") Alice Kester wrote to her sister, "It seems especially fitting to go to such a job now when Christianity and Democracy are being challenged around the world. It is really a part of what we are fighting for."[96] Howard Kester wrote that he had never had a job that "excited me more."[97] In the midst of World War II, Penn School had 274 students and 25 teachers. Teachers received less in salary than other underpaid African American teachers in the state. The school buildings and farm were run-down. The Kesters got right to work, starting with lectures against fascism.

Buck Kester was not the usual paternalistic white leader and was not willing to pander to those not ready for racial change, even if they were major funders. The Kesters and Francis Cope, who had been chairman of the board since 1924, did not agree on the ultimate mission of the school. Cope, like Cooley and House, saw Penn as a way to better the life of the people of St. Helena, a place to teach carpentry, wheelwrighting, canning, sewing, and cobbling. The Kesters wanted to prepare the students and the people of St. Helena for life in a more democratic society. The personal tensions between Cope and Howard Kester deepened, and Cope resigned from the board in 1946. Others in the Penn School community disapproved of the Kesters' work, too, including the African American stalwarts Joshua Blanton and York Bailey.[98] One resident of St. Helena wrote to Kester, "You and your dirty Georgia cracker wife is having Penn School going to hell ... You aint doing nothing but pulling confusion among many good people."[99]

The problems at Penn School went beyond educational philosophy; the school was threatened by an increasing deficit and the lack of a workable plan for the future. Realizing the difficulties, Kester recommended that the board invite Ira DeAugustine Reid, chairman of the Department of Sociology at Atlanta University, to undertake an evaluation of Penn School and to make recommendations for its goals and methods of operation. Reid had strong qualifications: he was a respected African American scholar, both as an educator and as an authority on race relations. He and Howard Kester had been friends since their work on an interracial conference in Birmingham in 1921.

If the trustees expected Reid to issue a positive plan of action, they were in for a shock. On February 19, 1948, his team's report was presented to the board of trustees at its meeting in New York City. Entitled "An Evaluation of the Facilities, Program, and Objectives of the Penn Normal, Industrial and Agricultural School," the report recommended that Penn cease to function as a school. Enrollment in January 1948 was 94 boys and 78 girls; in addition, 173 veterans were registered in the carpentry and auto mechanics courses.[100] Reid and his team wrote that the education provided at Penn School did not warrant its cost: $403 per pupil, when the average cost in Beaufort at that time was $136 for a white student and $38 for an African American student.[101] Penn's teachers, all African American, included six in the elementary school, five at the high school level, and twelve in the industrial and agricultural departments. Five community workers included a librarian, a farm-demonstration agent, a home-demonstration agent, and a nurse. The teachers' salaries were sadly inadequate.[102]

Citing excessive costs, an average curriculum, and the rising quality of public education, Reid concluded, "It seems wise and pertinent that Penn School discontinue its academic program." He credited "the pioneering of Penn School" with improving secondary education for African Americans in the area, but recommended that "Penn School withdraw from the field of academic education at the secondary level."[103] He noted that "the Beaufort County school bus now transports Negro children free of charge from St. Helena to the city high school."[104]

Reid indicated that numerous economic, social, and educational changes had occurred on St. Helena and throughout the South and that the war years had permanently changed the United States.[105] Looking forward, Reid recommended that Penn serve as a community agency to "promote, stimulate and cooperate in programs designed to provide guidance, mobile library service, recreation and social welfare programs and adult education in this area." Penn could also provide a "valuable service" as a place for interracial groups, particularly "agencies and organizations in the region now in need of a meeting place for its white and colored constituents."[106]

While the Reid report was under consideration, Howard and Alice Kester were happy to tender their resignations. Leaving in March 1948, Howard Kester returned to his job at the Fellowship of Southern Churchmen. The Kester years had not been easy, not for them and not for the community. Nevertheless, the Kesters helped St. Helena and the Penn Community look outward.

Whether to accept the Reid evaluation was a critically important decision for the Penn School Board of Trustees. The board itself was in the midst of a changeover. Traditionally, the board was made up of northerners, and it held its meetings in New York or Philadelphia or Boston. Only two members of the board were southerners. J. R. Macdonald, a merchant, had moved to St. Helena Island in the 1870s and become a good friend of Towne and of Penn School.[107] J. Nelson Frierson, a native of Sumter County and a faculty member of the Law School of the University of South Carolina, felt that his life and career should focus on his "opportunity and duty here in South Carolina."[108] The board now included two African Americans; both were college presidents and both owed their places on the board to Howard Kester. They were the renowned educator and president of Morehouse College, Benjamin E. Mays, and the former Penn School teacher and supervisor Joshua Blanton, who had left Penn in 1922 to become president of Vorhees College in Denmark, South Carolina.

In May 1948, the board of trustees accepted the Reid report. On May 6, 1948, the Penn Normal, Industrial, and Agricultural School gave up its academic responsibilities and turned its students over to the public schools. When the local public schools consolidated, the school district leased the school building from Penn. The new principal, an African American named Jonathan Francis, maintained a good relationship with Penn Center.[109] When Penn School closed, St. Helena Island lost its library.[110] As in so many rural areas, a book mobile carried the lending library to the people.

Penn needed a new executive director to implement its new mission, and the board instituted a search that took about eighteen months. The director would be in charge of the new Penn Community Services, Inc.

CHAPTER FOUR

Penn Center and the
Civil Rights Movement

The rebranding of Penn Community Services paralleled the new direction the nation took following World War II as African Americans in South Carolina, throughout the South, and across the nation demanded the rights of citizenship. Penn Center both promoted and reflected the demand for equal rights. A number of iconic leaders of the civil rights movement in the South attended meetings and workshops at Penn Center. The 1950s and 1960s were decades of immense social change. While Penn Center continued its abolitionist legacy, it was no longer led by progressive, paternalistic white northerners. Instead, central to Penn were progressive white southerners willing to work with African Americans to promote racial justice and equality and to dismantle Jim Crow.

In addition to his recommendation that Penn School become Penn Center, Ira Reid mentioned the idea of hiring Courtney Siceloff as the new director of Penn. Siceloff began his tenure in the spring of 1950. Born in Texas, the son of a Methodist minister, as a youth he became involved in the Methodist Student Movement, an organization whose goal was to teach young Christians how to live and apply their faith in the real world. He began college at Southwestern Methodist College in Dallas. When he was drafted into the military during the Second World War, he went to a work camp with other conscientious objectors, especially Quakers. After the war, Siceloff was "anxious to get involved in overseas work." With the American Friends Service Committee, he helped in a retraining program for refugees of the Spanish Civil War. He then returned to the United States and attended Haverford College near Philadelphia, a school founded by Quakers, where he worked with Ira Reid and learned about Penn Center.[1]

Siceloff came to Penn Center with his wife, Elizabeth Taylor Siceloff, who was born in North Carolina and had studied at North Carolina State University in Raleigh. Following college, she worked in Atlanta at the Southern Regional Council (SRC), an organization working to eradicate racism in the South. She went to Finland as a missionary with the American Friends Service Committee. Elizabeth and Courtney met on the steamer back from Europe. They were married that year, and only a few months later began their tenure at Penn Center, starting in the spring of 1950.[2] Both of their children, John and Mary, were born in Beaufort and reared at Penn Center with African American playmates as their best friends.[3]

The Siceloffs came to Penn Center at a time when the islanders were resentful over the closing of Penn School and distrustful of its new direction. The Siceloffs worked diligently to mend the relationship between Penn Center and the people of St. Helena. When islanders formed a local branch of the NAACP and a Saint Helena Community Council, the Siceloffs became involved. Local African Americans' initial resistance to Courtney Siceloff and the new Penn Center changed when he listened attentively to the concerns of the residents and demonstrated that he wanted local African Americans to determine the program needs at Penn. With the advice of the community, Penn continued its training of midwives, opened South Carolina's first day care center for African Americans, and began the Teen Canteen for local teenagers. Providing for a community health care clinic required more work. Siceloff made two strategic hires. First, in 1961, he hired Thomas Barnwell, an active leader in the Hilton Head NAACP, as director of community development. Barnwell was the first African American professional manager at the new Penn Center. Joseph McDomick joined the staff in 1964 and focused on islanders' self-help. McDomick, originally from West Feliciana Parish in Louisiana, had learned of Penn Center after a stint in Brazil with the Peace Corps. A Peace Corps brochure advertised the position at Penn.

With funding from the Field Foundation (Marshall Field), Siceloff sent Barnwell and McDomick to Puerto Rico to study the possibilities of community organization, and they discovered how community activism could contribute to the creation of health clinics. Working closely with medical professionals in the St. Helena area, they were instrumental in the creation of the new Beaufort-Jasper Comprehensive Health Services, a satellite of which was located at Penn Center. The clinic harked back to early days of Penn's role in health concerns on the island. The clinic became a "signature program" and a model for similar efforts in other areas.[4]

In an article celebrating the centennial of Penn, the North Carolina Mutual Life Insurance Company described Barnwell: "Inasmuch as he was born on the islands and is well-known among the residents, he has been able to inspire and maintain their confidence and spirited pride." In his work as the director of the Beaufort County Pilot Project in 1961, he helped the people build privies and informed islanders about voting, civil service jobs, and rural home loans.[5]

When the Siceloffs listened to the islanders' concerns, it marked a break with practices dating to Penn's origins. Penn's founders believed the local black community needed to be "taught" citizenship—in the most condescending terms, to become "civilized" and "Americanized." But the new leaders of Penn, including the Siceloffs and board members, thought otherwise. Instead of teaching citizenship, white leaders learned from the African American community. They came to an understanding of the Christian commitment and theological worldview of southern African Americans before Martin Luther King Jr. brought it to the attention of the world. These southern whites believed that African Americans might save the South and democracy from the sins foisted upon it by white southerners' commitment to segregation and disfranchisement.[6] Penn's new role was "to guide, not determine, the community development." In 1957, Marion Wright, an attorney from Conway, South Carolina, and a member of the Penn Center board of trustees, wrote to white funders, "This is a way you can relate yourself directly to the progress toward eliminating prejudice and fear from men's lives."[7] Penn began taking steps to honor island traditions by interviewing aging islanders and working to preserve the tradition of the praise houses.

In the mid-1950s, Penn Center underwent major renovations to reflect its new direction. The Siceloffs oversaw the remodeling of old buildings into new residences, large conference rooms, and a cafeteria. Penn had spent $18,000 on the renovations by 1956.[8] Penn became the only location in South Carolina—and one of the few anywhere in the South—where interracial organizations could stay overnight in integrated facilities.[9] Wright wrote to each member of the Penn board to "search his mind for contacts" with "organizations which might be interested in meeting at Penn."[10] A group that met there in May 1960 was the Consultation on Human Relations Programming in Rural South Carolina. Penn Center convened the meeting and hosted the group. Attending sociologists and rural economists noted that South Carolina "was one of the more discouraging areas from the standpoint of progress in human relations," being one of four states "with no public school desegregation of any kind at the elementary, secondary, or college level." The group recommended that "a major priority should be given to the need to increase Negro voting and political consciousness." The group also requested better access to libraries, health services, and agricultural extension services, improvements that might encounter "less local resistance to progress" than the "more emotionally-charged area of school desegregation." Attendees acknowledged that Penn Center had "already broken ground with local adult education offerings and other community work."[11]

Throughout the 1960s, Penn Center sponsored and hosted many conferences on aspects of human rights. The SRC, the World Peace Foundation, the NAACP, and many other institutions used Penn as a retreat site and as a pulpit for national and global concerns on human rights.[12] Penn Center had close ties to the SRC, which had been established in 1944 "to respond to African-American grievances and to win support for racial equality from sympathetic white business people." Guy Johnson, its first director, was part of the Woofter team that had studied St. Helena in the 1920s and was a very strong Penn supporter. Elizabeth Siceloff had worked for the SRC before coming to St. Helena Island, and George Mitchell, the next SRC director, was a close friend of hers.[13]

Penn Center was involved with the larger concerns of civil rights activism. Courtney Siceloff served as regional consultant for the U.S. Commission on Civil Rights, Southern Regional Office, and as secretary for the South Carolina Advisory Committee to the Commission on Civil Rights.[14] Siceloff wrote about the difficulty in forming that committee: "Neither the Governor [Hollings] nor the Congressional delegation would cooperate in its formation." South Carolina and Mississippi were the last two states to form state committees, and as Siceloff noted, "The reaction, particularly from elected officials in newspapers over the state, has been generally unfavorable." Before joining the advisory committee, Siceloff consulted with Marion Wright, "who gave his consent."[15]

Siceloff also served on the South Carolina Council on Human Relations (SCCHR) and was elected president of the group in June 1957.[16] In March 1960, the organization stated its defense of the sit-in movement. Sent by Siceloff to the *Columbia (SC) State* newspaper, the statement declared: "These actions express not merely the simple desire of these students to use public lunch counters, but are fundamentally, an understandable protest against continued unequal treatment in . . . public facilities and services."[17] Students committed to civil rights activities were often expelled from college, losing all that their families had conscientiously saved for their education.

White activists battling Jim Crow in South Carolina were often involved with the SCCHR. According to one of those activists, the director of the council, Alice Norwood Spearman, was a charmer; "she schemed, cajoled, and pushed her ideas with sweet reason."[18] Spearman saw how segregation hurt white students as well as African Americans, and she sometimes even wept over white students' misplaced attitudes of racial superiority.[19] Knowing the importance of collaboration, Spearman brought undergraduate and graduate students to biracial meetings in "safe" locales. In an offshoot of the council, more than 200 students from black and white colleges gathered at Penn Center in May 1961 in the immediate aftermath of the first violence against the Freedom Riders. Many students had been appalled at whites' viciousness when John Lewis and others stepped off a Greyhound bus earlier that month in Rock Hill, South Carolina. The Freedom Riders were set upon by a white mob while the local police did nothing to protect them.[20]

At the Penn Center conference, the group formed the Student Council on Human Relations. According to the historian Marcia Synott, "The collegial tone was set by its first president, Charles Joyner." Then a graduate student in history at the University of South Carolina, Joyner "attributed his election to his talent with the guitar and his knowledge of freedom songs."[21] Under the leadership of

Libby Ledeen, who became the council's program director, Penn Center became the group's meeting place over the next several years. The council sponsored integrated meetings and workshops and held "stay-ins" at Penn Center in the early to mid–1960s. In December 1962 the council invited Harvey Gantt, who was preparing for his enrollment in Clemson University in January 1963. Gantt was the first student to integrate any school in South Carolina, and as Ledeen reported, the council worked with Clemson students to make sure that "friendship and genuine acceptance" were a "natural and normal part of The Clemson Story."[22]

Another group that held meetings at Penn Center over the years was CORE, the Congress of Racial Equality, founded in Chicago in 1942. CORE held its national convention at Penn in June 1958.[23] The CORE activist David Dennis wrote that his relationship with Penn began in 1962, when he "attended a voter registration training session as a Field Secretary for CORE"; that relationship has continued through the present day.[24] Among other interracial groups that gathered at Penn Center because they needed a safe place to meet were the Baha'i, members of a religious movement that opposed segregation.

In the early years of Penn School, white South Carolinians had been willing to accept its role in the area because "its benign image as a project of white Yankee spinsters helping the poor island blacks helped to keep the suspicious eye of segregation turned the other way."[25] That changed in the mid-1950s. In a 1985 interview, Siceloff explained the white community's changing relationship with Penn Center. He said that after the school closed:

> We began trying to see it first as a community organization. But in '55 the decision had been made that we would make this available for integrated groups and this was in time for the Supreme Court Decision and we brought an AFC (American Friends Committee) group down there. That changed the whole attitude in the white community toward what we were doing. Before, it had been a black operation which they could tolerate for a hundred years. These northern ladies and so forth. It was the only place of its kind where we could stay integrated and stay overnight.[26]

College students had come to Penn Center for work camps and service projects before, but over Easter weekend of 1954, Penn hosted its first interracial camp for South Carolina college students.[27] This was only weeks before the rise of white massive resistance following the Supreme Court ruling in *Brown v. Board of Education*. That weekend, twenty-five students came to Penn from the black colleges of Allen University, Benedict College, and South Carolina State University and from the all-white University of South Carolina and the Citadel. During their time together, the students broke down racial barriers. Following the *Brown* decision, more groups of young people came to Penn, even as racial tensions across the South intensified. During a work camp in the summer of 1955, white Quaker students from northern universities and local black residents worked together for eight weeks. After a particularly hot day, Siceloff took several of the campers to nearby Hilton Head Island, which was not yet a posh beach resort. While the interracial group enjoyed the beach together, a highway department official observed them. He stopped Siceloff's truck and informed him that in the future his group would have to use the "colored" beach.[28]

After that beach incident, white residents in the area began to look distrustfully at the Siceloffs and at Penn Center.[29] In the autumn of 1957, the University of South Carolina's YMCA-YWCA planned a retreat at Penn. Although the Y occasionally hosted integrated retreats, this particular one was planned for whites only. Still, when the *Charleston News and Courier* ran an article about the retreat, white residents, believing the meeting would be integrated, signed petitions against the retreat and complained to the president of the university. In the face of such opposition, the Y canceled the retreat. In trying to find out where the opposition had originated, Siceloff found that "the letter of protest was at the County office building, in the hands of a member of the citizens' council." White citizens' councils throughout the South opposed integration. Siceloff noted that the leadership of this group did not come from Beaufort, but from "some ten miles away"; the group had "not been able to draw leading Beaufort people." Siceloff noted that Penn's determination to be a place of refuge for interracial groups was undiminished: "Rather than curtailing our activities in this respect, it teaches us another valuable lesson about the type of publicity we are to use, and particularly the timing." The Siceloffs quoted a letter they had received from Koinonia, an integrated religious organization founded in 1942 by two white

Baptist ministers. Unlike the more isolated Penn Center, Koinonia in Georgia faced continual harassment, including bombings and shootings. Koinonia wrote to the Siceloffs: "Let us all keep the faith together during these troubled times for our nation. Do not despair or become cynical." Calling for perseverance, Koinonia continued, "The Lord God has the whole world in His hands, and His truth shall surely prevail. Stand, therefore, and having done all, stand."[30]

The Ku Klux Klan was not active on St. Helena Island. Siceloff recalled, "Early on there had been a rally on Lady's Island of the Klan, of which Penn was the focus, but . . . we never felt threatened personally."[31] Nevertheless, Penn Center and the Siceloffs came increasingly under white South Carolinians' scrutiny. When Siceloff was named to the South Carolina Advisory Committee to the Commission on Civil Rights, the Charleston affiliate of a national television network asked to interview him. Siceloff thought it would be an opportunity to let others know the good work that Penn Center was doing. Instead, when the episode aired, it was obvious that the station had deliberately distorted what was happening at Penn and taken deliberate jabs at Siceloff, suggesting he was a communist.[32] According to Elizabeth Siceloff, "They said he had been brought in from Texas to head up the Community Services Program. It sounded like he was some sort of dangerous alien. . . . They organized a special meeting of the Klan. The purpose was to expose Courtney as a communist."[33]

In spite of spurious charges of communism and other types of white backlash, grassroots civil rights activities were picking up momentum throughout the South, including on other sea islands. In the early 1950s, on Johns Island, near Charleston, Esau Jenkins drove local African Americans to and from work and used that time to teach the riders to read and write so they could pass the state's literacy tests and vote. Jenkins himself was perhaps the only African American on Johns Island who had registered to vote, and he stressed the importance of voting to his riders.[34] This modest beginning evolved into what Aldon D. Morris, a sociologist of the civil rights movement, proclaimed to be "the most profound contribution of all those made to the emerging civil rights movement," that is, the citizenship schools, in which Penn Center played a critical role.[35] One of the ideas behind the Citizenship Education Program was that the students would begin registration campaigns in their local communities, leading to widespread black registration across the South.

Andrew Young, who in his life was a friend and confidant of Martin Luther King Jr., a member of Congress, a mayor of Atlanta, and an ambassador to the United Nations, wrote in 1996 of the importance of the schools: "I knew that the citizenship schools were laying the foundation for a Southwide movement."[36] He saw the importance of empowering ordinary citizens to register, vote, and change their communities. Students would gain "a sense that people had power and could change things without guns and without money, drawing only on the power in their own souls."[37]

Jenkins's impromptu school attracted the notice of an experienced teacher in Charleston, Septima Clark, and she saw immediately the need for more efforts along those lines. Clark had been a schoolteacher in Charleston until spring 1956, when she was fired for belonging to the NAACP.[38] According to Young, "She wanted the school to be nontraditional, interesting, and aimed specifically toward voter education and the most immediate needs of the people."[39] Clark's cousin Bernice Robinson joined the endeavor. Clark picked Robinson because she was familiar with the sea islands and the local culture and had worked with the NAACP.[40] Moreover, as a beautician, Robinson was not economically dependent on whites, who often fired African Americans for working on civil rights matters. The first citizenship school opened in December 1956 and ran through February 1957, three months in which the agricultural calendar did not demand local blacks' labor in the fields. Robinson, as the first regular teacher of the citizenship school, "based her lessons on questions from the students, assuming correctly that they would learn most quickly what they most wanted to know, whether it had to do with language or counting."[41] The first citizenship schools were so successful in facilitating African American voter registration in Charleston that the Charleston county school board scrutinized areas where African Americans held the majority and, only in those particular areas, changed the structure from electing school-board trustees to appointing them.[42]

In her efforts to expand the citizenship schools, a powerful weapon against voter discrimination, Clark contacted Myles Horton, one of the founders of Highlander Folk School in Tennessee. During the civil rights movement, Highlander, which was founded in 1932 as a training school for social justice, came under white segregationists' scrutiny for its integrationist focus. Rosa Parks, legendary for refusing to give up her seat on a bus in Montgomery, Alabama, had visited Highlander before her famous act, and many others involved in the civil rights movement trained at Highlander in nonviolent direct action. Clark soon joined the Highlander staff and further developed citizenship schools.[43] Through her work with citizenship schools, and especially while recruiting for Highlander, Clark became increasingly aware that poor African Americans knew what they needed and wanted. She thought affluent and educated black leaders could serve as role models, but they had to be willing to listen to others.[44] Young also accepted an offer to join the staff at Highlander in 1961 to run the Citizenship Education Program.[45] Before he could begin at Highlander, however, police raided the facility on false charges of "bootlegging," and the school had to close temporarily.[46] Another home base was needed, and the United Church of Christ took up the mantle. Young's headquarters were located in the administrative offices of the Southern Christian Leadership Conference (SCLC in Atlanta, but he was not under their auspices. The SCLC was Martin Luther King Jr.'s organization, formed after the Montgomery bus boycott of 1955–56, and tended to be hierarchical in its organization. Young was grateful that the citizenship schools were financially independent of the SCLC's budget directors, who from time to time "were upset that I had money."[47]

When looking for a site for the citizenship education program, he narrowed his choices to either the Dorchester Cooperative Center in Georgia, or Penn Center in South Carolina. Young settled on Dorchester, although, depending on where students were coming from, sessions were occasionally at Penn.[48] The program's staff at the SCLC consisted of Young, Clark, Robinson, and Dorothy Cotton, a member of the SCLC executive staff. Although the citizenship schools began at the Dorchester Center, classes were moved to Penn Community Center in 1963. Penn was a more convenient location for students who came from

Virginia and the Carolinas.[49] When setting up the citizenship schools at Penn Center during the fall of 1963, Septima Clark lived in the community.[50]

At Penn Center, the citizenship schools meant that schoolwork was again the order of the day, and the St. Helena community felt reassured that Penn School was, in a sense, still functioning. Throughout the week, morning lessons covered political realities and organizing techniques. Afternoons were more casual, and evenings were given over to filmstrips or discussion. Discussions dealt with civics and citizenship, what those at school referred to as "practical civics." As in the Cooley-House days of practical education, lessons focused on practical reading skills for common reading materials, such as tax forms or job applications. The school added American history to its curriculum, especially African American history. History lessons on Reconstruction included the role that African Americans had played in creating an interracial American democracy before unreconstructed whites upended blacks' political advances and enacted Jim Crow laws. The citizenship schools at Penn Center challenged segregation as being contrary to the constitutional amendments passed during Reconstruction.

In 1964, Young became the executive director of SCLC, and Dorothy Cotton took charge of the Citizenship Education Program. In an interview, Cotton recalled, "Andrew Young thought the training program was the base upon which the whole civil rights movement was built."[51] The schools were so successful that funding was extended, and between 1961 and 1966, over six thousand students were educated by the Citizenship Education Program.[52] According to a scholar of the civil rights movement who interviewed activists "of various persuasions," they all "stated repeatedly that the Citizenship Schools were one of the most effective organizing tools of the movement."[53]

The citizenship school at Penn was aided greatly by Penn's remote location. It was isolated from white segregationists; white residents of the area seldom were aware of the classes taking place there. This was not the case for citizenship schools in other areas of the South. In stark contrast to Penn's peaceful conditions, violence plagued citizenship classes in Mississippi in 1964. Participants in the citizenship schools there faced at a minimum the loss of their jobs, and violence and death in some cases.

Citizenship schools laid a foundation, but numerous others were taking up the banner for civil rights, too. Boycotts continued after the Montgomery bus boycott; sit-ins occurred throughout the South. The campaign to desegregate public facilities in Birmingham, Alabama, led to jail time for Martin Luther King Jr. His "Letter from a Birmingham Jail" (sometimes called "Letter from the Birmingham City Jail" or "Letter from Birmingham Jail"), April 16, 1963, helped articulate the goals and means of the civil rights movement.[54] Other organizations also formed to take up the struggle. SNCC (pronounced "snick"; Student Non-violent Coordinating Committee) was formed in 1960 to organize grassroots activism. SNCC and the SCLC, as well as more established organizations such as CORE, the NAACP, and the Urban League, worked together on the March on Washington in August 1963, in the centennial year of the Emancipation Proclamation. One month later, on Sunday, September 15, 1963, four African American girls died in a bomb blast at the 16th Street Baptist Church in Birmingham, Alabama.

The following year, in March 1964, the SCLC held its first retreat at Penn Center. Penn Center had been recommended to King by Andrew Young.[55] The purpose of the retreat, which fifty delegates from southern states attended, was to organize a series of boycotts and to train local leaders in nonviolent methods of protest. The *Charleston News and Courier* ran an article calling SCLC members "radicals under orders from communist leaders."[56] Segregationists for decades had accused civil rights activists and organizations as being communists or communist sympathizers. The charge was an effective one, since the United States, still in the throes of the Cold War, saw itself as a bulwark against communist advance. Courtney Siceloff contended with a false accusation of being a communist, but the charge was especially serious and hurtful to the residents of St. Helena Island. They saw themselves as God-fearing, loyal, and patriotic citizens, and most were fiercely opposed to atheistic communism. As southern segregationists linked the advocacy of black civil rights with "communist" agitation, those involved in securing racial justice bore the brunt of the malicious allegations. That people persevered despite these claims, which often destroyed a person's career and reputation, spoke of their brave determination.

In December 1964, Martin Luther King Jr. received the Nobel Peace Prize. He accepted the honor, as he put it, "at a moment when 22 million Negroes of the United States of America are engaged in a creative battle to end the long night of racial injustice." Beyond civil rights, King called for human rights: "I have the audacity to believe that peoples everywhere can have three meals a day for their bodies, education and culture for their minds, and dignity, equality and freedom for their spirits."[57]

Over the next four years, the SCLC held four more retreats at Penn Center, in September 1965, November 1966, May 1967, and November 1967. During that period, the SCLC was plagued by internal conflicts about the direction of the civil rights movement and the organization's role in it. The retreats provided a place where the SCLC could address the serious problems it faced, but were also intended to refresh the staff. In addition to planning sessions, retreats included meals, philosophical discussions, and relaxation. Sing-alongs relieved tensions. And King always spoke. SCLC staff members stayed in the Benezet House (a former residence for Penn's female teachers and students, built in 1905), Arnett House (built in 1937 for student-teachers), or Lathers Dormitory (from 1922, a residence for Penn's male teachers and students). King and some senior staffers slept in Gantt Cottage (a 1940 structure built by Penn School students). Meetings were at Frissell Hall, built in 1925.[58] The staff at Penn treated King with reverence, but not too much. Thomas Barnwell remembered picking him up at the Savannah airport, about an hour's drive from Penn Center. Barnwell recalled the private disagreement they had. Barnwell thought that when changes came, a disproportionate number of blacks "would be displaced from their businesses such as service stations, hotels, restaurants and things of that type." According to Barnwell, King answered, "No, Brother Barnwell, you have to have faith in the Lord," to which Barnwell said, "O.K., we'll see."[59]

Before the SCLC retreat at Penn Center in September 1965, several crucial developments occurred in the civil rights movement. During Freedom Summer (1964), a number of civil rights workers were murdered. The nation reacted with outrage, and President Johnson signed the Civil Rights Act of 1964 into law on July 2. In March 1965, the march from Selma to Montgomery, Alabama, was seen on national television, and the footage of Bloody Sunday, which showed the vicious beating of peaceful demonstrators, including John Lewis and others, shocked the nation. On August 6, Johnson signed the Voting Rights Act of 1965.

In the midst of all the civil rights activity, the nation was embroiled also in demonstrations against the Vietnam War. The nonviolent King was vehemently antiwar. The SCLC was not officially antiwar, so King's statements against the war were his personal views, not those of the SCLC. The pacifist view was not the view of the many African Americans, especially those from the South, who were in the armed services, one of the few places in American society where they could find employment. Many southern African Americans, including those from St. Helena, were very supportive of a war that their family members were fighting. The negative publicity that King received for his statements against the Vietnam War weighed heavily on him. He questioned whether he needed to back off of his stance on Vietnam—was he stretched too thin and losing media support?[60]

On August 11, 1965, riots erupted in Watts, an African American neighborhood in Los Angeles. King visited Watts on August 17; he deplored the violence, but asserted that the violence came from economic conditions of ghetto life. In the aftermath of the riots, King felt a growing conviction that the civil rights movement should address the problems facing black people in the nation's urban areas. Doing so would mark a major shift from the SCLC's southern focus, but King saw the need to stress anew the importance of nonviolence in any effort to change discrimination throughout the nation.

Knowing that these issues needed solid deliberation, King wanted the SCLC to have time for discussion and debate. One reason the SCLC retreats at Penn were so important to King is that they gave him time away from the national spotlight. He had the rare opportunity to be honest and open about how he felt about the movement and its effects on him. The folk singer Joan Baez, who was at the 1965 retreat, recalled King stating that "he couldn't take the pressure anymore, that he just wanted to go back . . . and preach in his little church, and he was tired of being a leader."[61] Penn Center provided a necessary platform for King to express his frustration and feelings of being overwhelmed.

During the retreat held September 13–16, 1965, the SCLC focused on whether to take the civil rights movement to the Chicago area. Divisions appeared among the staff as the SCLC looked to broaden the civil rights movement from a regional movement to a national one. The split was largely along generational lines. Septima Clark and other older staffers, as well as the Penn staff, felt that education should be the main focus. They believed that protests and demonstrations had a place in the movement but that they were secondary to long-term and less glamorous groundwork. Younger staff members felt frustrated by the slow rate of progress. Over a decade after *Brown v. Board of Education* and almost ten years after the Montgomery bus boycott, younger SCLC members wanted more direct-action protests, which often led to quicker results.

At the retreat, the SCLC decided to take the movement to the North and to begin training staff for activism in the Chicago campaign.[62] At the same time, Diane Nash Bevel, a former Freedom Rider who had joined the SCLC staff in 1962, would continue to develop educational programs on nonviolence in the South.[63] The organization recommitted itself to nonviolence in both its northern and southern efforts.

In January 1966, the SCLC announced its "War on Slums." The campaign did not have clear goals, only a determination to overhaul the system that had created urban slums. Unfortunately, the War on Slums did not find support from the residents of Chicago's slums. In addition to the failure of the Chicago campaign, King was facing other major setbacks. The Vietnam War was escalating, and in the aftermath of the riots in Watts, some activists were turning away from nonviolence. King called for another retreat at Penn Center, to be held November 11–17, 1966.[64]

This retreat highlighted the expansion of King's mission from civil rights to human rights. When King gave a speech on the evening of November 14, he was aware of its importance. Typically, King gave impromptu speeches or spoke from rough notes, but for that evening's talk, he had written a full draft of the speech. According to the King biographer Adam Fairclough, it was "among [King's] most significant statements, for it staked out the radical position which guided him for the rest of his life."[65] The speech covered where the civil rights movement had been, where it was at the moment, and where it was going. He candidly informed his audience, in the safety that Penn provided, "I am still searching myself. . . . I don't have all the answers and I certainly have no pretense to omniscience."[66]

King went on to place the civil rights movement in a global context. It was part of a social revolution not only in the United States but also around the world. He also responded to younger African American activists, particularly from the North, and especially Stokely Carmichael, who had replaced John Lewis as leader of SNCC in January 1966. Although not the first to use the term, Carmichael popularized the phrase "black power" and proclaimed at Greenwood, Mississippi, on June 17, 1966, that African Americans were tired of not making progress: "We want black power!" According to King, "Black Power is a cry of pain. . . . It is in fact a reaction to the failure of White Power to deliver the promises and to do it in a hurry. . . . The concept of Black Power is something we are certainly able to understand and accept . . . I hope what we are seeking is black equality, not black domination."[67]

At Penn Center, King was able to be candid; he could make claims about the direction of the civil rights movement that he would not be able to voice publicly. The fact that forty million Americans lived in poverty contributed to King's belief that "something is wrong with capitalism." He once again stressed the importance of nonviolence in the movement, stating, "We must still believe that violence, in our struggle, is impractical and immoral. . . . I think the ultimate weakness of violence, practically, and morally, is the fact that it never really deals with the basic evil in the situation." He explicitly rejected younger leaders' calls for violence and committed the SCLC to continue to be a beacon of hope lighting the path of nonviolence. Tying together his antiwar stance and his wider focus on human rights, King explained the "three basic evils in America: the evil of racism, the evil of excessive materialism, the evil of militarism." He called them "inseparable triplets" and informed the SCLC that any movement would have to address all three of them.[68]

Some of the sessions and workshops offered at the retreat included Andrew Young's "SCLC & Strategy for Social Change" and "Personal Decorum & Group Discipline of SCLC Staff"; King's "SCLC & Foreign Affairs"; James Lawson's

"Practice and Training in Nonviolent Action"; and Hosea Williams's "Voter Registration Emphasis." Sessions addressed challenges the civil rights leaders faced in the movement, and attendees freely voiced disagreement and dissent. For example, staff members could air grievances over their pay and treatment, grumblings that would undermine the work of the SCLC and the civil rights movement if they become public knowledge.[69] Such discussions often led to arguments, and King would have to remind his staff, "Remember, we are a non-violent organization."[70] King's speech and the sessions from this retreat became the basis for his next book, titled *Where Do We Go from Here: Chaos or Community?*

The SCLC had its fourth Penn retreat only six months later, May 21–26, 1967. In a memorandum to all SCLC staff, Young made clear that attendance was mandatory: "No one will be excused from this retreat."[71] King again spoke his thoughts:

> It is necessary for us to realize that we have moved from the era of civil rights to the era of human rights. . . . You see when we think of civil rights we are referring to those rights that are clearly defined by the Constitution. The denial of those rights can be dealt with by going into court, by demonstrating to dramatize the denial, or by an Executive Order . . . But when you deal with human rights, you are not dealing with something clearly defined in the Constitution. They are rights that are clearly defined by the mandates of a humanitarian concern. . . . We are talking about a good, solid, well-paying job. We are talking about a good, sound, sanitary house. We are talking not merely about desegregated education, but we are talking about quality education.[72]

Human rights encompassed the Vietnam War, and King spoke about the criticism he had received for his antiwar stance: "Now I know the voices that are being raised against me," and "it's hurting the civil rights movement, to take a stand against the war in Vietnam." He asked for their help: "I want you to help me as God's prophets. And a prophet tells the truth. What is the truth? The war in Vietnam is doing much more to hurt civil rights than our standing against the war is doing."[73] This was a deeply personal speech, and King needed the safe and secure environment that Penn provided.

The SCLC held its fifth and final retreat at Penn from November 27 to December 2, 1967. While King and his staff were there, the *Charleston News and Courier* ran an article that described Frogmore as "a backwater of the South Carolina coastal plantation country," a place where "Emancipation and Reconstruction left its people to doze in the sunshine, unmolested by overseers and mildly guided from the Penn Community Center." The article wondered "whether any good thing can come out of Frogmore," and concluded that "only time will answer."[74] Ignoring the determination of the people of St. Helena from the Civil War days and throughout Reconstruction, the paper showcased the white sentiment that portrayed local black residents as content until King and his SCLC came to Penn and brought trouble.

At the fall 1967 retreat, King gave two speeches: an informal motivational speech, "Why A Movement?," and a longer, formal speech, "The State of the Movement." In the latter, King admitted, "The decade of 1955 to 1965, with its constructive elements, misled us," adding, "Everyone underestimated the amount of rage Negroes were suppressing, and the amount of bigotry the white majority was disguising."[75] According to the South Carolina archivist J. Tracy Power, these speeches "provide excellent illustrations of the ways in which these retreats gave SCLC opportunities to refocus." King reaffirmed the SCLC's role of offering hope, determination, and a commitment to nonviolence.[76]

The SCLC announced its Poor People's Campaign a few days after concluding its Penn retreat. At the retreat, King told the gathering, "I don't know if I'll see all of you before April, but I send you forth."[77] This was his great commission to his staff. But on April 4, 1968, King was assassinated in Memphis, Tennessee, where he had gone to speak on behalf of the city's striking sanitation workers.

The relationship between Martin Luther King Jr. and Penn Center was symbiotic. The retreats deeply influenced King, and King validated the special value of Penn Center. King and the SCLC needed a place where they could get away from the glare of publicity in order to safely air doubts and grievances as well as reaffirm their determination. During the May 1967 gathering at Penn, King explained the purpose of the retreat to his staff. "I think," he said, "we are having a very necessary and fruitful retreat here together. . . . In any movement, every now and then, you must take off from the battlefield and try desperately to see where you are going." He continued, "This . . . is why we are here. . . . We are trying to see where we are going and how we are going to get there."[78] According to King's biographer Adam Fairclough, Penn Center was where the "SCLC, in its most complete expression, analyzed large questions of philosophy, strategy, and politics in an atmosphere of convivial informality."[79] Because one of the purposes of the retreats was to give King some solitude, Penn had begun constructing a remote cabin on the marsh, specifically for King's visits, but he was killed before it was finished. The cabin is still referred to today as the Martin Luther King cabin.

Upon the news of King's assassination, Courtney Siceloff gave a statement about King's relationship with Penn. He said that King came to Penn "seeking a quiet retreat from the demands of his busy life."[80] Penn Center may have been remote, but it faced opposition from some local whites over King's visits. Walter Mack, future executive director of Penn Center, told of how Penn had tried to keep King's visits out of the public eye: "The record of him coming was kept secret, even from the local sheriff." Mack said, "They wouldn't tell anybody. You never knew who would want to hurt Dr. King."[81] Joseph McDomick concurred: "Even when he came here, it had to be kept secret." He said, "We couldn't notify any law enforcement people because we didn't know who would be in that little group that would be after doing him in."[82]

The isolation and quiet of Penn Center helped many in addition to Martin Luther King Jr. and the SCLC. Elizabeth Siceloff, asked in a 1985 interview whether she and her husband had been "isolated" or removed from the civil rights movement while at Penn, responded straightforwardly, "It came there."[83] Luminaries of the movement, as well as many foot soldiers and unsung heroes, gathered at Penn Center. Rodney Hurst, president of the Jacksonville, Florida, youth NAACP, told of his first civil rights conference, one held at Penn in September 1960: "The civil rights movement embraced several different philosophies, and we needed to get together from time to time to discuss them."[84] Hurst came to discuss the events of "Ax Handle Saturday," August 27, 1960, when white thugs in Jacksonville attacked peaceful black and white demonstrators. At the conference, held at "that bastion of racial agitation in Frogmore, South Carolina," were attendees from SNCC, the NAACP, and the SCLC.[85] Groups held separate meetings at Penn Center, too; members of SNCC, for example, attended their own and other conferences at Penn Center, such as the National Sharecropper's Fund conference on September 27, 1963.[86] The SNCC leaders Cleveland Sellers and Stokely Carmichael were guests of Penn Center at Christmastime 1967.[87]

Vernon Jordan's memoir discusses a meeting he attended at Penn Center in August 1961. Ruby Hurley's NAACP field directors were there to discuss strategies for the coming year. But there was one serious difficulty: "The only problem was that along with the Quaker commitment to progressivism and equality came Quaker-type meals. In keeping with the will to simplicity, the center's menu was spare, and we only got two meals a day: breakfast early in the morning and supper at about four o'clock. This was nowhere near enough for a young man of my size or, as it turned out, for any of my colleagues. By around seven o'clock, we were all starved." The black café on St. Helena was closed, so Jordan drove several of them to Beaufort. When he stopped at a white truck stop, Hurley as well as Medgar Evers and the Reverend I. DeQuincey Newman, the South Carolina field director, objected. NAACP policy prohibited the staff from using the back door to establishments where African Americans were not allowed to use the front door. Nevertheless, Jordan continued. At the back door, he spoke to the chef, "an imposing-looking black man": "I'm Vernon Jordan. I'm the Georgia field director of the NAACP. We're meeting over at the Penn Center."

The chef replied, "Oh yeah, we know you all are over there. How's it going?"

Jordan said, "Well, fine, except the food is really bad, and we're hungry. We've been driving around trying to find something to eat. I want to know if you can do something about it."

The chef had a simple question: "How many are you?" In fifteen minutes the chef brought out a box with "eight T-bone steaks, lettuce, tomatoes, fried onion rings, french fries, and rolls." There was no charge: "The white man is going to pay for dinner tonight," the chef said.

Back in the car, Hurley was outraged. The Reverend Newman helped the situation by politely mentioning, "Ruby, I don't know what Vernon has, but it sure smells good." Jordan reported that no one dared laugh—"That would come later."[88]

Many activists have stories about Penn Center. Chuck McDew, the first chairman of SNCC, said that Penn Center was "a very important place in my life." McDew's father taught at Penn School before moving to Ohio. Chuck McDew had never been to South Carolina before attending South Carolina State University in Orangeburg, and he remembers vividly his first trip to Penn Center. His history teacher, Terry Sanford, introduced him to what he called an "underground South, where there was integration, where blacks and whites got together." McDew found Penn Center was always welcoming. After the formation of SNCC, its members were "treated well [at Penn], and they felt safe, protected, and at home." McDew remembers meetings there with Ella Baker, Bob Moses, John Lewis, Septima Clark, DeQuincy Newman, Jesse Jackson, and Constance Curry.[89] At the Penn Center in May 2013, U.S. representative John Lewis recalled visiting Penn Center for meetings with fellow civil rights leaders.[90]

Constance Curry remembers how she and others met and relaxed with Martin Luther King Jr. in the 1960s at a beach cottage on Hunting Island, not far from St. Helena. When the state of South Carolina offered to lease some of the lots on the island to private owners in the early 1960s, Courtney Siceloff applied for a lease to build a cottage. He wanted an ocean retreat that could be used by his family and by some guests at Penn. The state refused to give him a lease because he was known as an "n-loving communist." Siceloff sued the state and won. He leased the lot and built the cottage.[91] In the 1970s, Curry purchased the beach house from the Siceloffs, and Chuck McDew remembers how his father enjoyed that cottage: "He stood on the deck and cried as he looked out at the ocean."[92] McDew remembers that on a visit to Connie Curry at the cottage three white men on the beach allowed their two rottweilers to chase him. He managed to get to the cottage and "dove into the house just seconds before the rottweilers." Lying on the cottage floor, he remembered that his father used to say that Frogmore was one of the most beautiful places on earth, but that "people just cannot live there because of whites."[93] Curry donated the cabin to Penn Center, and in 2012 she and others tried to have it moved to the Penn Center property to save it from further flood damage, but it was too late. The weakened cottage fell apart and could not be moved.

John Reynolds, a young activist from Alabama, wrote of learning about nonviolent activism at Penn Center. He stated that there he met, for the first time, white people who were nice. Reynolds went on to conduct workshops based on the training he had received from Septima Clark at Penn Center.[94] Millicent Brown reported that her family "went regularly to Penn." Brown's father, J. Arthur Brown, an African American real estate agent and activist in Charleston, became president of the Charleston NAACP in 1955 and led court battles to desegregate the Charleston public schools. In 1963, Millicent Brown was in the first group to integrate South Carolina elementary and secondary public schools, after Clemson College had admitted Harvey Gantt earlier that year. Like Reynolds, Brown thought that her visits to Penn Center "introduced [her] to white 'progressives.'"[95]

White progressives in South Carolina likewise benefited from their experiences at Penn Center, which gave them the opportunity to work with African American leaders and students in the civil rights movement. Much has been written about Penn Center's importance to African Americans on St. Helena, other coastal islands, and the nation as a whole, but less attention has been paid to Penn's importance to non–African Americans. For young white activists, meetings at Penn were often the gateway to their first meaningful relationships with African Americans. Hayes Mizell remembers that the first time he met, ate, lodged, talked, and socialized with African American college students was at Penn Center under the auspices of the South Carolina Student Council on Human Relations when he was a graduate student at the University of South Carolina. He explained its importance to him: "Every awakening begins with opening one's eyes, and Penn was the venue where I caught my first glimpse of a wider world." Penn Center is where he met and began to develop relationships with such civil rights activists as Connie Curry, Andrew Young, Will Campbell, and James McBride Dabbs. Mizell considered his time at Penn as an initiation: "I became one more member of Penn's growing constituency who regarded it as both a sanctuary and a center of hope."[96]

In the 1950s and 1960s, the incipient civil rights movement in South Carolina included some whites who were army veterans. They had returned to the University of South Carolina to do graduate work in history, looking for a usable past to influence the state for a better tomorrow. Charles Joyner recalls that James McBride Dabbs introduced him to Andrew Young and Will Campbell at Penn Center.[97] Selden Smith appreciated that Penn Center "showed the potential for the new society without segregation," adding that at Penn "you could actually experience this world."[98]

While Penn Center strove to maintain contacts between African American and white activists, race relations were never an easy concern. The Sieloffs were honest about the difficulties of loving others as a way to form a beloved community. They wrote to Charles Joyner, "The conviction that we brought back from some Friends' conferences recently is that we must continually keep open to those who differ with us, and not just 'write them off' because we know they disagree. This has tightened considerably for us in the area around here. It is a real problem for me—loving creatively those who are opposed. We have to strengthen one another."[99] This reflection recalls an interaction between Dr. King and a Penn staff member, Frieda R. Mitchell. Mitchell was a pioneer in early childhood education and one of the first black school board members in Beaufort County (the other was also a Penn staff member). She felt determined to ask King one question: "How can you tell me to love people who treat me as if I were not human?" She remembered his reply, "He said we are created in God's image. So you love the image of God in that people."[100]

Penn Center's goal was to empower African Americans in their own communities. The Sieloffs had vowed that intention would be part of a new direction for Penn. Joseph McDomick recalled how Penn participated in pickets, boycotts, and sit-ins of local whites-only businesses. One demonstration he remembers took place in 1969 or 1970. At the time, the South Carolina Department of Social Services did not have any African American employees in its outreach program in the Beaufort area. When confronted about the lack of African American employees, the director defiantly insisted that no one would tell him whom to hire. Penn responded by organizing the Welfare Rights Organization and encouraging older people to picket the Department of Social Services. During a sit-in, a very tall and very large woman—over 300 pounds—sat in the doorway. The people inside were unable to get out of the building. Police who came to remove the woman begged her to move. She informed them that she had a paralyzed leg and was unable to move from the doorway. The police had to gather a large group of people to move her from the doorway. They carried her to jail, but Penn's lawyers immediately posted bail. The protest was successful; the department hired black caseworkers and a minority secretary, and the director was reassigned out of the area.[101]

Penn Center continued to pressure businesses and governmental agencies to hire African American employees.[102] McDomick remained a committed activist, and he continues his work with Penn Center. His four children were born while he worked at Penn, living on campus in Jasmine Cottage. When his wife, Nersene, went into labor, they traveled to the Savannah hospital because of segregated facilities in Beaufort, and because they felt safer going there, his activism having angered some locals.[103]

Sometimes progress meant taking small steps and seeing a situation in new ways. When the public schools in Beaufort were desegregated in the early 1970s, the school bus had to pick up African American children as well as the Siceloff children on St. Helena. Since the bus came first to Penn Center and St. Helena, the island children could sit at the front of the bus, an option not allowed during Jim Crow, when African Americans were forced to sit at the back. When it stopped to pick up white children on Lady's Island, some of them resented having to sit at the back.[104] Many whites in Beaufort responded as whites throughout the South did: they started a segregated private academy. For the academy's first graduation ceremony, the Marine band from nearby Parris Island agreed to play and also to lend the school some extra bleachers. Courtney Siceloff called the Marine base to remind the commander that federal law prohibits federal funds to be expended in discriminatory facilities. When the call to the base did not bring about a change in plans, Siceloff called the Pentagon. Suddenly, the Marine band and bleachers were no longer part of the segregationist academy's graduation festivities.[105]

Such small steps felt good, but it was becoming clear to many that in health care, education, voting, and citizenship, black leaders needed to be at the forefront of change. While it was hard for many well-meaning whites to give up their leadership positions, the role of progressive southern whites—whites willing to work under African American control—became especially important.

In 1968, activists organized a meeting at Penn Center, the "Citizens' Conference on Education in South Carolina." Funded by the American Friends Service Committee with the help of the South Carolina Council on Human Relations director Hayes Mizell, the participants discussed the importance of black history.[106] According to William Saunders, the conference chair and editor of the *Low Country Newsletter* on Johns Island, Cleveland Sellers was unable to attend because, as he told Saunders on the telephone, "If I come down there, a lot of people here [in Orangeburg] are going to die."[107] Even so, Sellers was not able to stop the mayhem; on February 8, 1968, police killed three peaceful demonstrators and wounded twenty-eight in what became known as the Orangeburg Massacre.[108] The conference at Penn Center also was to include Stokely Carmichael, who was scheduled to speak about the need for "all black people to work together on problems of education." But Carmichael did not attend because whites threatened to arrest him if he showed up. Instead, he sent a letter that was read at the gathering. Carmichael encouraged an alliance of all black people to work on matters they could agree on, such as the need for better schools. He declared, "I don't care if you're a Baptist preacher, a school teacher, a farm worker, or a SNCC worker—you've all got many things in common—one thing is we're black and we're oppressed."[109]

Tensions were running high throughout the nation. At the conference, African American leaders decided that whites would not be allowed to attend the workshop meetings but could attend the session summaries. According to Saunders, "the presence of whites would have inhibited discussion."[110] Jack Bass, one of the few reporters in the United States covering civil rights and one of the very few who tried to be objective rather than negative about the movement, reported, "A group of black power advocates attended, but did not dominate the conference."[111]

As black power increasingly became the goal of SNCC, reorienting the civil rights movement, whites were pushed out. At Penn Center, however, SNCC leaders continued to meet with and cooperate with whites sympathetic to black rights. Penn welcomed all and remained committed to interracial harmony and an interracial democracy. An African American activist could feel pulled in several directions. Working with whites could mean putting up with white patronization. It could also mean putting up with black accusations of not being "black enough." Courtney Siceloff recognized the rights and desires of SNCC and other groups to focus on African American leaders and to build a feeling of empowerment. He saw that people have to feel comfortable with themselves before they can feel comfortable with others. Working with the staff at Penn Center, Siceloff began sensitivity training to help Penn staff members understand their personal prejudices and become more sensitive to others.[112] One Beaufort county resident expressed Penn's work in 1968: "Penn is currently expanding this new consciousness that 'we are somebody' to communities throughout the southeast. Black leaders from Mississippi, Georgia, Alabama, and South Carolina are receiving concrete, relevant training in the techniques and processes of community development . . . This is pioneering, profoundly important work . . . This is education at its best and where it is most needed."[113]

At the same time, Penn Center never stopped working on ways to alleviate poverty. When U.S. senator Fritz Hollings of South Carolina made his expedition around the state in January 1968, it was the first time, as he put it, that he "really saw hunger."[114] On his journey, he drove to St. Helena Island, where he encountered Penn Center's Tom Barnwell. Barnwell told him, "If you are here simply to look, just turn around and drive away, because these people need help!"[115] When Hollings held Senate hearings on poverty, he wanted an African American to testify before the committee. According to Jack Bass, Hollings demanded that they find someone willing to challenge the whites in D.C.; he did not want an accommodationist "kerchief head." Hollings requested Barnwell.[116]

Barnwell testified in 1969: "Pure water is also a problem in some areas of the county. Warsaw Island, a small island on St. Helena, has been without pure drinking water since 1959. Water has to be carried for drinking purposes a distance of over a mile." The Farmers Home Administration had been set up to offer loans to establish water districts, but according to Barnwell, some residents had difficulty affording "the $25 fee requirement to sign up." Barnwell also testified about the problems of entrepreneurship: "When residents have tried to secure Small Business Administration loans to purchase vessels for fishing and shrimping, as well as other small business ventures, the red tape has swallowed them up."[117] During the heyday of President Lyndon Johnson's Great Society programs to eliminate hunger and poverty, Penn Center took a role in helping the people to know what was available to them.

In 1969, more than a century after the founding of Penn School, black and white leaders on the board of trustees agreed that African Americans should run the center. Siceloff and other whites working at Penn, people who had worked hard for social justice, people who believed in black leadership, were not prepared for the new turn of events. According to a Penn board member at the time, "Penn Center got caught off guard. It was doing its thing and not looking in the mirror."[118]

Courtney Siceloff resigned as executive director, reasoning thus: "For a program directed primarily at the black community, I could no longer as a white person remain as agency director." The board accepted "with reluctance" and unanimously voted a resolution recognizing that Courtney Siceloff was "a person of unusual integrity, ability, and commitment with whom one could disagree, even radically, without losing his friendship."[119] Over the course of the Siceloffs' two decades at Penn Center, Courtney and Elizabeth became integral members of the St. Helena community and remain beloved in the memory of the island. Courtney urged the board to move quickly to find an African American executive director, and the board agreed. He believed that putting African Americans in leadership positions at Penn would result in "creative, innovation leadership" and that the center would retain its "relevancey [sic] and effectiveness in all programs, goals, and commitments."[120] The Siceloffs went to work for the U.S. Information Agency in Afghanistan, where they taught English to Afghans who wished to study in the United States. They moved to Atlanta in 1973, headquarters of the Southern Regional Council, where Elizabeth worked in media relations for the organization. Both Elizabeth and Courtney continued to advocate for racial equality and peace.[121]

During the Siceloffs' tenure at Penn Center, the board gradually replaced its northern members with southern ones, white and black. In 1961, Marion Wright became chairman of the board. He was born and reared in Edgefield, South Carolina, where as a youngster he read in the library of South Carolina's leader of disfranchisement and segregation, governor and senator Ben Tillman. Wright did not agree with Tillman and instead became an eminent white liberal and president of the Southern Regional Council.[122] When Wright left the Penn board chairmanship in 1965, James McBride Dabbs, another white southern liberal, and another past president of the Southern Regional Council, became the new chairman. A retired English professor and lay theologian from Sumter, South Carolina, Dabbs was the distinguished author of *The Southern Heritage* (1958), in which he sought to arouse the conscience of southern whites.[123] Both Wright and Dabbs enthusiastically endorsed integration. When King wrote his letter from the Birmingham City Jail in April 1963, he offered the names of "some of our white brothers in the South" who saw the necessity of the civil rights movement. He wrote, "They are still all too few in quantity, but they are big in quality." Among those he called by name was James McBride Dabbs, crediting him and others with writing "about our struggle in eloquent and prophetic terms."[124] After the death of James Dabbs in 1971, the Penn board chose, for the first time, an African American as chair: the noted sociologist Herman Blake. Among Blake's research areas was the Gullah culture. Additionally, Blake served as scholar in residence and director of the Sea Island Institute at the University of South Carolina, Beaufort, an institute that promotes the study of Gullah culture.

During the 1950s and 1960s, Penn Center was a vehicle for change in the South Carolina Lowcountry—and the nation. The citizenship school at Penn Center was a vital tool in building a civil rights movement. In addition, black and white civil rights and human rights leaders came to Penn to meet and work together. The center provided a secluded and secure location where they could discuss strategy. The retreats that Martin Luther King Jr. and the SCLC held at

Penn gave him and the organization a chance to unwind and to have important discussions and voice dissent away from the media and the national spotlight.

Penn Center was pivotal to a remarkable movement in America. Like the abolitionist legacy after the Civil War, like its educational legacy during the bleakest years of segregation, the legacy of equal rights permeated Penn Center during the civil rights movement.

CHAPTER FIVE

Penn as a Center of Preservation and Sustainability

When the Siceloffs left Penn Center, the board of trustees hired John W. Gadson Sr. as its first African American executive director. Gadson, a graduate of South Carolina State University, with a master's degree from Fisk University in Nashville, had been a chemistry and physics teacher at Robert Smalls High School in Beaufort and the director of the Beaufort-Jasper Neighborhood Youth Corps. His organizing ability was an asset to Penn Center, and his dedication to Penn's mission of service continued his whole life.[1]

Gadson immediately went to work on a significant problem on St. Helena: between 1965 and 1970, landowners on St. Helena lost 350 acres through tax sales.[2] In 1972, Penn Center, under the direction of Gadson and with the help of Charles Washington Jr., a Beaufort lawyer, established Black Land Services, Inc., an organization whose purpose was to save black land ownership in Beaufort, Jasper, Hampton, Colleton, Charleston, and Dorchester Counties. Land ownership had always been an important matter on the sea islands.[3] During Reconstruction, Laura Towne lamented attempts by white landowners to regain the land they had abandoned; in the early 1900s, Rossa Cooley warned black landowners about the perils of losing their land. Through it all and against the odds, African American landowners on St. Helena struggled to keep their land. During the Depression, if family members could find employment off the island, they sent money to pay property taxes. According to the county tax collector, no other group of people in Beaufort County was so regular in paying their yearly taxes.[4]

In the late twentieth and early twenty-first centuries, Penn Center continued to support black land ownership. But whites also continued to covet land on the sea islands, and the advent of modern air-conditioning—window units in the 1950s, and central air-conditioning in the 1970s—made coastal areas increasingly valuable. Land on the sea islands became a valuable commodity. In 1956, the completion of the Hilton Head–Bluffton Bridge attracted recreational developers, and in 1959 the Sea Pines Corporation bought about a fourth of the island, including most of Hilton Head's coastline, to develop a posh residential resort. Plans for Hilton Head did not take into consideration the indigenous population or traditional land use.[5] Before the bridge, African Americans owned 3,000–7,000 of the 26,000 acres on Hilton Head. Now they own about 700 acres.[6]

Increased land values brought increased taxes thereon, and the inequity of tax laws heavily burdened low-income property owners who happened to live adjacent to wealthy land developments. Land belonging to people living near a new development, often small farmers or low-income workers, was so highly assessed that they either had to sell their land or face eviction for nonpayment of taxes. These taxes, as well as voluntary sales and some fraud, meant that many African Americans on the sea islands lost their ancestral homes. It is not easy to determine black land ownership on St. Helena Island. Best-guess estimates from the 2010 census are that approximately 38 percent of the 42,000 acres on St. Helena Island is owned by African Americans. That is about 15,960 acres of land, much of which is marshland, swamp, and tidal creeks.[7]

In the late 1980s, the Freewoods Foundation studied African American farmers who owned their own land. The study included six African American farm owners on St. Helena Island.[8]

Harold Rivers had farmed since he was a youngster of "about 12 or 13." He reported: "[I] moved from where I was born, and I bought my own land and built my own house." Rivers's father owned a farm, too, some land "handed down from his father," and he bought an additional twenty acres.[9]

Marion Bailey owned sixteen acres, farming ten of them. When asked about how he had acquired it, he replied: "I don't know how my grandparents got the land. I assume they inherited it like I did."[10]

James Washington farmed two acres, which his father had received from his father.[11]

Ace Johnson owned almost ten acres, which he had purchased: "I asked Mr. Dubose from up north to sell me a piece of land because I wanted to get married. Dubose used to come down here to hunt quail."[12]

George Seabrooks's father had a farm of eight to ten acres.[13]

Leroy Browne farmed about five acres, some purchased from his uncle, who had inherited it. According to Browne, "It was in the family all the while."[14]

These landowners often had something to say about Penn School and Penn Center. Bailey took classes at Penn Center. He said, "I brushed my knowledge up when I came to Penn. I learned many things in addition to the instruction for planting seeds and cultivation right there from Penn Center." His grandmother had attended Penn School: "I learned more from my grandmother than my mother." The interview with Bailey was cut short "due to difficulties in understanding." (It is likely that Bailey spoke Gullah.)[15] Rivers spoke of Penn School when asked about home demonstrations: "We had all that when the school was open." The interviewer asked whether "a lot of things were centered around the school," and Rivers replied, "Well, that was the place it was created."[16] Washington mentioned the fairs held "right here at Penn Center," adding, "It was a lot of fun at these fairs."[17] Johnson also recalled the social gatherings at Penn Center: "We did a lot right here at Penn Center. Once a year we had a cookout and the whole island was invited. We'd kill 2 or 3 cows and cook them. We had a social hall where we met and danced."[18]

Browne, who attended Penn School, said about the activities there, "It's hard for me to tell you, 'cause so much went on here at Penn. See[,] this institution was the head of the community. Everything that happened here radiated out into the community, and the school and the community was so close it was woven."[19]

Overall, the farmers grew cotton ("Cotton was the money: that was the crop") and foodstuffs—peas, corn, sweet potatoes, okra, peanuts, and rice. They composted. They had horses, cows for milk and butter, and hogs. They made syrup out of white and ribbon cane. They made soap. With fishing, they were self-sufficient. But they needed money to pay taxes. Bailey worked various jobs to pay the taxes. Seabrooks said, "We sold cows and turkeys to pay taxes. We also sold chickens."[20]

To assist native sea islanders in preserving their land in the midst of sweeping change and higher tax assessments, Joseph McDomick, who had come to Penn Center in 1964 to do community organizing, began to direct Black Land Services in 1972. McDomick designed a program of education, legal services, individual consultations, and strategic loans. He helped with wills and boundary disputes, a common problem, since many people who had held land since the late 1800s had not recorded plats and boundaries at the county courthouse. In a memo to a group of paralegals, McDomick laid out several priorities: "locate what is called abandoned land in Beaufort County"; get all the information on forthcoming tax sales from the courthouse "at least bi-weekly"; and notify those people who were listed as not paying their taxes.[21] McDomick knew the laws regarding land ownership and preservation and "all of the intricacies of heir's property."[22] In 1972, the New York–based Black Economic Research Center gave the program a $1,500,000 grant, with which Penn Center sponsored regular seminars for local landowners. Seminars dealt with the problems, as well as the long-term family benefits, of land ownership. Penn published a landowner's manual to be used in conjunction with the seminars.[23] This program succeeded in clearing complicated titles to family estates and helped about a hundred families each year avert confis- cation of their land during county tax sales. The land services at Penn Center have helped slow the rate at which families on St. Helena are losing their land.[24]

Penn Center continues to advocate for African American families who want to keep their land. Some may be delinquent in paying the land tax. Some owners may have passed away without a will, and the descendants are working to put the land into a single heir's possession. Representing Penn Center, McDomick attends the annual tax sales, and there has been "a great turnaround" in local own- ers' ability to keep the land. Over the course of the years, the county treasurer has established a routine. Because of Penn Center's diligence and its value within the community, the treasurer first declares that before the bidding begins, Penn Center would like to make a statement. McDomick then requests that others do not bid against the current owner. To date, only one person has ignored that request. The county paused the bidding at that point, and the other whites in the auction sternly admonished the errant bidder. In 2013, the county treasurer, a white Republican named Douglas Henderson, declared that Penn Center and the county had been working together at the annual tax sales over the course of many years "for the purposes of saving heirs' property." He stated, "It's a worthy cause."[25] The county treasurers have been so supportive of Penn's ideals that once the treasurer held up the auction until McDomick arrived. McDomick had been delayed because the bridge to Beaufort was closed to allow a ship to pass; the treasurer told the group that they would wait for Mr. McDomick before proceeding.[26]

McDomick was well respected in the community. Louis Dore, an African American attorney who worked with McDomick on land issues, thought that McDomick would make a good judge and wanted to submit his name to white state senator James Waddell, head of the local legislative delegation. Judges had been elected until the Voting Rights Act allowed a black majority to elect black judges; then the system moved to appointed magistrates, allowing whites to control the process. When McDomick said he needed time to think about it, Dore replied, "Don't think long; we need someone good."[27] McDomick was appointed magistrate in 1980, but also continued working at Penn Center on land issues.

As Penn Center continued to address hands-on, practical matters of land and taxes on St. Helena, John Gadson also understood the cultural significance of Penn Center's history. Realizing that culture needs preserving as much as land does, Gadson supported the idea of a cultural museum. Opened in 1971 and dedicated to the memory of the African American physician who served on St. Helena from 1906 to 1956, the York W. Bailey Cultural Museum at Penn Center houses archives and cultural collections, some of which go back to Civil War days. The museum benefited from some funding from the U.S. Department of Health, Education and Welfare and most especially from the direction of Agnes Sherman, "a legend at Penn Center," who had also been instrumental in getting the Beaufort County bookmobile to come to St. Helena Island.[28] Born and raised on St. Helena Island, she and her family had been in the mortuary business on the island for a good many years, helping the bereaved during traumatic times. Sherman was "a kind woman, a no-nonsense woman, and showed an appreciation for people."[29] Early on she was the major organizer of the museum and helped accumulate artifacts from the sea islands.

Simple and direct, the Bailey is "a powerful museum."[30] It displays St. Helena lifestyles from the nineteenth and early twentieth centuries. The museum's first permanent exhibition was titled Education to Freedom. It focused on the history of Penn School and the institution's continuing effect on southern education, especially that of African Americans from Reconstruction to the present. The museum microfilmed the Penn Center Papers and recorded more than a hundred oral-history tapes covering islanders' remembrances of the past.

Despite Penn Center's achievements, its financial situation was grim. The child care program, which had started under Courtney Siceloff in 1950, was "one of the first in the state, certainly the first in this [Beaufort] county."[31] Yet in the 1970s, Penn had to turn the day care facility over to United Communities for Child Development, which used Penn Center facilities and some Penn Center resources. Dwindling grants for Black Land Services forced Penn to cut the staff to the bone. Penn continued to host small conference groups, but Penn remained, as had been true so often in the past, on shaky financial ground.

And again, as had been true so often in the past, the director of Penn continued to pursue funding and good programming. A major effort by Gadson was to get the U.S. Department of the Interior to designate Penn Center a national historic landmark district. Several applications were denied, but Gadson did not give up. When he emphasized the unique history of Penn Center and the natural environment, particularly the magnificent live oaks that dominated the campus, Gadson's application was approved. On September 9, 1974, the Penn Center Historic District in the township of Frogmore and the county of Beaufort, South Carolina, became a reality. The district included Penn Center's seventeen historic structures and forty-seven acres.[32] According to Gadson, that was "one of the most significant objectives that we accomplished during my regime."[33] In crediting Gadson with this accomplishment, congressman James E. Clyburn, an African American Democrat from Sumter, South Carolina, remarked, "There is no limit on what one can accomplish if one does not get hung up on who gets the credit."[34]

Cabin on slave row, St. Helena.

Enslaved children, St. Helena.

Mothers and babies, St. Helena.

Founder of Penn School, Laura Towne, with students.

Ellen Murray
with students.

Charlotte Forten, first
African American
teacher at Penn School.
Public domain.

The Oaks Plantation, where Towne and Murray began teaching on St. Helena Island.

The Brick Church, where Penn School began.

First Penn School building, 1864.

Penn School
students with teacher.

Penn School teacher and students in field.

Basket making class.

Woodworking class.

Two-mule plowing by Penn student Elting B. Smalls.

Outdoor classroom with teacher Linnie Lumpkin.

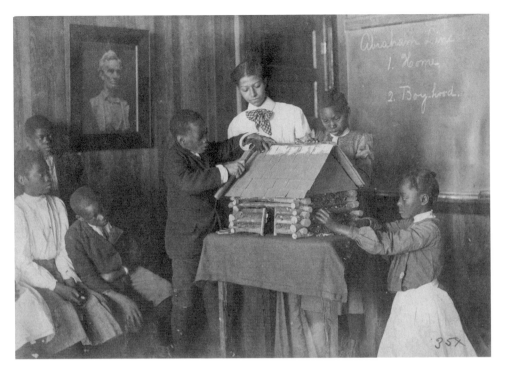

Penn School students learning about Lincoln.

Principals Rossa Cooley and Grace House on horseback.

Penn School nurse weighing children.

Dr. York Bailey.

Penn School canning club.

St. Helena residents examining "Better Homes" entry.

Penn School midwives celebrating graduation.

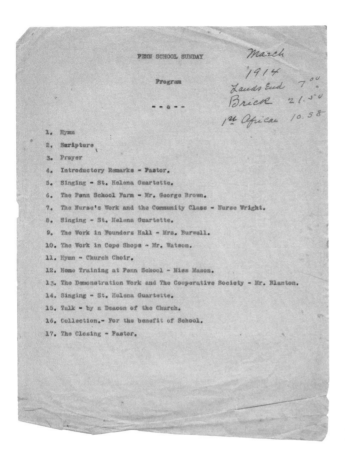

PENN SCHOOL SUNDAY

Program

--o--

March
'1914
Lands End 7.00
Brick 21.50
1st African 10.58

1. Hymn
2. Scripture
3. Prayer
4. Introductory Remarks - Pastor.
5. Singing - St. Helena Quartette.
6. The Penn School Farm - Mr. George Brown.
7. The Nurse's Work and the Community Class - Nurse Wright.
8. Singing - St. Helena Quartette.
9. The Work in Founders Hall - Mrs. Burwell.
10. The Work in Cope Shops - Mr. Watson.
11. Hymn - Church Choir.
12. Home Training at Penn School - Miss Mason.
13. The Demonstration Work and The Cooperative Society - Mr. Blanton.
14. Singing - St. Helena Quartette.
15. Talk - by a Deacon of the Church.
16. Collection.- For the benefit of School.
17. The Closing - Pastor.

March 1914 Sunday Program.

Principal Howard Kester
and his wife Alice Kester.

Martin Luther King Jr., with first executive director of Penn Community
Services Courtney Siceloff, and his wife Elizabeth and son John.
© Dave Duffin.

Penn Center Staff, circa 1960, with two guests. Standing from left:
Leroy Browne, Chad Lee (conscientious objector), Frieda Mitchell,
Elizabeth Siceloff, Jessie Mae Warren, Everett Gill (visiting minister).
Seated: Tom Barnwell, Courtney Siceloff, Joe McDomick.
© Dave Duffin. Courtesy of Mary Siceloff.

Jesse Jackson, Joan Baez, Ira Sandperl, Martin Luther King Jr.,
and Dora McDonald, on Penn Center campus.

Bob Fitch Photo Archive © Stanford University Libraries.

James Lawson and Ira Sandperl leading a workshop at Penn Center.

Bob Fitch Photo Archive © Stanford University Libraries.

Andrew Young, speaking at a Penn Center workshop.
Bob Fitch Photo Archive © Stanford University Libraries.

Joan Baez singing to the group, including King.
Bob Fitch Photo Archive © Stanford University Libraries.

Hosea Williams in group sing-a-long (King is in the background).
Bob Fitch Photo Archive © Stanford University Libraries.

Martin Luther King Jr. singing with the group (including Andrew Young, Ralph Abernathy, others).
Bob Fitch Photo Archive © Stanford University Libraries.

Martin Luther King Jr., Fred Shuttlesworth, and others singing "We shall overcome."

Bob Fitch Photo Archive © Stanford University Libraries.

Martin Luther King Jr. with staff in Penn Center cafeteria.

© Dave Duffin.

Left to right: John Gadson, first African American executive director of Penn Center; Tim West, former director of the Southern Historical Collection at Wilson Library, University of North Carolina, Chapel Hill; Louis Dore, Beaufort, South Carolina, attorney and strong supporter of Penn Center, photographed in 2012. Gadson and Dore were inducted into the Penn Center "1862 Circle." West was receiving the honor on behalf of the Wilson Library, which is the depository for many of the Penn School Papers.
Courtesy of Penn Center, St. Helena Island.

Former executive director of Penn Center Bernie Wright.

© Cecil Williams, www.cecilwilliams.com.

Former executive director of Penn
Center Emory Campbell.
Courtesy of Penn Center, St. Helena Island.

Joseph McDomick and Michael Campi, former executive directors of Penn Center.
Photo by Georganne Burton.

Walter Mack, former executive director of Penn Center, and Victoria Smalls, Penn Center director of history, arts and culture.

Courtesy of Penn Center, St. Helena Island.

Participants in the Program for Academic and Cultural Enrichment (PACE).

Courtesy of Penn Center, St. Helena Island.

Heritage Days Parade, 2007.
Courtesy of Penn Center, St. Helena Island.

Gullah flags parade.
Courtesy of Penn Center, St. Helena Island.

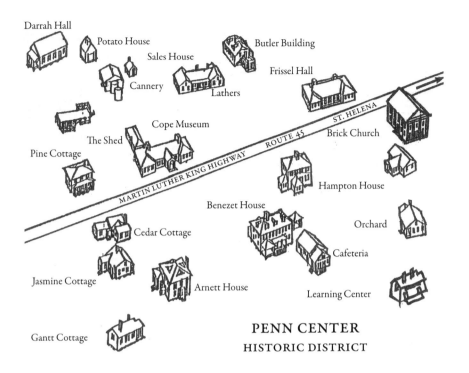

Darrah Hall
Potato House
Sales House
Cannery
Lathers
Butler Building
Frissel Hall
The Shed
Cope Museum
Pine Cottage
Brick Church
Hampton House
Benezet House
Cedar Cottage
Orchard
Cafeteria
Jasmine Cottage
Arnett House
Learning Center
Gantt Cottage

ST. HELENA
ROUTE 45
MARTIN LUTHER KING HIGHWAY

PENN CENTER
HISTORIC DISTRICT

Disheartened by the need to raise funds constantly while simultaneously running an organization, John Gadson left Penn in 1976; Joseph McDomick was asked to serve as interim director. The board found its next executive director in John Bluffington, an African American from Mississippi. Bluffington had fundraising experience and was expected to help the financial situation. He began his work at Penn in August 1976, but made no progress whatsoever. He was not able to establish new programs, and he brought in no additional income. At the end of 1977, the board realized that the new director had spent $200,000 of Penn's endowment just to pay current bills.[35] The situation was dire. Penn Center was in debt for $27,846.93 for such necessary items as fuel oil, insurance, water, and Social Security taxes. The 1977 audit had not been done because there were no funds to pay for it; moreover, Penn could not get its ledger books back from the accountants until it paid them for past services.[36] The situation was untenable, and Bluffington resigned in February 1978. Tom Barnwell was serving on the board when he learned that the endowment had been spent. Looking to the future, Barnwell stressed the importance of building a strong endowment and then protecting it.[37]

Joseph McDomick again stepped up as interim chief executive. McDomick and the maintenance supervisor, Leroy Browne, held Penn Center together. Browne, a graduate of Penn School and Hampton University, had been supervising facilities at Penn for twenty years, and his wife taught at the nursery school. Browne was the first African American since Reconstruction to run and win a seat on the Beaufort County Council (then called the Board of Directors).[38] He won that election in 1960, running in a multimember district against a white person from St. Helena. This was before the 1965 Voting Rights Act, but Browne had wide support from the African American population of St. Helena. Browne commented on a photograph taken on the day of the election: segregation was the law of the land, so the whites were "all on that side," while Browne sat "on this end of the table"; he added, "That's the way it was back in those days."[39]

McDomick and Browne could barely maintain services at Penn, but they managed to keep the organization afloat. Bluffington had applied to several national foundations for emergency grants, but all his requests were refused—except one. This was a donation from the New World Foundation in New York, which specified that the funds were to pay for limited technical assistance, in other words, for a management consultant to assess Penn's current status and provide professional advice about its future. The board asked for help from Karl Mathiasen, a consultant with expertise in nonprofit organizations. Mathiasen had worked with a variety of groups from his early career at the United States Agency for International Development.[40]

As Reid had done when writing his report thirty years earlier, Mathiasen studied Penn Center diligently before issuing his evaluation. At the October 1978 annual meeting of the board of trustees, Mathiasen began by noting that Penn should expect no new grants from foundations, for they were often "fickle and arbitrary."[41] He outlined three serious problems at Penn Community Services: leadership, finances, and programs. He thought that no single problem would destroy the organization, but problems in all three areas could be life threatening.

Mathiasen suggested ways to save Penn. First, the board had to become more committed and more effective, perhaps by choosing local members available to attend to Penn's affairs. The new board would have to move promptly and energetically on a plan for improvement. And the board would need to take immediate steps to locate and hire a new executive director. Mathiasen suggested that the most effective director would be a local person trusted in the community and familiar with Penn's history. The director should have a record of accomplishment in educational and sociological endeavors.

On the never-ending question of how Penn could become solvent, Mathiasen proposed that the board take steps to enlarge and increase the number of individual contributions. He suggested that Penn raise money by renting the campus to outside organizations as a conference center. Penn's buildings, although generally run-down, were available except when Peace Corps volunteers, as they had since the Siceloff days, periodically trained on campus.

Mathiasen's evaluation posed difficult choices for Penn Center. Over its history, Penn had always had to struggle against the odds: during the Civil War and Reconstruction; in days when white southerners rejected any education for African Americans; through world wars and a depression. There were always those who opposed helping poverty-stricken people, especially the low-income African Americans whom Penn Center served. Now the cultural forces arrayed against Penn Center were allied with real estate developers. Developers wanted the land, and there were many white leaders in the area who were not, and had never been, supportive of the Penn mission.

The board itself was divided on whether Penn Center was worth the effort to save it. Change was an enormous challenge for an organization that had too long been understaffed and undersupported, and often too set in its ways. Some members of the board felt that the institution should be shuttered and the land and buildings turned over to the county or the state for some kind of public use. But a number of trustees felt otherwise. Herman Blake, the board's first African American chairperson, and board member Thomas Barnwell lobbied hard to convince fellow members that one of the South's most prestigious institutions, with a remarkable history spanning more than 116 years, should be given one more chance to survive. According to the best-selling southern novelist John Jakes, a fervent supporter, "Penn Center is one of the great historic sites in America. This school, born in the era of fire and struggle that produced the Emancipation Proclamation, stands as a major milestone on the road to freedom, equality, and education for all. Penn Center absolutely must be saved!"[42]

Over the next two years, rumors persisted that Penn would close, but in January 1980 the board proudly announced that it had found a new executive director for Penn Community Services: Emory Shaw Campbell.

Campbell came to the post with eminent qualifications. An African American with community roots, born and raised on Hilton Head Island, Campbell had worked in the sea islands for most of his life. His parents and maternal grandparents were teachers. Campbell was familiar with Penn School, since his older sisters, brothers, and cousins had attended there. As a teenager, he became familiar with Penn Community Services, which provided local families with practical information about farming practices and land issues affecting the island communities. Campbell earned his bachelor of science degree in biology at Savannah State College, and his master's degree at Tufts University in Massachusetts in 1971. While earning his degrees, Campbell assisted with antipoverty programs in inner cities. In addition, he and his future wife, Emma, served as tutors in afterschool programs, finding them to be effective in improving the grades of participants and motivating them to seek higher-level careers. Campbell was active in the NAACP, and after the passage of the Voting Rights Act in 1965, he worked on civil rights, registering voters and monitoring boycotts in Savannah.[43]

After graduating from Tufts, Campbell was recruited by Tom Barnwell to join Beaufort-Jasper Comprehensive Health Services. Campbell and his family were happy in Boston, but as he put it, "Barnwell was a force to be reckoned with."[44] He returned to his native state to address environmental and health issues, including pleas for better outhouses and safer wells for drinking water. Crediting Lyndon Johnson's War on Poverty for starting these efforts, Campbell worked to build "a small army trying to address these issues that poverty presented."[45] Campbell was offered a position at Penn Center, whose independence he liked.

Looking back on that decision, he had to laugh: "So why not go over there and make a go of it, not knowing that I'd be starving."[46]

Though Penn's problems were severe, Campbell felt that by generating new local interest in Penn's activities, the institution could be revitalized. Campbell was pleased that the board of trustees had established priorities. Besides working to keep Penn's existing programs alive, which they now felt was possible, the board had decided to make Penn a nationally known conference center. It would not be a resort, for nearby Hilton Head and Fripp Island filled that need. Rather, Penn would try to attract groups that needed comfortable accommodations set in a rural atmosphere and steeped in history, with recreational facilities available. Groups that avail themselves of Penn Center include churches (for things such as youth mission trips), as well as organizations interested in black history and culture, community development and organization, cooperatives, and leadership training. Occasionally, a well-heeled group will book a time of retreat and reflection at Penn; one such foundation felt the need to renovate Frissell Hall for their meetings and to donate newer dishes for the kitchen.[47]

Within the first five months of Campbell's tenure, he announced some positive steps. The Peace Corps continued to supply income, since its volunteers used Penn as a training center for their overseas agricultural workers. Moreover, Campbell asked the Peace Corps to pay past-due invoices, which it did.[48] The Rockefeller Foundation gave a Small Farmers' Grant for a collaboration between Penn Center and the Clemson Extension Service. Clemson helped the farmers on St. Helena plan new crops of strawberries and broccoli. The New World Foundation, which had funded the Mathiasen consultation, gave an additional $90,000 grant to improve staff and program development.

In the 1980s, Penn Center continued its educational focus with PACE, the Program for Academic and Cultural Enrichment. Under the leadership of a local African American teacher, Mary Sweetenburg, the program worked with children from ages two to seventeen on teaching and learning, social stability, understanding the land and natural habitats, preserving the environment, cultural development, and personal enrichment. It also provided young people with a better understanding of their heritage and culture. Teens received job training and were encouraged to volunteer in their communities by helping individuals and families in need. In a typical year, all the participants in PACE advanced to the next grade level, and one-third received academic honors.

In another major undertaking, the director, the trustees, and the staff established the Land Use and Environmental Program. Economic development for the local residents too often meant minimum-wage jobs; Penn Center, however, wanted development that fosters a good quality of life. Penn's program worked in three areas: citizen education, land-use planning and policy reform, and sustainable community development. Campbell realized that the preservation of land and culture on St. Helena and the sea islands required a process of sustainability. As Michael C. Wolfe wrote in his book about St. Helena Island, "Campbell dreams of creating a 'sustainable community,' one that is not dependent on tourist dollars as a panacea."[49] With his expertise in environmental engineering, Campbell was able to articulate the importance of a sustainable environment to the culture. "I was one of the first Earth Day people," Campbell said. "The culture has always been able to sustain itself because we have consecutiveness among families. We live on the land a certain way."[50]

Sustainability is based on a simple principle: everything that people need for survival and well-being depends, either directly or indirectly, on the natural environment. Sustainability helps ensure that people will continue to have the water, materials, and resources needed to protect human health and the environment.[51] At Penn Center, sustainability included the preservation of land and culture in the midst of one-sided economic development. Throughout the history of the sea islands, a sense of place has been important, whether it was a large oak where the people went to meditate while seeking spiritual guidance, or the landings where fishermen kept their bateaux until the tide was right to "go casting." The love of a place carries the responsibility to maintain it, and Penn Center hoped to counter the disastrous upswing in pollution caused by resort development. That pollution meant that some of South Carolina's coastal shellfish beds had been closed because of runoff from new roads, golf courses, parking lots, and large expanses of chemically treated lawns.

By working with national foundations whose missions are to provide financial and other help to organizations active in education and the preservation of the environment and native land and cultures, Campbell created the Penn School for Preservation to unite environmentalists, historical preservationists, and concerned citizens to discuss problems and take action. Penn staff members joined with the county planning staff to devise a "bottom-up planning," that is, a program for what the community wanted regarding future land use, rather than what governmental planners said land use should be.[52] One of the most notable achievements of Penn School for Preservation graduates was their involvement in the Low Country Consensus Building Campaign. The participants assumed leadership roles and assisted state officials in drafting ordinances to protect property for individuals and families. The rich cultural history of sea islanders has given them a distinct way of viewing the world, and their vision is necessary to good regional community planning. In his study of Gullah culture, the anthropologist William Pollitzer found that values "based on harmony with nature and their fellow man, contrast with the frantic pace of the consumerism of today and deserve to be more widely known and appreciated."[53]

The efforts of Penn Center and the St. Helena community evolved into the Beaufort County Comprehensive Plan, which was South Carolina's first mandated land-use plan. The project involved the local environment, economic development, population growth management, zoning, and land planning. The installation of two traffic lights on St. Helena required hard lobbying on the part of Penn Center. The Penn School for Preservation continues to grapple with how to maintain some of the community's traditions while trying to build a sustainable economy.[54] For example, St. Helena has no chain grocery stores and no golf courses, and gated communities are not allowed on the island.[55] But opposition to any and all development is not the answer; lack of economic opportunity means that young people may have to leave the island. One development project that is ecologically friendly is a food-processing plant that converts local vegetables for use in the community schools. This plant is an example of local people using local food, such as collards, to help local school children.[56]

Good development requires community dialogue, and Penn Center has been helpful in bringing people together. The cooperation of local supportive whites has been instrumental throughout the history of Penn Center. One such family of local supporters is the Keyserlings. Dr. Herbert Keyserling was the first white person from Beaufort to join the Penn Center Board of Trustees, serving from 1992 until 1998.[57] His wife, Harriet Keyserling, a South Carolina state legislator from 1977 until 1993, was also a firm advocate for Penn Center. As a member of the Ways and Means Committee, she almost single-handedly adjusted the budget to grant one million dollars for Penn School building renovation. She wrote in her autobiography, "I felt it was now or never for Penn; these historic buildings could collapse without immediate help, and the local community had no hope of raising the needed funds."[58] Their son, Billy Keyserling, elected the mayor of Beaufort in November 2008, worked with Penn on fund-raising.[59] The Keyserlings sparked the interest of Senator Fritz Hollings, who then spearheaded work to refurbish some of the Penn Center buildings, calling Penn "a remarkable landmark of African-American history."[60] Hollings, Representative James Clyburn, state senator James Waddell, Penn Center's Thomas Barnwell, and the Keyserlings helped gain the interest of the National Park Service.[61] The park service gave special attention to Penn Center's Sea Islands Preservation Project and its plan to conserve the natural environment on St. Helena and the sea islands and to protect the most vulnerable areas from flooding, erosion, drought, and overdevelopment.

These efforts continued under the new executive director of Penn Center, Bernie L. Wright, who came on board in 2001. From St. Matthews, South Carolina, near Orangeburg, Wright graduated from South Carolina State University with a bachelor of science degree in agricultural economics and business. He earned his master's degree in applied financial management at American University in Washington, D.C. One of Wright's goals was to stabilize finances at Penn Center by retiring its mortgages. He accomplished this by establishing an easement on 190 acres of Penn land. The easement, financed by the U.S. Department of Agriculture (USDA), meant that the land cannot be developed for any use except agriculture or green space. For these development rights, Penn Center received $849,000, just more than enough needed to pay off the mortgage debt. Wright also undertook a renovation project at Penn. Among the improvements was the innovative use of a particular kind of sand particle that packs very tightly as surfacing material for the roads through the campus. The look remained rustic, but the roads could accommodate vehicular tonnage.

Next, Wright wanted to make Penn Center's income sources more structurally sound. Penn Center received an incredibly generous business offer from Joe Mix, a local white man. "A good friend of Penn Center," Mix was willing to sell his hotel and restaurant on St. Helena to Penn for less than one-fourth of the market value. The generous offer would have been worthless, however, without needed funding from the USDA and the Beaufort County Council. Wright began to work on a business partnership that required a close-working collaboration among all parties: Wright as executive director of Penn Center; the Penn Center Board of Trustees under the encouragement and guidance of its chairman, Delores Pringle; and the Beaufort County Council.[62] That all went well was a superb accomplishment and must be credited to the trust that Penn Center had earned in the community. Money to refurbish the property came from public sources: the U.S. Department of Commerce and a South Carolina grant sponsored by state senator Scott Richards from Hilton Head.[63]

Wright retired in 2007, before his project came to fruition. It was fully accomplished under the leadership of Walter Mack, who had been deputy director. Mack, a native of St. Helena, a chemist working with Beaufort-Jasper Comprehensive Health Services, had come to Penn in 1985 to lead the demonstration farm. That farm, funded by the Save the Children Foundation to show children the basics of farming, began the first, and very popular, "U-Pick Strawberries," which allows customers to pick the berries. In all, Mack served Penn Center for twenty-nine years. When he stepped down as executive director in 2013, he received thanks from many in the community. One grateful person was David Dennis, a former CORE member who had joined Bob Moses's Algebra Project. Dennis worked with students at Penn Center to improve their skills in math. He wrote to Mack, "Thank you for your commitment and patience. It has been great working with you over the years and the participants in the Algebra Project workshops held at Penn over the years have expressed their gratitude and are still sharing the wonderful experiences. Many of the students are now doctors, lawyers, ministers, teachers, college professors and professionals in their communities. Over 90% of the 250 youth participants finished college. You played an important role in this success."[64]

Another note was from Dr. Joseph Opala, an anthropologist who studies western Africa. He remembered how Mack had helped a group of distressed children from Africa, stranded in Washington, D.C., in 2000. Opala was dealing with families that had just arrived from the civil war in Sierra Leone, traumatized by the violence they had witnessed and worried about providing food and shelter for their children. Mack's answer was immediate. He brought the children to Penn Center and enrolled them in Penn's summer enrichment program. Each child stayed with a local family, happy to eat "the Gullah- (and African-style) rice dishes they craved every day."[65]

Looking at his tenure at Penn Center, Mack listed three accomplishments that he thought were especially good for Penn: he eliminated all credit lines; he finalized the renovation of the Quality Inn and Luna Restaurant (started under Wright), and he led the efforts to bring to St. Helena a branch of the county health department and a branch of the public library. These two public services now sit in a complex on land donated by Penn Center.[66] Mack continued his work at Penn Center, concentrating his efforts on land preservation.

Michael Campi began as executive director of Penn Center on June 17, 2013. A native of Conway, South Carolina, Campi looked forward to using his training as a psychologist with experience in supervising residential facilities and health services. The appointment of a white man was the first since 1969, after six African American directors. Campi worked to put Penn on a firmer financial base, and he gave credit to Victoria Smalls, director of history and culture at Penn Center, for her work on person-to-person relationships with the visitors to Penn. In June 2014 the Board of Trustees accepted Campi's resignation and began to put together a search committee for the next executive director and the next step in the history of Penn Center.

CHAPTER SIX

Penn as a Center of Gullah Preservation

On St. Helena and the sea islands, the people preserved their culture for centuries under the harshest of conditions, "reflecting both continuity with Africa and creativity in America."[1] Every executive director at Penn Center since the 1980s has noted the essential mission of preservation, which also involves culture. Scholars and preservationists alike are coming to see the importance of such efforts: "Preserving a culture is akin to preserving an ecosystem. There are many interlocking parts to the whole."[2]

The Gullah culture has a language, history, religion, and economic system unlike any other, so historians and preservationists want to know how to preserve this rich heritage in the midst of modernization.[3] One thing all agree on is that the Gullah culture is manifest in its relationship to the land.

Gullah ancestry and heritage are a distinct part of St. Helena Island.[4] Their roots are strong, and today Gullah is as much a part of Penn Center as its ancient oaks and nineteenth-century buildings. There one can hear talk of *benyas*, those whose domicile can be traced back to plantation life, and *cumyas*, those who are recent arrivals to the area. And yet before the late 1970s, Penn Center was not interested in Gullah. From the days of Laura Towne and Rossa Cooley, Penn School was transformative; teachers wanted to imbue the islanders with a knowledge of Standard English language and Eurocentric customs. It was under the leadership of John Gadson, the center's first African American director, that Penn began the Sea Island Language Project in 1976. The project was to teach both Gullah and English to counteract the failure of the public schools to teach either.

In public schools in coastal South Carolina, students who were Gullah speakers had long been humiliated for speaking and writing "bad English." As late as the 1970s, few beyond linguistic scholars recognized Gullah as, in Gadson terms, "a separate language with its own form and structure." The Sea Island Language Project emphasized that Gullah was "a legitimate language that should and could be spoken without criticism" as well as a cultural trait worthy of being preserved. Gadson cautioned, however, that the workplace environment required the use of Standard English: "There comes a time when you have to communicate with your fellow workers, most of whom use standard English."[5] The pilot project, funded by a government grant from the Department of Labor, was to last three years, but was not renewed after its first year.

A major boost to the preservation of the Gullah language was the translation of the New Testament in the 1980s. Gullah is an oral language, and generations of Gullah preachers had been reading and teaching the Bible, but two missionaries, Claude and Pat Sharp, who did not speak Gullah, wanted a literary biblical translation.[6] The American Bible Society agreed, hoping to achieve a written translation of Gullah pronunciation. The Bible project might not have continued, but the Reverend Ervin Greene, pastor of the Brick Baptist Church near Penn Center, began to promote the project. For the estimated 125,000 Gullah speakers in the United States, of which 7,000–10,000 speak no other language, the translation of the New Testament into Gullah meant they could read scripture in their native tongue. The Gospel according to Luke, entitled *De Good Nyews Bout Jedus Christ Wa Luke Write*, was translated into Gullah in 1994. The American Bible Society has published seven editions and 32,000 copies.[7] On first hearing or reading the Gullah version, some people feel a sense of pride and joy. One wrote, "Love, love, love it. The New Testament in Gullah speaks to my core." Another wrote, "When I heard the Gullah Bible I felt a personal connection to it. It just went right inside me, to the deepest part of me."[8]

In 1980, when he took over the leadership of Penn Center, Emory Campbell was not an enthusiast for Gullah preservation. It was Herman Blake, then chairman of the board of trustees, who arranged for Campbell to meet Joseph Holloway, an expert on Africanisms in America.[9] Holloway arranged for Campbell to meet with other linguists, and newly converted, Campbell became an ardent and dedicated ally. Campbell wrote about his "personal eureka moment" when he read a pamphlet by Herman Blake, *The Sea Islands as a Cultural Resource* (1974).[10] Under Campbell's guidance, Penn Center then became the focus of Gullah preservation and its greatest promoter.[11] Campbell saw that the times had changed since the early teachers and missionaries tried to force people to give up the language and culture to become "Americanized." He thought Penn should play a critical role in developing methods to preserve and enhance the unique and rich Gullah heritage in the face of advancing tourism and construction along the seacoast. *Ef oona ent kno weh oona da gwuine, oona should kno weh oona kum from.* (If you didn't know where you are going, you should know where you come from.)

Many credit the African American linguist Lorenzo Dow Turner as being the father of Gullah studies. His classic work *Africanisms in the Gullah Dialect* (1949) precipitated academic investigation of the Gullah language.[12] Charles Joyner studied Gullah in his research on a slave community in Georgetown, South Carolina. Since his publication of *Down by the Riverside* (1984), scholarship on Gullah has been growing.[13] Joyner found that "the verbal system of Gullah was considerably more complex than that of English."[14] Another professor, Daniel Littlefield, studied the extent to which rice planters in coastal South Carolina sought slaves from rice-growing areas of Africa.[15] St. Helena produced cotton rather than rice, but the Gullah connections occurred in cotton-producing areas as well as rice-producing ones. When the anthropologist Joseph Opala conducted research at the University of Sierra Leone from 1985 to 1991, he noted the significant cultural connection between the Gullah people and the Sierra Leoneans.[16] Opala's research dovetailed with Campbell's interests. Campbell and Opala led an effort to reconnect the Gullah community to its family roots in Sierra Leone. In 1988, Sierra Leone's president, Joseph Momoh, visited Penn Center, and the next year Campbell took a group from the Gullah community to Sierra Leone for a reunion with their ancestral families. In 1990, South Carolina Educational Television produced a documentary, *Family Across the Sea*, that chronicled these events.[17]

Veronica Davis Gerald, an African American professor of English, has pointed out the importance of the Gullah people to much of our culture, including music, folkways, moral values, rituals, and agricultural products.[18] Gerald has made extensive studies of the Gullah language and its origins, and has found that many erroneously believed Gullah to be "broken English."[19] She wrote that few realized that the Gullah language originated in Africa, where people from different linguistic and cultural groups and geographic regions needed a common language in which to conduct business and intertribal affairs. During the slave trade, when Africans from different tribes were captured and housed together in holding cells, the language spoken in freedom became their method of communication in captivity, a West African Coast Creole English. In the United States, white deprecation of the Gullah language may have begun with utter confusion, such as when Laura Towne realized in 1862 that she could not understand what some of her schoolchildren were saying.[20] Then, according to William S. Pollitzer, whites in the 1920s and 1930s were condescending and incorrect in describing the language as an imperfect English dialect. Pollitzer's work was pioneering in his use of DNA analysis in Gullah studies.[21]

The origin of the word *Gullah* is said to derive from the enslaved Angolans who survived the journey to the sea islands.[22] Thousands of captured Africans constituted the population in the coastal communities of South Carolina and Georgia. As late as 1858, years after the 1808 ban on the slave trade, smugglers brought enslaved Africans from Angola to the sea islands. The *Wanderer* brought 409 captives to Jekyll Island, Georgia, in November 1858.[23] Enslaved workers were responsible for cultivating cotton. In all their activities—planting, hoeing, ditching, pounding, plowing, basket making, winnowing, picking, and threshing—they, of course, had to cooperate and communicate with one another, and they spoke Gullah.

The Gullah people enslaved on the sea islands developed communities on isolated plantations. Whites were few and did not interfere with the cultural practices of the enslaved people. As late as 1862, Charlotte Forten, the first African American teacher at Penn School, noticed that very few of the children were of mixed race: "Indeed in our school, with one or two exceptions, the children are all black." She wrote of one mixed-race student whose mother was "a good-looking woman, but quite black." Forten did not go into the details, but wrote, "Thereby, I doubt not, 'hangs a tale.'"[24] The tale, of course, was the widespread sexual abuse of enslaved African American women by white men, common throughout the South, but rare on St. Helena, with its very low proportion of whites. In the absence of white interference, enslaved blacks developed and maintained their own hybrid West African culture. The Gullah language allowed the people to remain one expansive family with a real sense of community, helping keep them intellectually, collectively, and ethnically protected.

Gullah is a language of cadence and accents, intonations as well as words. Gullah "shouts," for example, so strongly associated with the spiritual lives of the Gullah people, are rhythmic translations of old spirituals and songs and were oftentimes used as codes for transmitting meeting times and places, and as messages of freedom. The shout evokes African drum rhythms; as mentioned in the introduction, the State of South Carolina forbade drums after the 1739 Stono Rebellion.[25]

Gullah is living evidence of a remarkable transformation of African to African American culture. People speaking Gullah provide testimony to one of the great acts of human endurance in the history of the world, the survival of enslaved African people away from home. West Africans not only survived, they thrived—spiritually, intellectually, and physically—mainly because family members and families bonded with one another. After slavery, Gullah speech and customs continued because of the isolation of the sea islands. Access to the islands was only by water until the Beaufort River Bridge was built in 1927.[26] A close-knit community flourished, drawing on individual and collective strengths.

Not only did the language cross the Atlantic, but dress, food preparation, art forms, spirituality, and medicinal practices did as well. Gullah folktales resonate with all peoples everywhere. In 2000, the University of Georgia Press brought again to the public Charles Colcock Jones Jr.'s collection of folktales, originally published in 1888.[27]

Gullah culinary traditions abound on St. Helena. According to *The Ultimate Gullah Cookbook*, "Gullah food is older than the South, and as ancient as the world."[28] Food customs reached out from Africa: sweet potatoes, collards, turnips, peanuts, okra, melons, and eggplant. People added African foods to food grown in America such as tomatoes and corn. They added others such as peas, which came from the Mediterranean. Cuisine, like other aspects of culture, mixes up and changes. In addition to produce from their gardens, people relied on small game that lived in abundance all around them, including opossums, rabbits, raccoons, squirrels, wild turkeys, quails, and terrapins. The creeks, lagoons, and bays had seemingly endless quantities of shrimp, crabs, turtles, oysters, clams, mussels, and fish of many sizes and species. Forests yielded nuts, berries, and seeds, as well as syrups, roots, and barks that were useful for flavoring and medications. From their farm livestock came pork and other meats, as well as bacon, eggs, and liver.

Among the most popular Gullah foods are hoppin' john, a combination of peas and rice cooked in a greased iron skillet that makes the ingredients "hop"; hoecake, a pan bread made out of corn meal or flour dough mixed with salt and water, originally cooked over a fire on a hoe; gumbo made with either meats or fish or leftovers of any kind, and often including okra; perlo, a one-pot meal of rice with a vegetable and meat or shrimp or fish; and swimp 'n grits, made from shrimp simmered in a brown gravy and grits. Traditionally, many dishes are prepared in a single pot similar to the stew pots native to West Africa. Typical of St. Helena Island, for example, is Frogmore stew, which combines shrimp, potatoes, sausage, and corn. Another is conch stew, which contains smoked pork neck bones, bacon, drippings, pig tails, onion, peppers, celery, garlic, lard, and cooking oil, as well as shellfish.

During slavery, when many of the recipes originated, plantation owners did not want some parts of slaughtered pigs, such as the feet, jowls, ears, and intestines (chitlins). These ingredients had food value and, when properly cooked, provided not only nourishment but also in many cases came to be preferred over more appetizing-looking foods. Pot liquor, the liquid that is left over after boiling collard and other greens, was available for the enslaved workers. It has a strong taste usually flavored by the fatback cooked in the pot with the vegetables. Often the vegetables were overcooked, and many of the vitamins and minerals in the greens ended up in this pot liquor.[29] As Gerald says in her Gullah cookbook, "*Love* is one of the best kept secrets and main ingredients in Gullah food. However, of all the ingredients, it is most difficult to explain and to pass on in a recipe."[30]

Traditional food has been an important ingredient in Gullah celebrations. Festivals, feasts, holidays, and other events recognizing Gullah culture have been increasingly popular. Beaufort holds its Gullah Festival on Memorial Day weekend along the waterfront park, where there are multitudes of booths for food, art, folklore, publications, music, and other goods, and music, dancing, and dining all along the historic quay.[31]

Gullah folk medicine continues to hold interest today.[32] Plants known to people from coastal West Africa, many of which are also available in the coastal corridors of America, heal aches and pains. Combinations of certain herbs and seaweeds, when boiled together, relieve abdominal and pulmonary complaints. Some plants are dried and smoked to assuage asthma, or chewed to ease toothache. Among those mentioned in Laura Towne's diaries and letters, and those of her compatriots, were sweet gum, myrtle, blackberry, swamp grass, sassafras tea, galax (an evergreen), and kidney weed. The application of spider webs to the skin, most often to the face and neck, alleviated sores and painful insect bites.[33] While many sea islanders recognize the benefits of herbal remedies, a knowledgeable few were recognized as "root doctors" or herbalists, an esteemed position in Gullah society.

Gullah culture has a strong religious component.[34] Always a central aspect of the community, religion continues to be a powerful force. Gullah religious belief on St. Helena Island is Christian, yet Gullah spirituality is grounded in an African cosmology and worldview that transcends traditional religions and denominations.[35] On the plantation, away from white supervision, the praise house was the focus of community worship and was the official site for legal and social matters, including conflict resolution. Religious elements of shouting, dancing, spirit possession, and foot stomping, which astonished Laura Towne and Charlotte Forten in the 1860s, continue as African traditions in a Christian framework.

Enslaved Africans brought with them an African tradition of call-and-response. During praise-house meetings, the song leader calls a new verse of a spiritual, immediately after which the assembled parishioners respond. Call-and-response provides direction during the service and establishes a bond between the congregation and the religious leader. Worship, song, and religious dance reflect the African rhythms of sea island spirituals. Songs were a form of self- and group expression, a way to communicate the oppressions and hardships of slavery as well as a mental release. Songs such as "Gwine t'res from all my labuh" and "Somebody een yuh, it mus' be jedus" represented the spiritual devotion of the community.

Many parts create a culture: the Gullah culture has a language, history, economic system, and artistic vision found nowhere else. It is a heritage too valuable for a price tag. In 1990, the National Trust for Historic Preservation placed Penn School and its historic buildings on the list of "America's 11 Most Endangered Historic Places."[36] In 2004, the same organization added the Gullah Geechee coast of South Carolina and Georgia to the list. According to the group's website, "this stretch of coastline is home to one of America's most distinctive cultures: the Gullah or Geechee people, descendants of slaves who have stoutly maintained lifeways, crafts, traditions—even a language—whose origins can be traced back over the centuries to their homelands in West Africa." Preservationists fear that if the culture is lost to developers, "our nation's unique cultural mosaic will lose one of its richest and most colorful pieces."[37]

Some who hear about "the Gullah Geechee culture" are confused about the term *Geechee*. Historians have credited the name *Geechee* to the many West Africans who were smuggled into Georgia waterways and settled along a river named the Ogeechee. Gullah people, then, tend to live on the sea islands of South Carolina, and the Geechee in coastal Georgia.

James E. Clyburn became an advocate for the preservation of the coastal area of South Carolina, including the Penn Center property. Clyburn is one example of the efficacy of the Voting Rights Act of 1965. The law opened opportunities for qualified people willing to serve the country. Clyburn, one such person, was interested in political activism from an early age, and at twelve was elected president of his NAACP youth chapter. A student organizer at South Carolina State College, he led civil rights demonstrations.[38] Clyburn was elected to Congress in 1993, and in 2006 with his leadership Congress created the Gullah Geechee Cultural Heritage Corridor.[39] Clyburn wrote, "As a former history teacher and a vocal advocate of historic preservation, I believe the work of the Gullah/Geechee Cultural Heritage Corridor Commission is imperative to saving culture. The Gullah/Geechee way of life is an integral part of the Southern heritage."[40] With the support of the local Gullah Geechee communities of North Carolina, South Carolina, Georgia, and Florida, the Gullah Geechee Cultural Heritage Corridor works to "preserve, protect and sustain the vitality of Gullah Geechee Culture in the 21st Century."[41]

The purpose of the corridor is to create "an environment that celebrates the legacy and continuing contributions of Gullah Geechee people to our American heritage." Its mission is fourfold:

- To nurture pride and facilitate an understanding and awareness of the significance of Gullah Geechee history and culture within Gullah Geechee communities.
- To sustain and preserve land, language, and cultural assets within the coastal communities of South Carolina, Georgia, North Carolina, and Florida.
- To promote economic development among Gullah Geechee people.
- To educate the public on the value and importance of Gullah Geechee culture.[42]

Vital to this mission is the work of Penn Center. Emory Campbell, its former executive director, was appointed to the twenty-five-member commission charged with promoting and preserving Gullah cultural assets. In addition to work with the Gullah Geechee Cultural Heritage Corridor, Penn Center works to preserve cultural icons such as the praise houses as well as folklore and music. Moreover, Penn Center continues to facilitate dialogue among local sea islanders, real-estate developers, governmental officials, and newcomers. According to Campbell, "Unless we get both developers and newcomers to recognize the value inherent in our culture," economic development will overtake a culture where a sense of place and a relationship to the land are so vitally important. Penn Center has helped show the business community that Gullah culture is to be valued, and now the local chamber of commerce shares an appreciation of Gullah food, basket making, music, and storytelling. Some small businesses specialize in cultural items, including gift and dress boutiques, art galleries, specialized groceries, music marts, and bookstores. Local businesses that cater to tourists can see the monetary value, but as Campbell says, "One also needs the human value."[43]

Human value is depicted in art. If a picture is worth a thousand words, then a look at Gullah art is a worthwhile enterprise. Cassandra Gillens, although born and reared in the North, resides in Beaufort and cherishes her childhood memories of the South Carolina Lowcountry. Self-taught, Gillens is an artist whose work shows a love of Gullah culture.[44] The artwork of Jonathan Green also shows the human value of Gullah culture. Green uses the Gullah sense of place and identity to portray in rich detail the elements of Gullah life. "I wanted to go back to my roots," Green explained. "The older people were dying, and I began to see [the Gullahs] differently. I saw them as a people with a strong link, probably the strongest link with Africa of any of the black American people. I had studied African Art, and I began to appreciate a certain uniqueness."[45] Jeanne Moutoussamy-Ashe, a noted photographer, has been fascinated by Gullah culture: "Beginning with my first visit to the South Carolina Sea Islands, I immediately fell under the spell of the low country." She appreciates that "Gullah culture stands as a unique and distinct, yet integral part of American history."[46]

To acknowledge that Gullah culture was a vital part of U.S. culture and something to be celebrated and preserved, Penn Center instituted Heritage Days. Held on the Penn Center campus, Heritage Days also celebrates the role that Penn Center has played in the life and culture of individuals and institutions of the sea islands over many generations. Visitors often go to Penn Center's Bailey Museum, which has a permanent exhibition on the Gullah culture of the sea islands. This exhibition, which traces the transfer of West African cultural traditions to South Carolina, was a pioneering venture in publicizing the Gullah language and heritage. The museum continues as a drawing card; despite its modest size, it attracts people from all over the country—and abroad—who want to see

Penn Center and the culture of St. Helena, one of the few locations where they can see Gullah culture with little contamination by the outside world.

Inaugurated in 1982, the Heritage Days celebration was held on one afternoon, with about three hundred in attendance. According to Campbell, "The first few years were very slow."[47] Heritage Days now spreads across five days with thousands in attendance. Often beginning with an educational component, the festival ends with Sunday worship at the Brick Church, where Penn School began in 1862. Heritage Days features music, songs, meals, performers, displays, dance, theatre, art, education, and much more to celebrate Gullah culture. Entertainers have included the Hallelujah Singers, Ron and Natalie Daise, and Aunt Pearlie Sue and her Gullah Kinfolk.[48] On the grounds are authentic presentations of basketry, storytelling, net making, braiding, quilting, and bateau (boat) construction. Heritage Days also offers an old-fashioned prayer service, an art exhibition, a cultural symposium, educational seminars, a fish fry, an oyster roast, blues performances, a fashion show, a student talent show, films, and a traditional craft fair. Heritage Days attracts all races and nationalities. All visitors are encouraged to participate in every way possible and share the programs, displays, and events to the fullest extent. There is something for all ages, including a special section called "Fun Fuh De Chillun."

The Heritage Days celebration highlights a different Gullah theme each year. Some past themes include the following:

1982 What Penn Center Means to My Heritage
1985 Bend to the Oar, although the Tide Be against You
1994 The African American Family: Preserving Leadership through Cultural Involvement
1998 The Black Seminoles: Gullah Pioneer Freedom Fighters
2002 Lest We Forget: 140 Years of Education for Freedom
2004 De Ole Sheep Done Know de Road! De Young Lamb Mus Find e Way
2013 Eyes Still on the Prize

Preserving a culture is vastly different from preserving a cultural artifact. Living cultures and living languages continually change and evolve. The Gullah people shaped their culture and were in turn shaped by it, all the while "reflecting both continuity with Africa and creativity in America."[49] Emory Campbell pointed out that Gullah culture involved "people who were using their African know-how, people who were using their stamina to survive in this environment."[50] This resilience often went along with poverty. Preservationists have to struggle with ways to preserve cultural resilience even as they try to eliminate poverty. Development can mean better wages, better health, and less isolation, but it can bring an end to traditional ways of life. Furthermore, marketing Gullah culture may be a means of preserving it, but it also could mean its demise.[51]

The loss of Gullah culture and language would mean the loss of an integral component of American heritage and way of life. If we homogenize our coastal areas, we cut down part of our nation's cultural treasure. Because the issues are complicated, it takes all interested persons to discuss what should be preserved and why, as well as how preservation can be accomplished. The questions have no easy answers, but Penn Center will continue its role in bringing groups together for needed dialogue. Through it all, the indomitable spirit of Penn School/Penn Center, a spirit nourished by the idealism of black and white men and women, will persevere.

APPENDIX

Beaufort County and St. Helena
Subdivision Population Data

Created in 1769, Beaufort District (designated a "County" in 1868) in 1860 had
a population of 40,053, 83 percent of whom were African Americans, of whom
only 809 were free (see table 1). Between 1790 and 1865, Beaufort District comprised three parishes: St. Peter on the west, St. Luke in the middle (covering
what is now Bluffton and Hilton Head), and St. Helena to the east (covering
St. Helena Island, the town of Beaufort, and other places). In 1878, Beaufort
County lost territory in the creation of Hampton County, and again in 1912 in
the creation of Jasper County. The last change came in 1951, when Jasper County
received a strip from Beaufort County along the Savannah River. According to
census reports, the total population of Beaufort County declined in each decade
from 1860 (with the exception of the 1890 and 1900 reports, both of which
showed increases in whites and blacks) until 1950, when there was a substantial
increase among white citizens. The census of 1960 reported that for the first time
whites were a majority; African Americans were 38 percent of the population
of Beaufort County. By the 2010 census, although the African American population of Beaufort had increased dramatically, nearly doubling from the 1960
figure of 16,969 to 30,662, the non–African American population had exploded.
Whites numbered 107,279, and other ethnicities such as Hispanic and Asian
accounted for another 2,238. African Americans were only slightly more than a
fifth of the total population (less than 22 percent).

Migration statistics from the American Community Survey (ACS), com-
bined with IRS tax data, reveal massive migration into the South. Table 2 displays where Beaufort County's residents were born for each census year between
1970 and 2010. South Carolina's sea islands and beaches attract retirees, and the
Parris Island Marine Base brings in more people from out of state. In 1970, 40.6

TABLE 1. Population of Beaufort County, South Carolina, 1860–2010

Year	Whites	African Americans	% African American	Other	Total
1860	6,714	33,309*	83.2		40,053
1870	5,309	29,050	84.5		34,359
1880	2,442	27,732	91.9	2	30,176
1890	2,695	31,421	92.1	3	34,119
1900	3,349	32,137	90.5	9	35,495
1910	3,963	26,376	86.9	16	30,355
1920	4,801	17,454	78.4	14	22,269
1930	6,243	15,571	71.4	1	21,815
1940	7,255	14,781	67.1	1	22,037
1950	11,472	15,504	58.1	17	26,693
1960	27,083	16,969	38.4	135	44,187
1970	33,864	16,848	32.9	424	51,136
1980	42,454	21,504	32.9	1,406	65,364
1990	59,843	24,582	28.4	2,000	86,425
2000	85,451	29,005	24.0	6,481	120,937
2010	107,279	30,662	21.9	2,238	140,179

Source: U.S. Census
*The figure for 1860 includes 809 free persons of color.

percent of all residents of Beaufort County were South Carolina natives. In 2010, although the absolute number of native South Carolinians living in Beaufort County had more than doubled, they accounted for a little more than a quarter (28.1 percent) of the population. Some 14,908 of the newcomers were foreign born (9.6 percent), and of the 94,728 born in states other than South Carolina, the largest proportion, more than a third (37.4 percent), were from the other fifteen states defined by the census as being part of the South, and represented a little more than a fifth (22.8 percent) of the total population of Beaufort County. Together, native-born South Carolinians and those from the other fifteen defined southern states now account for barely a majority (50.9 percent) of Beaufort County's population. In contrast, southerners accounted for more than two-thirds (67.8 percent) of all the county's inhabitants in 1970. The population of Beaufort County is changing rapidly, and St. Helena Island, part of the county, is as well, but has been more slowly affected.

Table 3 is a compilation of published population figures for St. Helena Island. From studying only the published census figures from either the census itself or

TABLE 2. Nativity for Beaufort County, South Carolina, 1970–2010:
Number and percent of total population

Census Year	1970		1980		1990		2000		2010	
	No.	%	No.	%	No.	%	No.	%	No.	%
Total population	51,136		65,364		86,425		120,937		155,550	
Native born (in U.S.)	50,561	98.9	63,342	96.9	84,131	97.3	113,341	93.7	140,642	90.4
Born in state of residence	20,768	40.6	25,940	39.7	30,075	34.8	37,960	31.4	43,736	28.1
Born in a different state	26,771	52.4	36,784	56.3	52,786	61.1	73,541	60.8	94,728	60.9
Northeast	6,810	13.3	10,605	16.2	15,191	17.6	24,495	20.3	32,054	20.6
Midwest*	4,029	7.9	6,875	10.5	11,600	13.4	15,489	12.8	20,386	13.1
South	13,926	27.2	16,592	25.4	22,233	25.7	28,279	23.4	35,467	22.8
West	2,006	3.9	2,712	4.1	3,762	4.4	5,278	4.4	6,821	4.4
Born outside the U.S.**	395	0.8	618	0.9	1,270	1.5	1,840	1.5	2,178	1.4
Foreign born***	na		2,022	3.1	2,294	2.7	7,596	6.3	14,908	9.6
State of birth not reported (1970 only)****	2,627	5.1								

Sources: 1970 Census of Population, chapter C, table 119; 1980 Census of Population, chapter C, table 174; 1990 Census of Population, CP-2, table 143; 2000 Census of Population, QT-P22; 2010 American Community Survey, 5-Year Data (2006–10), B05002.

* Region listed as Midwest was called North Central in the 1970 and 1980 Censuses.

** Called "Born Abroad" or "Born Outside United States"; indicates persons who are native American citizens who were born outside the territory of the United States.

*** The 1970 Census had a section entitled "foreign stock," but included people born in the United States whose parents were foreign born, hence it was impossible to determine a number for this category for 1970.

**** The 1970 Census numbers are based on all responses to the census, and some did not report their state of birth; the 1980 Census and later censuses used sampling to determine proportions, which were applied to the total population.

by using *Social Explorer*, it appears that African Americans have been a minority of St. Helena since 1990. It is difficult, however, to get the precise population figure for St. Helena Island, and several scholars have not distinguished between St. Helena Island (the actual island where Penn Center is located), and St. Helena Island Division, a census designation that includes all the islands to the south and east of the Coosaw and Beaufort Rivers. According to a South Carolina Department of Transportation map, the St. Helena Island Division includes St. Helena Island as well as Morgan, Judge, Dataw, Lady's, Pine, Warsaw, Gibbs, Cane, Cat, Pola Wana, Fig, Phillips, Bay Point, Capers, Pritchards, Fripp,

TABLE 3.   St. Helena Census Subdivision Population, 1930–2010

	Population	African Americans	% African Americans	Whites
1930	4,626	4,458	96.4	168
1940	4,266	3,961	92.9	305
1960	6,048	4,994	82.6	1,054
1970	5,718	4,278	74.8	1,440
1980	8,134	4,934	60.7	3,200
1990	11,524	5,443	47.2	6,081
2000	18,273	7,242	39.6	11,031
2010	20,932	7,486	35.8	13,446

Sources: Information on 1930–1980 is from Patricia Jones-Jackson, *When Roots Die: Endangered Traditions on the Sea Islands* (Athens: University of Georgia Press, 1987), 11, citing the U.S. Census. Information on 1990–2010 is from *Social Explorer* on the U.S. Census website.

Note: See text on why these figures should be used with caution.

Huntington, and Harbor Islands. Some of these other areas, such as Fripp Island and Lady's Island, are more developed and have more white residents. Thus, while St. Helena Division changed from nearly all–African American in 1930 (96.4 percent) to 60.7 percent African American in 1980, in 2010 it was only slightly more than a third (35.8 percent) African American.

Beginning with the 2000 Census, it is possible to look at individual census tracts for Beaufort County. These tracts allow a good estimation of the population on just St. Helena Island, since Lady's Island and Fripp Island are excluded. Table 4 shows interesting trends. It indicates that African Americans still make up a majority of the population on St. Helena, but their share of the population has shrunk from 63 percent to 59 percent in the last decade. Although African Americans still occupy most homes, that proportion also declined from 2000 to 2010, from 58 to 55 percent. The percentage of African American–owned homes has also dropped (from 58 to 52 percent), while the percentage of homes owned by whites has gone up (40 to 46 percent). Though African American home ownership has decreased, still three-quarters (78.3 percent) of African Americans on St. Helena Island live in homes that they own. The African American population on St. Helena has fared better at keeping their land than people on other islands, such as Hilton Head, or in other areas along the coast. Penn Center and the programs it sponsors have made a huge difference for the African American population on St. Helena Island.

TABLE 4. St. Helena Island Census Track Area Population and
Home Ownership (%), 2000 and 2010

	2000			2010		
	Black	White	Other	Black	White	Other
Total population	63.17	34.60	2.22	59.23	36.53	4.25
Total housing units occupied by group	58.39	40.05	1.56	54.57	42.73	2.70
Total owned housing units owned by group	58.49	40.36	1.15	51.89	46.30	1.81
Total rented housing units rented by group	57.80	38.07	4.13	67.08	26.05	6.86
Group living in owned homes	86.56	87.09	64.00	78.29	89.23	55.10
Group living in rented homes	13.44	12.91	36.00	21.71	10.77	44.90

Note: All figures are percentages. The St. Helena Island Area is defined as Beaufort Census Tract 11 for the 2000 Census and as Beaufort Census Tracts 11.01 and 11.02 for the 2010 Census.

NOTES

Introduction

1. Additional photographs are available in the Penn School Papers (hereafter cited as PSP) in the Southern Historical Collection at the University of North Carolina, Chapel Hill.

2. Bill Saunders, interview by Vernon Burton, October 9, 2013.

3. Rowland, Moore, and Rogers, *History of Beaufort County*, 1:16–17. Hispaniola is the island shared today by Haiti and the Dominican Republic.

4. Ibid., 18. The precise location remains in doubt.

5. According to Rowland, Moore, and Rogers (*History of Beaufort County*, 18), the colony's location is still debated among historians. Some have said Wynah Bay, others Port Royal. Most recent scholarship suggests that it was closer to the Savannah River (Lawrence Rowland, e-mail to the authors, September 19, 2013). See also Joyner, "San Miguel de Gualdape."

6. Hoffman, *New Andalucia*, 78; Rowland, Moore, and Rogers, *History of Beaufort County*, 1:19.

7. Rowland, Moore, and Rogers, *History of Beaufort County*, 1:23.

8. Hoffman, *New Andalucia*, 139.

9. Rosengarten, *Tombee*, 41–47.

10. Ibid., 50–51.

11. Utsey, *Who's Who in South Carolina, 1934–35*, 251; Ochiai, *Harvesting Freedom*, 24.

12. Smith, *Stono*; Burton, *In My Father's House*; Hoffer, *"Cry Liberty"*; Thornton, "African Dimensions of the Stono Rebellion"; Wood, *Black Majority*, 308–26.

13. See Williams, *Self-Taught*. W. E. B. Du Bois reminds us that public education in the South was the idea of freed African Americans; see his *Black Reconstruction in America*, 638. See also Span, *From Cotton Field to Schoolhouse*, 4.

14. Rose, *Rehearsal for Reconstruction*.

15. Finnegan, *A Deed So Accursed*.

16. Cooley, *School Acres*, 157.

17. The classic statement on the "long civil rights movement" is Hall, "Long Civil Rights Movement"; see also Lawson, "Long Origins of the Short Civil Rights Movement"; for a critical reading of the long civil rights movement thesis, specifically with regard to timing and place, see Cha-Jua and Lang, "The 'Long Movement' as Vampire," and especially Lang, "Locating the Civil Rights Movement."

18. Power, *I Will Not Be Silent*, 24.

19. Stokely Carmichael, speech read at the Citizens Conference on Education, Penn Center, January 28, 1968. Ethel Minor delivered the speech on behalf of Carmichael. The manuscript of the speech is in the possession of Cleveland Sellers.

20. NET news, Fall 2013, brochure.

21. "Penn Center: History Overview," accessed January 30, 2014, www.penncenter .com/history.

22. National Park Service, Gullah/Geechee Cultural Heritage Corridor, http://www .nps.gov/guge/index.htm. The corridor extends from Wilmington, North Carolina, to Jacksonville, Florida. See chapter 6 for more information.

23. Hugh Gibson, "Dateline Columbia: Frogmore Agenda Presages Trouble," *Charleston News and Courier*, March 15, 1964.

CHAPTER 1. Penn School Begins amidst War

1. The 1860 U.S. Census Slave Schedules for Beaufort District, South Carolina, which included St. Helena and more, show a total of 32,530 slaves, the second-highest county total in the country, behind Charleston; see table 1 in the appendix. Ninety-eight slave owners held 80 or more slaves in Beaufort County, accounting for 14,858 people, or 45 percent of the county total (NARA microfilm series M653, Roll 1231). Census data can found at the University of Virginia Library, Historical Census Browser, http:// mapserver.lib.virginia.edu. See also "The Port Royal Experiment," accessed April 8, 2013, http://drbronsontours.com/bronsonportroyalexperiment.html. The Beaufort District became Beaufort County in 1868.

2. Rosengarten, *Tombee*, 55.

3. Ibid., 213, 215.

4. James McPherson, e-mail to Burton, August 22, 2013; see also Rosengarten, *Tombee*, 211–12. This was the first major battle involving steam-powered ships, which were more difficult to hit than sailing ships (Stephen R. Wise, e-mail to Burton, September 3, 2013).

5. Many then regrouped to form an organized Confederate retreat (Rosengarten, *Tombee*, 215–17).

6. Rose, *Rehearsal for Reconstruction*.

7. Ibid., 16. She cites *Official Records of the War of the Rebellion*, series 1, 4:4–6.

8. Rose, *Rehearsal for Reconstruction*, 107–10.

9. Ibid., 115, 105.

10. Ibid., xii. See also Butchart, "Laura Towne and Ellen Murray," 2:16.

11. Smalls quoted by the historian Bernard Powers in "Into the Fire (1861–1896)," an episode of *African Americans: Many Rivers to Cross*, a PBS television documentary narrated by Henry Louis Gates, http://www.pbs.org/wnet/african-americans-many -rivers-to-cross/video/into-the-fire.

12. *Charleston Daily Courier*, May 14, 1862.

13. Burton, *Age of Lincoln*, 151–52; see also Billingsley, *Yearning to Breathe Free*; Uya, *From Slavery to Public Service*; Miller, *Gullah Statesman*.

14. *Collected Works of Abraham Lincoln*, 5:132.

15. *New York Tribune*, February 14, 1862.

16. In addition to the classic work by Willie Lee Rose, *Rehearsal for Reconstruction*, other useful sources on the Port Royal Experiment include Ash, *When the Yankees Came*, 76–92; Gerteis, *From Contraband to Freedman*, 49–62; Ochiai, *Harvesting Freedom*, 51–144; Richardson, *Christian Reconstruction*, 17–19.

17. Rose, *Rehearsal for Reconstruction*, 26–27.

18. Towne diary, October 19, 1862. This passage is not included in Holland's edited version of the Towne letters and diary. The complete set is in PSP.

19. Rose, *Rehearsal for Reconstruction*, 49.

20. In 1849, McKim was the recipient of a package containing Henry "Box" Brown, who shipped himself to freedom.

21. Butchart, "Laura Towne and Ellen Murray," 17–18.

22. *The Letters and Diary of Laura M. Towne, Written from the Sea Islands of South Carolina, 1862–1884*, ed. Rupert Sargent Holland, x (hereafter cited as Towne, *Letters and Diary*). When a quotation from Laura Towne's diary is not included in Holland's edited version, the citation is to Towne Diary, PSP.

23. Wolf, "Towne and the Freed People," 380. Wolf cites Hiram Barney to Laura M. Towne, April 3, 1862, Custom House, New York, "Circular of the Port Royal Relief Committee [Philadelphia]," March 7, 1863, Papers of Arthur Sumner, vol. 4, PSP.

24. Rose, *Rehearsal for Reconstruction*, 77.

25. Towne, *Letters and Diary*, April 17, 1862, 6.

26. Ibid.

27. For more on the Gullah culture and language, see chapter 6.

28. Towne, *Letters and Diary*, April 17, 1862, 7.

29. Ibid., April 27, 1862, 18.

30. People did not know that mosquitoes carry the parasite that causes malaria.

31. Emory Campbell, Gullah Tour, Hilton Head, October 18, 2013. Conservationists are trying to preserve the breed.

32. Towne, *Letters and Diary*, October 28, 1877, 281.

33. Ibid., April 27, 1862, 22, 20.

34. Ibid., April 28, 1862, 23.

35. Ibid., December 18, 1884, 144.

36. Ibid., February 7, 1864, 127.

37. Ibid., March 27, 1864, 135.

38. See Schwalm, *Hard Fight for We*, 70.

39. Ochiai, *Harvesting Freedom*, 64.

40. Towne, *Letters and Diary*, August 25 1862, 26.

41. Ibid., 57. The letter was dated May 23, 1862, and Ellen Murray arrived on June 8 (65).

42. Butchart, "Laura Towne and Ellen Murray," 18.

43. Towne, *Letters and Diary*, April 17, 1862, 8.

44. Ibid., June 18, 1862, 70. They sometimes had extra students. For instance, when a schoolteacher at another school on the island visited the North, Murray took her students into her own classes. (Towne, *Letters and Diary*, 92). St. Helena was home to thirty little schools, most of which did not continue long; see Edith Dabbs, *Walking Tall*.

45. Towne Diary, September 22, 1862, PSP. Kurt J. Wolf discusses some of the discrepancies around the actual founding date of the school; see "Towne and the Freed People," 390.

46. Towne, "Pioneer Work on the Sea Islands," 399–400.

47. Ibid., 400.

48. Towne Diary, October 3, 1862, PSP.

49. Cooley, *School Acres*, 12. Cooley was quoting Murray.

50. *Journal of Charlotte Forten Grimke*, 17. See also *Journal of Charlotte L. Forten*, 24, hereafter cited as Forten, *Journal*.

51. Charlotte Forten, "Life on the Sea Islands," 587.

52. *Journal of Charlotte Forten Grimke*, 389; see also Forten, *Journal*, October 28, 1862, 144.

53. Forten, *Journal*, 146.

54. Bennett, *Before the Mayflower*, 212.

55. Forten, *Journal*, 148.

56. Ibid., 149.

57. Ibid., 150.

58. Ibid., 150, 152.

59. Billingsley, *Yearning to Breathe Free*, 109.

60. Towne Diary, October 28, 1862, PSP.

61. Ibid., November 4, 1862.

62. Forten, *Journal*, 146.

63. Ibid.

64. Towne Diary, October 29, 1862, PSP.

65. Rose, *Rehearsal for Reconstruction*, 161.

66. Forten, *Journal*, 156.

67. Ibid., 154. Although Abraham Lincoln did not proclaim Thanksgiving a national holiday until 1863, many people were already celebrating the fourth Thursday in November for that purpose.

68. Edward S. Philbrick wrote on November 16 1862: "I had a talk with General Saxton. He was feeling very blue, had just been to Hilton Head to get some tents for his new recruits of which he enlisted about a hundred on his recent expedition to St. Mary's. There are some 3000 tents in warehouse there, but General Brannan refused to open it for him, alleging the advice of the Medical Department, which closed it because yellow fever had been near it. Now it is notorious that whenever one of General Brannan's men wants anything from the same warehouse, he gives a special order and it is opened for him, but not for General Saxton, the Abolitionist" (available at http://www.drbronson tours.com/bronsongeneralrufusbsaxton.html).

69. Forten, *Journal*, 154–55.

70. Ibid., 155–56.

71. Ibid., 165.

72. Ibid., 165–66.

73. Ibid., 152, 167; Towne, *Letters and Diary*, December 25, 1862, 97.

74. Forten Grimké, "Personal Recollections of Whittier." See also Bob Hester, "Origin of the 'St. Helena Hymn': Words, Music, and Spirit," unpublished paper, December 2012, in possession of Burton.

75. Stevenson, introduction to *Journal of Charlotte Forten Grimké*, 32–33. One of Weld's coauthors was Angelina Grimké, future aunt of Charlotte Forten Grimké. Towne

had first learned in October 1862 about Lincoln's plan for emancipation: "Our first victory worth the name."

76. *Journal of Charlotte Forten Grimké*, 374.

77. Ibid., January 1, 1863, 428–35.

78. Forten, *Journal*, 171, 172.

79. Morris, "'We Are Verily Guilty concerning Our Brother.'" See also McNulty, "William Henry Brisbane."

80. *The Complete Civil War Journal and Selected Letters of Thomas Wentworth Higginson*, ed. Christopher Looby, available on the University of Chicago Press website, accessed April 6, 2013, http://www.press.uchicago.edu/Misc/Chicago/333302 .html. In addition, the passage refers to "Corporal, later Sergeant, Prince Rivers, later a member of the South Carolina Constitutional Convention, and a member of the state legislature; Corporal, later Sergeant, Robert Sutton, later court-martialed for an alleged act of mutiny (which, however, Higginson and his officers disbelieved), then pardoned and restored to his place in the regiment)." See also Burton, *In My Father's House*; and Burton, "Whence Cometh Rural Black Reconstruction Leadership."

81. Forten, *Journal*, 172–73. Towne had earlier written about Prince Rivers as a "gifted sergeant" (Towne Diary, November 2, 1862, PSP).

82. Forten's diary suggests her friendship with Dr. Rogers during their time on St. Helena was more than platonic; see *Journal of Charlotte Forten Grimké*, 46–48, and especially 454–55, Forten's entry for February 19, 1863.

83. Forten, *Journal*, 149–50.

84. Towne, *Letters and Diary*, August 26, 1862, 87.

85. Anderson, *Education of Blacks in the South*, 28.

86. Towne, *Letters and Diary*, July 17, 1862, 78.

87. Towne Diary, September 24, 1862, PSP.

88. Towne, *Letters and Diary*, July 20, 1862, 78.

89. Ibid., August 26, 1862, 88–89.

90. Towne Diary, September 26, 1862, PSP.

91. Towne, *Letters and Diary*, July 20, 1863, 114.

92. Ibid., October 24, 1862, 93.

93. Ibid., November 28, 1862, 96.

94. The Union lost 1,515 men (246 dead, 880 wounded, and 389 missing) out of a total of 5,264, compared with a Confederate total of only 174 (36 dead, 133 wounded, and 5 missing); see Burton, *Age of Lincoln*, 182–83. The movie *Glory* (1989) tells the story of

this battle. Lewis Douglass, son of Frederick Douglass, was in this regiment and fought at Fort Wagner.

95. *Journal of Charlotte Forten Grimké*, 497.

96. William C. Kashatus, "America's Civil War: 54th Massachusetts Regiment," *American History*, October 2000, available at HistoryNet.com, accessed April 8, 2013, http://www.historynet.com/culture/african_american_history/3029086.html?showAll=y&c=y.

97. J. Rickard, "Battle of Fort Wagner, 11 and 18 July 1863" (September 3, 2007), HistoryOfWar.org, accessed April 8, 2013, http://www.historyofwar.org/articles/battles_fort_wagner.html; see also Burton, *Age of Lincoln*, 183.

98. *Journal of Charlotte Forten Grimké*, July 22, 1863, 495.

99. Towne, *Letters and Diary*, July 27, 1863, 115–16.

100. *Journal of Charlotte Forten Grimké*, 34.

101. Forten, *Journal*, June 30, 1863, 211.

102. Towne would purchase Frogmore in 1868 and live there until her death in 1901.

103. Forten, *Journal*, July 26, 1863, 217–18.

104. Forten came back for visits in 1868, 1869, and 1872; see Wolf, "Towne and the Freed People," 392. In 1871, she returned to South Carolina to teach at the Shaw Memorial School (*Journal of Charlotte Forten Grimké*, 43).

105. Towne, *Letters and Diary*, January 7, 1864, 122.

106. Ibid., March 14, 1864, 134.

107. Ibid., March 25, 1864, 135.

108. Ibid., October 23, 1864, 140.

109. Ibid.

110. The Freedman's Aid Society of Pennsylvania would be one of the few sources of income for the school over the ensuing years, other than what the Towne family and their close friends contributed when the financial situation became desperate; see Towne, "Pioneer Work," 398.

111. The military used prefabricated buildings during the war. The author is grateful to Steven Wise for pointing out an article by Charles E. Petersen, "Early American Prefabrication," *Gazette des Beaux Arts* 53, no. 6 (1948): 37–46, and to Alex Moore for pointing out Burnham Kelly's *The Prefabrication of Houses* (Cambridge, Mass.: MIT Press, 1951), available online at https://archive.org/stream/prefabricationfooalberich#page/n7/mode/2up.

112. Edith Dabbs, *Sea Island Diary*.

113. Goodwine, "Penn Center," 711.

114. Towne, *Letters and Diary*, January 21, 1865, 151.

115. Ibid., January 8, 1865, 148, 147.

116. Cooley, *Homes of the Freed*, 106–7.

117. McPherson, *Battle Cry of Freedom*, 826.

118. Burton, *Age of Lincoln*, 188.

119. Towne, *Letters and Diary*, January 8, 1865, 148. Union forces took Columbia, South Carolina, on February 17, 1865, and Charleston on February 18.

120. Towne, *Letters and Diary*, January 8, 1865, 148–49.

121. See Bell, *Major Butler's Legacy*. During the Civil War, Kemble published her *Journal of a Residence on a Georgian Plantation in 1838–1839*; see *Fanny Kemble's Journals*.

122. "Great Auction of Slaves at Savannah, Georgia", *New York Tribune*, March 2-3, 1859, available at Antislavery Literature, accessed January 30, 2013, antislavery.eserver .org/travel/thompsonauction/thompsonauction.html.

123. Towne, *Letters and Diary*, September 12, 1862, 92.

124. Ibid., January 21, 1865, 150.

125. General Kirby Smith surrendered his army on May 26, and on June 23, General Stand Watie and the last of the Confederate armies surrendered in Indian Territory (now Oklahoma).

126. Quoted in Billingsley, *Yearning to Breathe Free*, 92.

127. Towne, *Letters and Diary*, April 29, 1865, 162.

CHAPTER 2. Penn School from Reconstruction to 1901

1. For the history of Reconstruction, see Burton, *Age of Lincoln*, 234–322; Du Bois, *Black Reconstruction in America*; Foner, *Reconstruction*. For Reconstruction in South Carolina, see Williamson, *After Slavery*; Zuczek, *State of Rebellion*; Josephine Martin, "Educational Efforts of Freedmen's Aid Societies"; Saville, *Work of Reconstruction*. Reconstruction and its legacy have been traced in Baker, *What Reconstruction Meant*.

2. Richardson, *Christian Reconstruction*, 143.

3. *Papers of Andrew Johnson*, 8:263–64.

4. Ibid., 8:317–19.

5. Towne, *Letters and Diary*, March 9, 1866, 172.

6. Quoted in Uya, *From Slavery to Public Service*, 35; see also Burton, *Age of Lincoln*, 254.

7. Towne, *Letters and Diary*, June 13, 1865, 163.

8. Ibid., June 13, 1865, 164.

9. *Pennsylvania Freedmen's Bulletin* 3 (April 1867): 5, published as part of *American Freedman* 2 (April 1867); Butchart, "Laura Towne and Ellen Murray," 21.

10. Towne, *Letters and Diary*, December 13, 1868, 202–3. *Normal* referred to norms, the idea being that teacher training would follow a standardized curriculum. Some early normal schools evolved into colleges.

11. Butchart, "Laura Towne and Ellen Murray," 21.

12. Towne, *Letters and Diary*, November 27, 1870, 221.

13. Cooley, *School Acres*, 19. Cooley actually found these subjects less than adequate; see chapter 3.

14. Towne, *Letters and Diary*, February 1, 1863, 100.

15. Ibid., February 24, 1863, 103.

16. Lincoln made that suggestion on February 10, 1863; see Lincoln, *Collected Works*, 6:98. For more about Brisbane, see chapter 1.

17. Ochiai, *Harvesting Freedom*, 119.

18. Rowland et al., *History of Beaufort County, South Carolina*, 1:417. The librarian in Beaufort wrote on Brisbane's biographical sketch, "*Not exactly an activity that would endear one to one's former neighbors, relatives and childhood associates.*" See also Wallace Alcorn, "William Henry Brisbane, 1806–1878," accessed April 26, 2012, http://www .wallacealcorn.org/main/Tentative_biographical_sketch_Brisbane.html.

19. Chesnut, *Diary from Dixie*, 540; see also *Private Mary Chesnut*.

20. Towne, *Letters and Diary*, September 1, 1865, 167.

21. Ibid.

22. Ibid., October 15, 1865, 167–68.

23. Ibid., October 15, 1865, 168.

24. Ibid., September 1, 1865, 166.

25. Ibid., February 8, 1863, 102.

26. Historians have examined the tension over economic policy and the differing attitudes of whites and African Americans toward labor; see, for instance, Foner, *Nothing but Freedom*.

27. Towne, *Letters and Diary*, February 23, 1866, 171.

28. Ibid., January 10, 1868, 187–88.

29. Ibid., February 10, 1867, 175.

30. Ibid., January 10, 1868, 188.

31. Ibid., April 11, 1869, 207.

32. Ibid., December 3, 1869, 214.

33. Ibid., May 12, 1867, 182.

34. Rose, *Rehearsal for Reconstruction*, 78. The judge who convicted Hunn was Roger Taney, later the chief justice of the U.S. Supreme Court who issued the infamous opinion in *Dred Scott* (1857) that African Americans had no rights whatsoever.

35. Towne, *Letters and Diary*, March 3, 1867, 178.

36. Ibid., March 3, 1867, 179.

37. Ibid., January 10, 1868, 187–88.

38. Ibid., February 20, 1868, 190.

39. Ibid., April 3, 1868, 192.

40. Billingsley, *Yearning to Breathe Free*, 82–85.

41. South Carolina General Assembly, 117th Session, 2007–2008, H. 3695; see also Uya, *From Slavery to Public Service*, 35; Burton, *Age of Lincoln*, 254; Miller, *Gullah Statesman*.

42. Towne, *Letters and Diary*, May 29, 1870, 220.

43. Kristen Adkins, "Benezet, Anthony," on LearningToGive.org, October 10, 2012, http://learningtogive.org/papers/paper77.html.

44. Towne, *Letters and Diary*, July 6, 1871, 223.

45. Ibid., February 12, 1873, 228.

46. Many members of the Cope family were philanthropists, and many supported Penn School. Francis Cope's son, Francis R. Cope Jr. (1878–1962), would become chairman of the Penn School Board of Trustees; see chapter 3. The papers of Francis Reeve Cope are in the Historical Society of Pennsylvania, Collection 1847, Cope Family Papers.

47. Towne, *Letters and Diary*, April 6, 1873, 230.

48. Ibid., September 27, 1874, 237–38.

49. Ibid., June 20, 1875, 242.

50. Ibid., May 21, 1876, 247. Grits cost $1.05 a bushel, about 26 cents a peck.

51. Ibid., July 2, 1876, 250.

52. The industry declined in South Carolina in the late 1880s; see Shuler, Bailey, and Philips, "Phosphate Mining in South Carolina"; Shick and Doyle, "South Carolina Phosphate Boom."

53. Simkins and Woody, *South Carolina during Reconstruction*, 89. Eric Foner found that between 1865 and 1876 about two thousand blacks held elective and appointive

offices in the South. A few are relatively well known, but most became obscure after being omitted from official state histories after Reconstruction. Foner profiles more than 1,500 black legislators, state officials, sheriffs, justices of the peace, and constables in *Freedom's Lawmakers*.

54. Burton, "'Black Squint of the Law,'" 167.

55. Resolution honoring "members of the South Carolina executive, legislative, and judicial branches of government and the members of the state's congressional delegation who heroically served the people of this state following the Civil War until the early twentieth century," South Carolina General Assembly, 117th Session, 2007–2008, H. 3695. See also Carolina Heart Strings, "The Penn Center: From the Civil War to Civil Rights and Beyond," accessed February 22, 2011, http://www.carolinaheartstrings .com/?p=2292.

56. *New South Newspaper*, 1862–65, available online and searchable at the University Libraries Digital Collection. http://library.sc.edu/digital/collections/newsouthabout .html.

57. Towne, *Letters and Diary*, July 2, 1876, 249.

58. Burton et al., "South Carolina," 192.

59. "Plan of the Campaign of 1876," in the Papers of Martin Witherspoon Gary, South Caroliniana Library; quotation from Benjamin R. Tillman, "The Struggle of 1876: How South Carolina Was Delivered from Carpet-Bag and Negro Rule," speech at the Red-Shirt Reunion at Anderson, S.C., 1909; The campaign is discussed in Burton, *Age of Lincoln*, chapter 12.

60. Towne, *Letters and Diary*, October 29, 1876, 254.

61. Ibid., 254–55.

62. For an analysis of this election, see Burton, *Age of Lincoln*, 310–12.

63. Towne, *Letters and Diary*, April 15, 1877, 261.

64. Towne letters, May 6, 1877, scan 400–401, PSP.

65. Towne, *Letters and Diary*, May 27 and June 17, 1877, 265–67. A mil is one-tenth of one cent.

66. Towne, July 15, 1877, p. 270. In April 1877, Towne described Macdonald: "Mr. Macdonald has two stores now—the corner one, from which Walter R. has departed, ostensibly for his health, but really because he doesn't make enough, and the store that Edgell had, where Mr. M. has been these two years. Mr. M. is very nice, gets everything we want, either from Beaufort or Savannah, charges very moderately, and every way does all he can for us. I like him better and better. He is a noble, splendid fellow" (*Letters and*

Diary, 261). The Macdonald family has supported Penn School and Penn Center ever since; see Edith Dabbs, *Sea Island Diary*, 204.

67. Towne, *Letters and Diary*, July 15, 1877, 270.

68. Ibid., August 19, 1877, 272.

69. Ibid., 273.

70. Quoted in Burton, *Age of Lincoln*, 283; Uya, *From Slavery to Public Service*, 105.

71. Towne, *Letters and Diary*, November 6, 1878, 289.

72. Ibid., October 29, 1878, 288.

73. Ibid., 288–89.

74. Ibid., November 10, 1878, 292.

75. Ibid., November 6, 1878, 289.

76. Wolf, "Towne and the Freed People," 402.

77. "Hurricanes," *The South Carolina Encyclopedia*, ed. Walter Edgar (Columbia: University of South Carolina Press, 2006), 470.

78. Edith Dabbs, *Walking Tall*, 7.

79. Tindall, *South Carolina Negroes*, 88; Burton et al., "South Carolina."

80. Escott and Goldfield, *History of the American South*, 2:183; Burton, *Age of Lincoln*, chapter 12.

81. Burton, "'Black Squint of the Law,'" 170; Simkins, *Pitchfork Ben Tillman*, 57, 407; Tillman, inaugural address, South Carolina, *Journal of the House of Representatives, 1890*, 130–54.

82. Hegstrom, *Penn*, 84.

83. Towne, *Letters and Diary*, October 28, 1877, 281.

84. Ibid., July 9, 1884, 309–10.

85. Jacoway, *Yankee Missionaries*, 37.

86. For a history of Hampton Institute, written during a time of segregation, see Francis Greenwood Peabody, a member of the board of trustees, *Education for Life*.

87. Armstrong's parents began a school in Honolulu. Punahou continues today and is the school that Barack Obama attended as a young man.

88. Anderson, *Education of Blacks*, 37–38.

89. Frissell to Potter, 22 February 1899, Hampton Institute Archives; quoted in Anderson, *Education of Blacks*, 77.

90. Anderson, *Education of Blacks*, 33.

CHAPTER 3. Penn Normal, Industrial, and Agricultural School

1. Alfred Collins Maule to Penn School contributors, March 1909, in James M. Dabbs Papers, South Caroliniana Library, Columbia, hereafter cited as JMD; Jacoway, *Yankee Missionaries*, 41. This chapter relies heavily on Jacoway, whose work concentrates on the Hampton years.

2. "Armstrong League Association," *Southern Workman*, March 1899, 103. *Southern Workman* was the newsletter of Hampton Institute.

3. Jacoway, *Yankee Missionaries*, 50.

4. Ibid., 47, 52.

5. "Annual Report, 1903," 15, PSP; see also Jacoway, *Yankee Missionaries*, 49.

6. Jacoway, *Yankee Missionaries*, 50.

7. J. C. P. Miller to Cope, July 21, 1902, JMD; Jacoway, *Yankee Missionaries*, 51.

8. Buttrick to Peabody, July 15, 1903, JMD; Jacoway, *Yankee Missionaries*, 53.

9. Robert D. Jenks to Francis R. Cope Jr., July 6, 1903, PSP, reel one.

10. Robert D. Jenks to Francis R. Cope Jr., July 8, 1903, PSP, reel one; Jacoway, *Yankee Missionaries*, 53; see also McPherson, "White Liberals and Black Power."

11. Cooley, *School Acres*, 24.

12. Ohles, Ohles, and Ramsey, *Modern American Educators*, 74–75.

13. Kellogg, a graduate of Columbia University, was a journalist interested in social reform. He wrote the introduction to Cooley's *School Acres*. This quotation appears on page xvii of that book.

14. John Henry House family tree, http://www.cromwellbutlers.com/fam_tree/jhouse.htm.

15. John Dewey taught at Columbia from 1904 until his retirement in 1930. He had a profound belief in democracy for all, including women and Africans Americans; see Dewey, *Education and Democracy*. Dewey was surprised when encountering prejudice; see Stack, "Dewey and Race." When Alice Dewey invited African American women to their apartment in New York to organize for black rights and women's suffrage, they could hardly believe it when the owner of the building forbade them from holding integrated meetings; see Jay Martin, *Education of John Dewey*, 248.

16. Jacoway, *Yankee Missionaries*, 58.

17. Cooley, *School Acres*, 35; see also Hegstrom, *Penn*, 105; Jacoway, *Yankee Missionaries*, 61.

18. Cooley, *School Acres*, 36–37.

19. Ibid., 37.

20. Ibid.

21. Cooley, *Homes of the Freed*, 103.

22. Eleanor Barnwell, interview by Frank Martin, August 11, 1993, in Frank Martin, *Moments from the Past*, 62. Martin was the curator of exhibitions and collections at the I. P. Stanback Museum, South Carolina State University, Orangeburg.

23. Trustee Minutes, March 2, 1908, and "Annual Report, 1909," 17, PSP; Jacoway, *Yankee Missionaries*, 73.

24. Billingsley, *Yearning to Breathe Free*, 194.

25. Edith Dabbs, *Sea Island Diary*, 221.

26. "Orangeburg Cemetery," on the City of Orangeburg website, accessed January 30, 2014, http://www.orangeburg.sc.us/index.php?option=com_content&view=article& id=38&Itemid=75.

27. Cooley, *School Acres*, 27–28.

28. Ibid., 47.

29. Ibid., 71.

30. Ibid., 119–21. By the early 1900s, scientists knew that mosquitoes carried malaria-causing parasites.

31. Cooley, *Homes of the Freed*, 50.

32. Daise, *Sea Island Heritage*, 89.

33. Edith Dabbs, *Sea Island Diary*, 324.

34. Cooley, *Homes of the Freed*, 58–59.

35. On midwives, see Fraser, *African American Midwifery in the South*, 35–37; Jacobson, "Hospital Care and the Vanishing Midwife"; Butter and Kay, "State Laws and Lay Midwifery." See also South Carolina Licensed Midwives, http://www.sc-midwives.org/.

36. Cooley, *Homes of the Freed*, 60.

37. Ibid., 63.

38. On their continued idealism and support of black education, see McPherson, *Abolitionist Legacy*.

39. See chapter 1 for the origin of the "St. Helena Hymn" and the reaction to "Sweet Land of Liberty."

40. Wilbur Cross, "Penn Center: A History Preserved, a Culture Shared, a Future Changed," unpublished manuscript in possession of Cross.

41. Cooley, *School Acres*, 99–100.

42. Ibid., 101.

43. Hutchison, "Better Homes and Gullah"; Riney-Kehrberg, " Separation and Sorrow."

44. Cooley, School Acres, 43–44.

45. Ibid., 103.

46. Ibid., 161–62.

47. Robert Middleton, interview by Frank Martin, August 15, 1993, in Martin, *Moments from the Past*, 54–55.

48. Martin Luther King Jr. came to Penn in the 1960s in search of quiet and a place to work on strategy. He and his staff held retreats at Penn Center; see chapter 4.

49. Cooley, *School Acres*, 140–41; Jacoway, *Yankee Missionaries*, 124. Ballanta, *Saint Helena Island Spirituals*.

50. The Rev. Homer McMillan to Rossa B. Cooley. December 13, 1915, PSP, reel two.

51. Herbert Mills to Rossa B. Cooley. April 5, 1916, PSP, reel two.

52. Watkins, "Thomas Jesse Jones."

53. Thomas Jesse Jones, *Negro Education.*

54. Thomas Jesse Jones, *Education in Africa.*

55. Mabel Carney to Grace House, May 10, 1926, quoted in Jacoway, *Yankee Missionaries*, 171.

56. Glotzer, "Career of Mabel Carney."

57. Sibusisiwe Makhanya and Amelia Njongwana were already qualified teachers. Njongwana returned home, and Makhanya, cut off from Phelps-Stokes support, enrolled in a religiously oriented social welfare program at the Schauffler Training School in Cleveland, Ohio, financing her studies by cleaning bathrooms; see Glotzer, "Career of Mabel Carney," 328–29.

58. For more on the country life movement, see Danbom, "Rural Education Reform"; Danbom, *Resisted Revolution*; Bowers, *Country Life Movement in America*; Swanson, "The 'Country Life Movement.'"

59. Danbom, "Rural Education Reform," 462.

60. Carney, *Country Life and the Country School*, 1. When she wrote this book, Carney was the director of the country school department at Illinois State Normal University.

61. This conflict between urban and rural life has been part of American culture since early industrialization; see Burton, *Age of Lincoln*, esp. chapter 2.

62. Cooley, *Homes of the Freed*, 47.

63. Cooley, *School Acres*, 20.

64. Ibid., 129.

65. Ibid., 114–15.

66. Edith Dabbs, *Sea Island Diary*, 226–27.

67. Jacoway, *Yankee Missionaries*, 130–31.

68. Cooley, *School Acres*, 112.

69. Cooley, *Homes of the Freed*, 42.

70. W. H. Mills, "The Extension Service and Rural County Organization," 8, Mills Papers, box 3, file 14, Strom Thurmond Institute, Clemson University (hereafter cited as Mills Papers). William H. Mills was a professor of rural sociology at Clemson.

71. South Carolina could not have received federal funds for a white land grant school at Clemson unless it established a black land grant school.

72. Kyriakoudes, "T. J. Woofter," 2–3.

73. Members included leaders such as George Peabody, Harry Byrd, William Poteat, and John Eagan. In 1944 this organization merged with the Southern Regional Council. For more on the Commission on Interracial Cooperation, see McDonough, "Men and Women of Good Will"; Burrows, "Commission on Interracial Cooperation"; Krueger, *And Promises to Keep.*

74. Woofter, *Black Yeomanry*, v. The book is dedicated to Rossa B. Cooley and Grace B. House, "whose devotion to the realities of education has given vital leadership to St. Helena and its people."

75. Ibid., 103.

76. Ibid., 244.

77. T. J. Woofter to Howard W. Odum, January 24, 1928, folder 160, Howard W. Odum Papers, Southern Historical Collection, University of North Carolina at Chapel Hill; Kyriakoudes, "T. J. Woofter."

Woodson was Dean of the College of Liberal Arts and Sciences at Howard University and was active in scholarship and racial justice activities. He had earned his PhD at Harvard (the second African American to do so, after W. E. B Du Bois). Known as the "father of black history," Woodson founded the Association for the Study of Negro Life and History and established Negro History Week, which we now call Black History Month. On the favorable reaction to Woofter's report at Penn, and the unfavorable reaction by W. E. B. Du Bois, see Jacoway, *Yankee Missionaries*, 181–90.

78. Kyriakoudes, "T. J. Woofter"; Richards, *Race, Racism, and Psychology*, 102.

79. Woofter, *Black Yeomanry*, x. In addition to Woofter's book, three others came from this study: Kiser, *Sea Island to City*; Johnson, *Social History of the Sea Islands*; Johnson, *Folk Culture on St Helena Island.*

80. Parker, "Peabody Education Fund," 149.

81. West, "Peabody Education Fund and Negro Education," 4.

82. Ibid., 4, 13–16.

83. "Governor Blease's Inaugural Address," *House Journal of South Carolina, 1911,* 92–93.

84. Cooley, *School Acres,* 89.

85. Kiser, *Sea Island to City,* 211–12. Gardenia Simmons-White, president of the Penn Club in 2013, wrote that the club allows its members to "demonstrate appreciation for Penn Center's mission by supporting it financially and through service" ("The Penn Center 1862 Circle Gala, 2012," copy at Penn Center).

86. Dabbs, *Sea Island Diary,* 244.

87. Ibid., 242. See chapter 5 for the story of a Keyserling who was a future supporter of Penn Center.

88. Cooley, *Homes of the Freed,* 2.

89. See Jones and Richardson, *Education for Liberation.* McPherson discusses motivations and outcomes in "White Liberals and Black Power."

90. "Why Am I a Trustee of Penn School?," Mills Papers, box 4, file 14.

91. "Negro Education in South Carolina in Schools of Higher Grades," Mills Papers, box 2, file 21. Benjamin E. Mays details discriminatory funding for black and white children in his autobiography, *Born to Rebel,* appendix A. See Burton, "'Black Squint of the Law,'" 161–85.

92. Edith Dabbs, *Sea Island Diary,* 245, 247.

93. The leaders were Fred L. Brownlee of the American Missionary Association, Walter White of the National Association for the Advancement of Colored People, Liston Pope of Yale Divinity School, Benjamin E. Mays of Morehouse College, A. D. Beittel of Guilford College, Mordecai W. Johnson of Howard University, and Reinhold Niebuhr of Union Theological Seminary. Their letters are in PSP.

94. Egerton, *Speak Now Against the Day,* 125; see also Krueger, *And Promises to Keep.*

95. Burton, "Kester, Howard (1904–1977)."

96. Dunbar, *Against the Grain,* 209.

97. Ibid.

98. Jacoway, *Yankee Missionaries,* 245–46. Blanton had come to Penn School in 1906 and ably headed the farm and other projects, including the Cooperative Society (68, 145).

99. Quoted in Dunbar, *Against the Grain,* 211.

100. Ira DeAugustine Reid, " An Evaluation of the Facilities, Program, and Objectives of the Penn Normal, Industrial and Agricultural School," 9, PSP.

101. Ibid., 10.

102. Ibid., 8.

103. Ibid., 42–44.

104. Ibid., 6.

105. Ibid., 4–8.

106. Ibid., 48, 49.

107. Macdonald served for thirty years and was succeeded by his widow, Clare Peters Macdonald. She was then succeeded by her daughter, Margaret M. Sanders, who served until 1970, "a period of seventy years of dedicated family participation on the Board" (Edith Dabbs, *Sea Island Diary*, 204); see also Mary Macdonald Gaston and Paul Gaston, interview by Vernon Burton, June 8, 2013.

108. "James Nelson Frierson Papers, 1911–1959," South Carolinia Library, http://library.sc.edu/socar/uscs/2001/frier.html.

109. Francis's daughter, Omega Francis, currently serves on the board of trustees.

110. It was not until 2010 that the people got a library, built on land donated by Penn Center.

CHAPTER 4. Penn Center and the Civil Rights Movement

1. Courtney Siceloff, interview by Marvin Ira Lare, January 16, 2005, in Lare, *Champions of Civil and Human Rights;* see also, minutes, Penn Board of Trustees, January 25, 1950, PSP, reel 16. The minutes were taken by Grace House as acting secretary.

2. Minutes, Penn Board of Trustees, January 25, 1950, PSP, reel 16; see also the obituary of Elizabeth Taylor Siceloff, *Friends Journal*, October 2003, 51.

3. John Siceloff, interview by Georganne and Vernon Burton, May 25, 2013, Penn Center.

4. Thomas Barnwell, interview by Georganne and Vernon Burton, October 19, 2013. See also Hollings and Victor, *Making Government Work*, 133.

5. "Penn Celebrates Centennial: First Negro School in South," *Whetstone Education Issue*, North Carolina Mutual Life Insurance Co., 1962, Durham, North Carolina (in the possession of Thomas Barnwell and Vernon Burton).

6. See especially the powerful writings of James McBride Dabbs: *Haunted by God, Who Speaks for the South?, The Southern Heritage,* and *The Road Home.* For the text of

King's "Letter from a Birmingham Jail," see the copy maintained by the African Studies Center at the University of Pennsylvania, http://www.africa.upenn.edu/Articles_Gen /Letter_Birmingham.html. See also Wolfe, *Abundant Life Prevails*, 113–14.

7. M. A. Wright to Friends, March 25, 1957, in PSP, reel 16.

8. Howie, *Bluffton Charge*, 80–81. Howie was a white minister vitally interested in racial justice and equality.

9. PSP, last box, 2005 addition (from an *Atlanta Journal-Constitution* article, November 13, 1988). Another site was Highlander School, discussed later in this chapter.

10. Marion Wright to Board Members of Penn Community Services, Inc., June 19, 1957, PSP, reel 16.

11. Consultation on Human Relations Programming in Rural South Carolina, "Preliminary Report," May 13–15, 1960, PSP, reel 16.

12. Wolfe, *Abundant Life Prevails*, 121.

13. Ibid., 109.

14. PSP, 1862–2004 and undated (the bulk of them from 1862 to 1978), SHC description of collection.

15. Courtney Siceloff to Members of the Board of Trustees, memorandum, January 25, 1960, PSP, reel 16.

16. Wright to Board Members, June 19, 1957.

17. "Human Relations Council Defends Sit-In Students," *Columbia (SC) State*, March 7, 1960.

18. Selden Smith, interview by Vernon Burton and written comments, September 6, 2013.

19. Synott, "Moderate White Activists," 108.

20. Arsenault, *Freedom Riders*; see also Arsenault, "Five Days in May." Rock Hill was the locale of the Friendship Nine, where the students arrested at a sit-in chose "jail without bail." Governor Ernest Hollings sent state police to prevent further violence; see Bass and Poole, *Palmetto State*, 99–100. See also Lewis, *Walking with the Wind*.

21. Synott, "Moderate White Activists," 108; Joyner, "'One People.'"

22. Quoted in Synott, "Moderate White Activists," 113.

23. Lau, *Democracy Rising*, 218.

24. David Dennis to Vernon Burton, e-mail, October 9, 2013.

25. Howie, *Bluffton Charge*, 80.

26. Elizabeth and Courtney Siceloff, interview by Dallas Blanchard, July 8, 1985, 18–20.

27. "News-Letter," May 1954, PSP, reel 16.

28. Howie, *Bluffington Charge*, 81–82.

29. Ibid.

30. Courtney and Elizabeth Siceloff to "Dear Friends," Members of the Board of Trustees, December 5, 1957, PSP, reel 16. Mabel and Martin England and Florence and *Clarence Jordan* established Koinonia Farm on 400 acres in rural Sumter County, Georgia, in 1942; see *New Georgia Encyclopedia*, s.v., "Koinonia Farm," edited December 4, 2013, accessed February 9, 2014, http://www.georgiaencyclopedia.org/articles /arts-culture/koinonia-farm.

31. Courtney Siceloff, interview by Lare. John Siceloff, who was young at the time, recalls an episode with a burning cross; see John Siceloff interview.

32. John Siceloff interview.

33. Elizabeth and Courtney Siceloff interview, 20–21.

34. Young, *Easy Burden*, 139–40.

35. Morris, *Origins of the Civil Rights Movement*, 149–55, 237–39, quotation on 149; Burton, "'Black Squint of the Law,'" 163–64, 173–75; Burton et al., "South Carolina," 197; Wolfe, *Abundant Life Prevails*, 116; Branch, *Parting the Waters*, 263–64, 381–82, 575–78.

36. Young, *Easy Burden*, 143–44.

37. Ibid., 145.

38. Charron, *Freedom's Teacher*, 243.

39. Young, *Easy Burden*, 140.

40. Charron, *Freedom's Teacher*, 250.

41. Young, *Easy Burden*, 140.

42. On the change from elected to appointed majority–African American districts, see Burton, "'Black Squint of the Law'" and Report of Dr. Orville Vernon Burton (expert witness report), October 5, 2001, in *Moultrie v. Charleston County Council*, CA No. 9-01 562 11; see also Charron, *Freedom's Teacher*, 247.

43. Young, *Easy Burden*, 139; Wolfe, *Abundant Life Prevails*, 116.

44. Charron, *Freedom's Teacher*, 217.

45. Young, *Easy Burden*, 131–32.

46. Ibid., 133.

47. Ibid., 153.

48. Ibid., 133–35.

49. Ibid., 278.

50. Leroy E. Browne Sr. (1916–2007), interview by Marvin Ira Lare, September 27, 2005, in Lare, *Champions of Civil and Human Rights*.

51. Morris, *Origins of the Civil Rights Movement*, 238.

52. Young, *Easy Burden*, 153–54.

53. Morris, *Origins of the Civil Rights Movement*, 236–69, quotation on 239. See also, Cotton, *If Your Back's Not Bent*, 117.

54. King, "Letter from a Birmingham Jail"; Bass, *Blessed Are the Peacemakers*; Colaico, "American Dream."

55. PSP, last box, 2005 addition (from an *Atlanta Journal-Constitution* article, November 13, 1988).

56. *Charleston News and Courier*, March 13, 1964; Wolfe, *Abundant Life Prevails*, 118.

57. Martin Luther King Jr., acceptance speech for the Nobel Peace Prize, December 10, 1964, available at Nobelprize.org, http://www.nobelprize.org/nobel_prizes/peace/laureates/1964/king-acceptance_en.html.

58. Power, *I Will Not Be Silent*, 3–4.

59. Barnwell interviews, October 19, 2013, and November 8, 2013.

60. Garrow, *Bearing the Cross*, 443–46.

61. Quoted in Power, *I Will Not Be Silent*, 9.

62. Ibid., 8–9.

63. Garrow, *Bearing the Cross*, 446. Nash had helped organize the successful sit-ins in Nashville, was at the founding meeting of SNCC in 1960, had been arrested during the Rock Hill sit-in in 1961, and had reinvigorated the Freedom Rides in 1961; see her biography on the website of the Martin Luther King, Jr. Research and Education Institute, http://mlk-kpp01.stanford.edu/index.php/encyclopedia/encyclopedia/enc_nash_diane_1938.

64. Garrow, "Where King Was Going," 724; Power, *I Will Not Be Silent*, 12.

65. Power, *I Will Not Be Silent*, 12; Fairclough, *To Redeem the Soul of America*, 324.

66. Martin Luther King Jr., speech at Frogmore, November 14, 1966, SCLC Papers, King Library; quoted in Fairclough, *Martin Luther King, Jr.*, 139.

67. Carmichael quoted in Branch, *At Canaan's Edge*, 486. King quoted in Power, *I Will Not Be Silent*, 15. For more on black power, see Branch, *At Canaan's Edge*, 486–87, 494–95, 532–33, 539–40, and Ladner, "What 'Black Power' Means to Negroes."

68. Power, *I Will Not Be Silent*, 15. For more on King's speech at the retreat and the subsequent book, see Garrow, "Where King Was Going."

69. Power, *I Will Not Be Silent*, 16–17.

70. Quoted in ibid., 3.

71. Ibid., 19.

72. Martin Luther King Jr., "Speech at Staff Retreat, Penn Center, Frogmore, South Carolina, May 1967," King Papers, quoted in Power, *I Will Not Be Silent*, 19.

73. Ibid.

74. *Charleston News and Courier*, November 28, 1967; see also Power, *I Will Not Be Silent*, 23.

75. Garrow, *Bearing the Cross*, 581.

76. Power, *I Will Not Be Silent*, 21; Wolfe, *Abundant Life Prevails*, 120.

77. Martin Luther King Jr., "The State of the Movement," speech to SCLC staff, November 28, 1967, King Papers, series 3, Speeches, Sermons, Articles, Statements, 1954–1968 (August–December 1967), 1, quoted in Power, *I Will Not Be Silent*, 22.

78. King, "Speech at Staff Retreat, Penn Center," 1, quoted in Power, *I Will Not Be Silent*, 4.

79. Fairclough, *To Redeem the Soul of America*, 171, quoted in Power, *I Will Not Be Silent*, 3.

80. "McNair Extends His Sympathy," *Charleston News and Courier*, April 6, 1968, quoted in Power, *I Will Not Be Silent*, 23.

81. Quoted in Wayne Washington, "The Day the 'Big Gun Shoot' Brought Opportunity to Former Slaves," *Columbia (SC) State*, February 20, 2011.

82. Quoted in Dewan, "Through Trying Times for Blacks."

83. Elizabeth and Courtney Siceloff interview, 18.

84. Hurst, *Hot Dog and a Coke*, 148.

85. Ibid., 149, 150.

86. Minutes, SNCC Executive Committee, September 6–9, 1963, Atlanta, Georgia, 4, available at Civil Rights Movement Veterans, http://crmvet.org/docs/6309_sncc _excom.pdf.

87. Grose, *South Carolina at the Brink*, 201.

88. Jordan and Gordon-Reed, *Vernon Can Read!*, 151.

89. Charles Frederick (Chuck) McDew, telephone interview by Vernon Burton, August 8, 2013.

90. Allison Stice, "Georgia Congressman, Civil Rights Leader, Rallies Beaufort Voters," *Hilton Head (SC) Island Packet*, May 5, 2013, http://www.islandpacket .com/2013/05/05/2491604/georgia-congressman-civil-rights.html#storylink=cpy.

91. Constance (Connie) Curry, telephone interview by Vernon Burton, August 8, 2013.

92. McDew to Walter Mack, no date, at Penn Center; copy sent via e-mail to Vernon Burton, August 22, 2012.

93. McDew interview.

94. Reynolds, *Fight for Freedom*, 46–50.

95. Millicent Brown to Vernon Burton, e-mail, July 9, 2013; *Brown v. Charleston District Twenty School Board*, 226 F. Supp. 819 (EDSC 1963); Brown, "Civil Rights Activism in Charleston." Brown is now a senior research fellow and associate professor of history in the Department of History and Sociology at Claflin University (Orangeburg, S.C.), and serves as principal investigator for the "Somebody Had to Do It" Project (http://somebody.claflin.edu/).

96. Mizell was a member of the South Carolina Advisory Committee to the U.S. Commission on Civil Rights, which met at Penn Center. For a brief time Mizell served on the Penn board. His first professional job was to write a report on a regional rural-development conference at Penn Center; Paulo Friere, the noted Brazilian educator and philosopher, was the primary speaker (Mizell to Vernon Burton, e-mail, August 23, 2013). Connie Curry was the first white member of the SNCC's executive committee; see Curry, "Official Observer," 45–48. Will Campbell was on the National Council of Churches.

97. Charles Joyner to Vernon Burton, e-mail, August 10, 2013.

98. Selden Smith to Vernon Burton, e-mail, August 10, 2013.

99. Courtney and Elizabeth Siceloff to Charles Joyner, July 11, 1961, in possession of Joyner.

100. Quoted in Dewan, "Through Trying Times for Blacks." See also Frieda Mitchell, interview by Marvin Ira Lare, December 22, 2004, in Lare, *Champions of Civil and Human Rights*.

101. Joe McDomick, interview by Georganne and Vernon Burton, June 24, 2013, Penn Center, and telephone interview by Orville Vernon Burton, August 1, 2013.

102. Dewan, "Through Trying Times for Blacks"; Wolfe, *Abundant Life Prevails*, 116–17.

103. McDomick interview, October 18, 2013.

104. John Siceloff, interview by Orville Vernon Burton and Georganne Burton, June 25, 2013, Penn Center. Siceloff's good friends Craig and Rowland Washington attended white schools in Beaufort in 1964, before "full integration." Their father, Charles, who had attended Morehouse College with Martin Luther King Jr., was a local attorney,

and their mother, Juanita, was a schoolteacher; for the obituary of Craig Washington, see Erin Moody, "Beaufort Native, Musician, Who Helped Desegregate Local Schools Dies," *Hilton Head (SC) Island Packet*, May 2, 2012, http://www.islandpacket .com/2012/05/02/2056888/beaufort-native-musician-who-helped.html.

105. John Siceloff interview, June 25, 2013.

106. Jack Bass, "They Want Negro History: Conference Deplores Omission on Their History in Textbooks," *Charlotte Observer*, January 28, 1968.

107. Saunders interview, September 24, 2013.

108. Moore and Burton, *Meeting of the Waters*, 359–80, 433–39; Bass and Nelson, *Orangeburg Massacre*. Sellers was the only person arrested and jailed for the events in Orangeburg; he was not pardoned until twenty-five years later; see Sellers and Terrell, *River of No Return*.

109. Carmichael, speech presented at Penn Center, January 28, 1968;see also Jack Bass, "'Black Alliance,' Stokely Writes Frogmore Meet," *Charlotte Observer*, January 29, 1968.

110. "Carolina Negroes Ask School Power," *New York Times* January 29, 1968. William ("Bill") Saunders was an African American activist in Charleston. He helped organize and lead the Charleston hospital strike of 1969. In 1970 he established the Committee on Better Racial Assurance (COBRA) to address race-related community problems. From 1972 to 1998, he operated the AM radio station WPAL; see "Inventory of the William ("Bill") Saunders Papers, circa 1950–2004," on the website of the Avery Research Center for African American History and Culture, http://avery.cofc.edu./archives/Saunders _Bill.html. His show, called *The Informant*, stimulated local activists and gave them an opportunity to let others know about the movement; see Will Moredock, "Bill Saunders Remembered in Smithsonian Exhibit," *Charleston City Paper*, September 28, 2011, http://www.charlestoncitypaper.com/charleston/bill-saunders-remembered-in-smithsonian-exhibit/Content?oid=3592313. See also Saunders interview. William Saunders continues his activism and says that he is "still a trouble-maker." His organization COBRA continues to work with the Gullah community to fix problems before they become polarizing in the community (Saunders interview, September 24, 2013).

111. Bass, "They Want Negro History." Bass, who was also a stringer for the *New York Times*, was at the scene of the four Hollings "tours." He first met Cleveland Sellers at Penn when Sellers was shooting baskets on the outdoor basketball court. This began a lifelong friendship between the newspaper reporter and the black activist, who is now president of Voorhees College.

112. Siceloff, memorandum, October 28, 1968, PSP, folder 476.

113. PSP, addition of 2005, folder 469.

114. Hollings, *The Case against Hunger*, 5.

115. Jack Bass, interview by Georganne and Vernon Burton, October 19, 2013, at the SC Progressive Network meeting at Penn Center. Bass was the reporter accompanying Hollings.

116. Ibid.

117. "Hearings before the Select Committee on Nutrition and Human Needs of the United States Senate, Ninetieth Congress, 2nd Session and Ninety-First Congress, 1st Session on Nutrition and Human Needs, Part 4—South Carolina" (Washington, D.C.: U.S. Government Printing Office, 1969), pp. 1185–86.

118. John W. Gadson Sr., interview by Martin Ira Lare, September 14, 2005, in Lare, *Champions of Civil and Human Rights*, 37.

119. George Harmon, "Penn Center Director Resigns Position," *Charleston News and Courier*, April 22, 1969.

120. Ibid.

121. Elizabeth Taylor Siceloff obituary, *Friends Journal*, 51.

122. Marion Wright, oral history interview by Jacquelyn Hall, March 8, 1978; excerpts online at "Oral Histories of the American South," http://docsouth.unc.edu /sohp/B-0034/excerpts/excerpt_3974.html. In 1970 Wright, a widower, married Alice Spearman, to whom he had grown close during civil rights movement activities; see Synott, "Alice Buck Norwood Spearman Wright," 215.

123. Dabbs, *Southern Heritage*. His wife, Edith Dabbs, felt much love for the community and wrote a history of Penn Center and the island of St. Helena: *Sea Island Diary*. See Johnson, "James McBride Dabbs."

124. King, "Letter from a Birmingham Jail." Bass, *Blessed Are the Peacemakers*, 9, 127, 250; Colaico, "American Dream Unfulfilled."

CHAPTER 5. Penn as a Center of Preservation and Sustainability

1. In 1986, Gadson received the Order of the Palmetto Award, the highest honor that the governor of South Carolina can bestow. In 2012 he was inducted into the Penn Center 1862 Circle.

2. Wolfe, *Abundant Life Prevails*, 125. St. Helena has an area of about 42,000 acres.

3. Rowland, Rogers, and Moore, *History of Beaufort County*. See also the statistics

about St. Helena on City-Data.com, http://www.city-data.com/city/St.-Helena
-South-Carolina.html

4. Kiser, *Sea Island to City*, 76.

5. Emory Campbell, interview by Brian Rumsey, October 1, 2002, 3; transcript in possession of Burton.

6. Barnwell interviews, October 19, 2013, and November 8, 2013.

7. Penn Center's "best guess"; Walter Mack, e-mail Vernon Burton, October 23, 2013; see the appendix.

8. Freewoods Foundation, *African-American Family Farm*.

9. Ibid., 115–16.

10. Ibid., 167.

11. Ibid., 181.

12. Ibid., 268.

13. Ibid., 304.

14. Ibid., 25. Leroy Browne is the same man as Leroy Brown.

15. Ibid., 165, 166, 169.

16. Ibid., 129.

17. Ibid., 181.

18. Ibid., 271.

19. Ibid., 38.

20. Ibid., 119, 167, 304; quotation about cotton (119) was from Rivers. He mentioned Mr. Seabrook, who "graduated from here," went to college, and "came back and helped some" (129). Seabrook served as a "guide for the big man" but "didn't go to the poor man." Rivers added: "We had 2 classes of people—little class and big class" (129).

21. Joseph McDomick, memorandum to paralegals, ca. 1975, Penn Center Museum.

22. Emory Campbell, interview by Brian Rumsey, November 12, 2002, 9, transcript in possession of Burton.

23. Joseph McDomick, interview with Georganne and Vernon Burton, June 24, 2013.

24. Hegstrom, *Penn*, 178; Thomas, Pennick, and Gray, "What Is African-American Land Ownership?"

25. Douglas Henderson, Beaufort County treasurer, interview by Georganne Burton, July 31, 2013.

26. Emory Campbell, Joseph McDomick, Walter Mack, Michael Campi, Georganne

Burton, and Vernon Burton, meeting on June 24, 2013, Hampton House, Penn Center; tape recording of the meeting in possession of Burton (hereafter cited as Hampton House meeting).

27. Ibid.

28. Campbell, interviews by Rumsey, September 17, 2002, 11–12, and November 12, 2002, 4–7, quotation on 4.

29. Campbell, interview by Rumsey, November 12, 2002, 7.

30. Ibid., 6.

31. Campbell, interview by Rumsey, September 17, 2002, 9.

32. South Carolina Department of Archives and History, State Historic Preservation Office, *African American Historic Places in South Carolina* (June 2009), available at http://shpo.sc.gov/pubs/Documents/aframerhisplinsc.pdf.

33. Gadson, interview with Wilbur Cross, August 20, 1980.

34. James Clyburn, remarks at the funeral of John William Gadson Sr., January 11, 2013, First African Baptist Church, Beaufort, South Carolina. Gadson and Clyburn were friends and fellow students at South Carolina State. Gadson had offered Clyburn a job teaching, but Mrs. Clyburn did not like the marshes around Beaufort.

35. Wolfe, *Abundant Life Prevails*, 125.

36. Hegstrom, *Penn*, 180; Wolfe, *Abundant Life Prevails*, 125.

37. Barnwell interview, October 19, 2013. Barnwell, who has never ceased in his loyal support of Penn Center, is including Penn in his legacy. He understands the need for long-term commitment and has noted that the historical commitment of the Quakers and the Unitarians has diminished. He finds this sad because Penn Center is part of their heritage.

38. Sometimes the spelling is "Brown"; Campbell, interview by Rumsey, September 19, 2002, 1.

39. Browne, interview by Lare, September 27, 2005. When Browne retired in 1980, Governor Richard Riley awarded him the state's highest honor, the Order of the Palmetto, for his contributions to South Carolina; see Browne's obituary in the *Beaufort Gazette*, available at https://groups.google.com/forum/#!topic/alt.obituaries/WIKfvq9zdTs, and the resolution passed by the South Carolina General Assembly on January 25, 2007, extending sympathy to Browne's family after his death, http://www.scstatehouse.gov/sess117_2007-2008/bills/3361.htm.

40. Mathiasen's later work on various boards led to the establishment of the

Management Assistance Group. See Mathiasen, Gross, and Franco, "Steering Nonprofits."

41. Mathiasen, "Evaluation."

42. Brochure in PSP; Wolfe, *Abundant Life Prevails*, 129. John Jakes and Wilbur Cross discussed the origin of this quotation (e-mail, August 25, 1999, copy in possession of Burton). Barnwell served as chairman of the board from 1985 to 1994.

43. Campbell, interview by Rumsey, September 17, 2002, 17.

44. Campbell, interview by Vernon and Georganne Burton, October 18, 2013.

45. Campbell, interview by Rumsey, September 24, 2002, 3, 6.

46. Paul DeVere, "Emory Campbell: Coming Home," *Celebrate Hilton Head*, February 2009, http://www.celebratehiltonhead.com/article/1291/emory-campbell-coming-hom.

47. Hampton House meeting.

48. Wolfe, *Abundant Life Prevails*, 126. The Peace Corps used Penn Center for its training until 1992, when it found other venues.

49. Ibid., 127.

50. The first Earth Day was in 1970, the same year when Campbell got his master's; see DeVere, "Emory Campbell: Coming Home."

51. "Sustainability," on the website of the U.S. Environmental Protection Agency, http://www.epa.gov/sustainability/basicinfo.htm.

52. Campbell, interview by Brian Rumsey, October 1, 2002, 2.

53. Pollitzer, *Gullah People*, 4.

54. Campbell interview Dec 10, 2002.

55. "Gullahs v. Golfers: Preserving the Culture of the Sea Islands," *Economist*, January 31, 2008, available at http://www.economist.com/node/10608808.

56. Hampton House meeting.

57. The Keyserling family had been involved on St. Helena since the 1870s; See chapter 1.

58. The $1 million was reduced to $900,000, administered in partnership with the University of South Carolina; see Keyserling, *Against the Tide*, 362. Keyserling credits the people of St. Helena for helping her win her election (33).

59. "Meet Billy Keyserling," http://mayorbilly.com/about-billy.

60. "Sen. Hollings Sparks Fund Drive For Historic Penn Center Site In S.C.," *Jet*, September 28, 1992, 29.

61. Campbell, interview by Rumsey, November 12, 2002, 11.

62. Bernie Wright, interview by Georganne and Vernon Burton, July 31, 2013. A plaque at the county council office commemorates this achievement.

63. Ibid.

64. David Dennis to Walter Mack, e-mail, August 9, 2013.

65. Joseph Opala to Walter Mack, e-mail, August 9, 2013.

66. Hampton House meeting. The first exhibition at the new library was titled "Lincoln: The Constitution and the Civil War," a project of the National Constitution Center and the American Library Association. Penn Center was one of 200 sites nationwide selected to host this traveling exhibition, and the center's first guest speaker was Vernon Burton.

67. Hampton House meeting.

CHAPTER 6. Penn as a Center of Gullah Preservation

1. Joyner, *Down by the Riverside*, xliv.

2. "Gullah Culture," *Now*, PBS.org, January 24, 2003, http://www.pbs.org/now /arts/gullah.html.

3. See Cross, *Gullah Culture in America*; Wood, *Black Majority*, chapter 6.

4. About 750,000 Gullah people live on the coast between North Carolina and Florida (Campbell, interview by Rumsey, December 10, 2002, 10).

5. Quoted in the *Wilmington Star-News*, October 3, 1976.

6. Claude Sharp was from Columbia, and Pat Sharp was from New Hampshire (Hampton House meeting).

7. As of summer 2013, it is out of print.

8. Frank, "Gullah as a Language."

9. See Holloway, *Africanisms in American Culture*.

10. Emory S. Campbell, "Revelation of GullahGeechee Mystique"; see also Campbell, "A Sense of Self and Place."

11. Candice Glover from St. Helena won the American Idol contest in June 2013. Her speaking Gullah to the audience boosted national interest in the language.

12. Turner, *Africanisms in the Gullah Dialect*.

13. Joyner, *Down by the Riverside*, xlii; Nichols, "Creoles of the USA"; Wood, *Black Majority*, 167–91; Jones-Jackson, *When Roots Die*; Nichols, *Voices of Our Ancestors*;

Margaret Washington Creel, *A Peculiar People*; Powers, *Black Charlestonians*; Dusinberre, *Them Dark Days*; Clarke, *Dwelling Place*; Judith Carney, *Black Rice*; Ferguson, *Uncommon Ground*.

14. Joyner, *Down by the Riverside*, 199.

15. Littlefield, *Rice and Slaves*.

16. Opala's research on Bunce Island, the British slave castle in Sierra Leone that sent thousands of African captives to South Carolina and Georgia in the eighteenth century, helped lead to the preservation of that historic site.

17. Preview for *Family across the Sea*, http://www.youtube.com/watch?v=KnuB1o PO64k. See also Representative James Clyburn, "Tribute to Emory Campbell," 158 Cong. Rec. E318 (extension of remarks, March 6, 2012), available at CapitolWords .org, http://capitolwords.org/date/2012/03/06E318-3_tribute-to-emory-campbell. ETV did not include Gullah scholars in their documentary.

18. http://artsandsciences.sc.edu/afra/2001_lecture.html.

19. Gantt and Gerald, *Ultimate Gullah Cookbook*. Both authors are Gullah. Gerald is a professor of English at Coastal Carolina University, and Gantt, a retired restaurateur, is regarded as an expert on Lowcountry cuisine. In 2001, Gerald was an archivist at Penn Center.

20. See chapter 1.

21. Pollitzer, *Gullah People and African Heritage*.

22. Another source for the word *Gullah* is the Gola people from western Africa.

23. Wells, *Slave Ship "Wanderer"*; Calonius, *The "Wanderer."* The ship's owners and crew were prosecuted but not convicted.

24. Forten, *Journal*, 150.

25. Smith, *Stono*; Burton, *In My Father's House*; Hoffer, *"Cry Liberty"*; Thornton, "African Dimensions of the Stono Rebellion"; Wood, *Black Majority*, 308–26.

26. Many accounts of the sea islands distinguish between times "before or after the bridge."

27. Charles Jones, *Gullah Folktales*.

28. Gantt and Gerald, *Ultimate Gullah Cookbook*.

29. Burton, *In My Father's House*, 385.

30. Gantt and Gerald, *Ultimate Gullah Cookbook*.

31. This celebration was enhanced after the independent film *Daughters of the Dust* (1991), produced and directed by Julie Dash. The film won the Best Cinematography

award at the 1991 Sundance Film Festival. See also Julie Dash, *Daughters of the Dust: A Novel* (1997), set twenty years after the events in the film.

32. Pollitzer, *Gullah People and African Heritage*, 99–104.

33. Michael Ellison, a professor of polymer fibers at the School of Materials Science and Engineering at Clemson University, has studied the healing power of spider silk; see also Andy Extance, "'Spider Threads' Bring Great Self-Healing Power," *Chemistry World*, August 6, 2012, http://www.rsc.org/chemistryworld/2012/08 /spider-threads-bring-great-self-healing-power.

34. This is the central thesis of Wolfe, *Abundant Life Prevails*.

35. The Gullah people on rice plantations, however, were often Muslim; see Georgia Writers' Project, *Drums and Shadows*.

36. "11 Most Endangered Historic Places: Penn School," National Trust for Historic Preservation, http://www.preservationnation.org/issues/11-most-endangered /locations/penn-school.html.

37. "11 Most Endangered Historic Places: Gullah/Geechee Coast," National Trust for Historic Preservation, http://www.preservationnation.org/issues/11-most -endangered/locations/gullah-geechee-coast.html#.UY_4pEqjN8E.

38. Clyburn met his wife, Emily, while jailed for taking part in a civil rights demonstration; see his official biography at http://clyburn.house.gov/about-me/full-biography.

39. "Gullah/Geechee Cultural Heritage Center," National Park Service, http://www .nps.gov/guge/index.htm. The corridor extends from Wilmington, North Carolina, to Jacksonville, Florida.

40. James E. Clyburn, "We Must Protect Gullah/Geechee Culture," at the official site of the Gullah Geechee Cultural Heritage Corridor, http://gullahgeecheecorridor .org/pdfs/CongressmanJamesEClyburn.pdf; see also the account of Emory Campbell at Encore.org, http://www.encore.org/emory-campbell.

41. Allen, "Gullah Geechee Cultural Heritage Area."

42. Ronald Daise, "Gullah Geechee Cultural Heritage Corridor." Daise, whose parents attended Penn School, is chair of the commission. See also Daise, *Reminiscences of Sea Island Heritage*.

43. Emory Campbell, interview with Wilbur Cross, August 20, 2006; Campbell, interview with the Burtons, October 18, 2013. Since his retirement in 2002, Campbell has continued work on preserving the Gullah culture. He has written several publications, including *Gullah Cultural Legacies*. In 2005, he received the Carter G. Woodson

Memorial Award from the National Education Association for outstanding work. He is the president of Gullah Heritage Consulting Services; see his biography on History Makers: http://www.thehistorymakers.com/biography/emory-campbell-41. He and his family conduct Gullah heritage history tours on Hilton Head; see http://www.discoversouthcarolina.com/products/3696.aspx.

44. Cassandra Gillens's work is part of the collection of the Myrtle Beach Museum, Myrtle Beach, S.C., and the Harvey Gantt Center in Charlotte. Gillens's art was featured in the movie *Nights in Rodanthe*, based on the novel by Nicholas Sparks. See her work at http://cassandragillens.com.

45. See the account of Jonathan Green at Answers.com, http://www.answers.com/topic/jonathan-green#ixzz2W1Pu4Dhv; see also Green, *Gullah Images*.

46. The Penn Center 1862 Circle Gala, 2012, at Penn Center; see also three works by Moutoussamy-Ashe: *Daufuskie Island*; *Viewfinders*; and *Daddy and Me*.

47. Campbell interview by Rumsey, September 24, 2002, 11–12.

48. Ron and Natalie Daise created *Gullah Gullah Island* (1994–97), a television show to teach children about Gullah culture.

49. Joyner, *Down by the Riverside*, xliv; see also Joyner, "Endangered Traditions: Resort Development and Cultural Conservation in the Sea Islands," in *Shared Traditions*.

50. Campbell, interview by Rumsey, September 17, 2002, 13.

51. Charles Joyner to Vernon Burton, e-mail, August 9, 2013.

BIBLIOGRAPHY

Manuscript and Archival Materials

Papers of Thomas Barnwell, in his possession, Hilton Head Island, South Carolina.

Black Farmers Papers, Miscellaneous Files, South Carolina State Archives, Orangeburg.

Papers of Constance Curry, in her possession, Atlanta, Georgia.

Papers of Edith M. Dabbs, South Caroliniana Library, University of South Carolina, Columbia.

Papers of James McBride Dabbs, South Caroliniana Library, University of South Carolina, Columbia.

Papers of James Nelson Frierson, 1911–1959, South Caroliniana Library, University of South Carolina, Columbia.

Papers of Martin Witherspoon Gary, South Caroliniana Library, University of South Carolina, Columbia.

Papers of Charles Joyner, in his possession, Myrtle Beach, South Carolina.

Papers of Martin Luther King Jr., King Library, Atlanta, Georgia.

Papers of William H. Mills, William Hayne Mills Collection, Special Collections, Clemson University, Clemson, South Carolina.

Papers of Hayes Mizell, Hayes Mizell Collection, South Caroliniana Library, University of South Carolina, Columbia.

Papers of Howard W. Odum, Southern Historical Collection, Wilson Library, University of North Carolina, Chapel Hill.

Papers of the Southern Christian Leadership Conference, King Library, Atlanta, Georgia.

Papers of Laura Towne, including her complete diary, Southern Historical Collection, Wilson Library, University of North Carolina, Chapel Hill.

Penn School Papers, Avery Institute, College of Charleston, Charleston.

Penn School Papers, Southern Historical Collection, Wilson Library, University of North Carolina, Chapel Hill, and at Penn Center, St. Helena, South Carolina.

Records of the South Carolina Council on Human Relations, South Caroliniana Library, University of South Carolina, Columbia.

Southern Oral History Collection, Southern Historical Collection, Wilson Library University of North Carolina, Chapel Hill.

Oral Histories and Interviews

Barnwell, Thomas, interviews by Georganne and Vernon Burton, October 19 and November 8, 2013.

Bass, Jack, interview by Georganne and Vernon Burton, October 19, 2013.

Brown, Millicent, interviews by Vernon Burton, July 9 and September 4, 2013.

Browne, Leroy E., Sr. (1916–2007), interview by Marvin Lare, September 27, 2005.

Campbell, Emory, interviews by Brian Rumsey, September 17 and 24, October 1, November 12, and December 10, 2002; interview by Marvin Lare, September 27, 2005; interview by Wilbur Cross, August 20, 2006; interview by Vernon and Georganne Burton, October 18, 2013.

Curry, Constance (Connie), interview by Vernon Burton, August 8, 2013.

Dennis, David, interview by Vernon Burton, October 9, 2013.

Gadson, John W., Sr., interview by Marvin Lare, September 14, 2005; interview by Wilbur Cross, August 20, 1980.

Gaston, Mary Macdonald, and Paul Gaston, interview by Vernon Burton, June 8, 2013.

Henderson, Douglas, interview by Georganne Burton, July 31, 2013.

Joyner, Charles, interview by Vernon Burton, August 9, 2013.

Keyserling, Billy, interview by Georganne Burton, August 2, 2013.

Keyserling, Harriet, interview by Marvin Lare, September 27, 2005.

Mack, Walter, interview by Vernon Burton, October 23, 2013.

McDew, Charles Frederick (Chuck), interview by Vernon Burton, August 8, 2013.

McDomick, Joseph, interview by Marvin Lare, December 22, 2004; interviews by Georganne and Vernon Burton, June 24, August 1, and October 18, 2013.

Mitchell, Frieda, interview by Marvin Lare, December 22, 2004.

Saunders, Bill, interviews by Vernon Burton, September 24 and October 9, 2013.

Sellers, Cleveland, interviews by Vernon Burton, October 11 and 17, 2013.

Siceloff, Courtney, interview by Marvin Lare and Patricia Tyler Lare, January 16, 2005.

Elizabeth and Courtney Siceloff, interview by Dallas A. Blanchard, July 8, 1985, interview F0039, Southern Oral History Program Collection (#4007), Southern Historical Collection, Wilson Library, University of North Carolina at Chapel Hill.

Siceloff, John, interview by Georganne and Vernon Burton, June 25, 2013.

Smith, Selden, interview by Vernon Burton, September 6, 2013.

Spearman, Alice, interview by Jacquelyn Hall, February 28, 1976, Southern Oral History Program, Southern Historical Collection, Wilson Library, University of North Carolina at Chapel Hill.

Wright, Bernie, interview by Georganne and Vernon Burton, July 31, 2013.

Wright, Marion, interview by Jacquelyn Hall, March 8, 1978, interview B0034, Southern Oral History Program Collection (#4007), Southern Historical Collection, Wilson Library. University of North Carolina at Chapel Hill.

Books, Articles, and Unpublished Papers

Secondary sources are limited to works cited in the notes.

"African American Historic Places in South Carolina." South Carolina Department of Archives and History. http://shpo.sc.gov/pubs/Documents/aframerhisplinsc.pdf.

Allen, Mike. "Building the Gullah Geechee Cultural Heritage Area: A Personal and Professional Journey." Paper presented at the Association for the Study of African American Life and History annual meeting, Jacksonville, Florida, October 2013.

Anderson, James D. *The Education of Blacks in the South, 1860–1935*. Chapel Hill: University of North Carolina Press, 1988.

Arsenault, Raymond. "Five Days in May: Freedom Riding in the Carolinas." In *Toward the Meeting of the Waters: Currents in the Civil Rights Movement of South Carolina during the Twentieth Century*, edited by Orville Vernon Burton and Winfred B. Moore, Jr., 201–21. Columbia: University of South Carolina Press, 2008.

———. *Freedom Riders*. New York: Oxford University Press, 2006.

Ash, Stephen V. *When the Yankees Came: Conflict and Chaos in the Occupied South, 1861–1865*. Chapel Hill: University of North Carolina Press, 1995.

Baker, Bruce E. *What Reconstruction Meant: Historical Memory in the American South*. Charlottesville: University of Virginia Press, 2007.

Ballanta, Nicholas G. J. *Saint Helena Island Spirituals: Recorded and Transcribed at Penn Normal, Industrial and Agricultural School, Saint Helena Island, Beaufort County, South Carolina.* New York: Schirmer, 1925.

Bass, Jack, and Jack Nelson. *The Orangeburg Massacre.* Macon, Ga.: Mercer University Press, 1996.

Bass, Jack, and W. Scott Poole. *The Palmetto State: The Making of Modern South Carolina.* Colombia: University of South Carolina Press, 2009.

Bass, Jonathan S. *Blessed Are the Peacemakers: Martin Luther King, Jr., Eight White Religious Leaders, and the "Letter from Birmingham Jail."* Baton Rouge: Louisiana State University Press, 2001.

Bell, Malcolm, Jr. *Major Butler's Legacy: Five Generations of a Slaveholding Family.* Athens: University of Georgia Press, 1987.

Bennett, Lerone, Jr. *Before the Mayflower: A History of Black America.* 6th ed. New York: Penguin, 1993.

Billingsley, Andrew. *Yearning to Breathe Free: Robert Smalls of South Carolina and His Families.* Columbia: University of South Carolina Press, 2007.

Bowers, William L. *The Country Life Movement in America, 1900–1920.* Port Washington, N.Y.: Kennikat, 1974.

Brabec, Elizabeth, and Sharon Richardson. "A Clash of Cultures: The Landscape of the Sea island Gullah." *Landscape Journal* 26, no. 1 (January 2007): 151–67.

Branch, Taylor. *At Canaan's Edge: America in the King Years, 1965–68.* New York: Simon and Schuster, 2006.

———. *Parting the Waters: America in the King Years, 1954–1963.* New York: Simon and Schuster, 1988.

Brown, Millicent Ellison. "Civil Rights Activism in Charleston, South Carolina, 1940–1970." PhD diss., Florida State University, 1997.

Burrows, Edward Flud. "The Commission on Interracial Cooperation, 1919–1944: A Case Study in the History of the Interracial Movement in the South." PhD diss., University of Wisconsin, 1954.

Burton, Orville Vernon. *The Age of Lincoln.* New York: Hill and Wang, 2007.

———. "'The Black Squint of the Law': Racism in South Carolina." In *The Meaning of South Carolina History: Essays in Honor of George C. Rogers, Jr.,* edited by David R. Chesnutt and Clyde N. Wilson, 161–85. Columbia: University of South Carolina Press, 1991.

———. "Expert Witness Report of Orville Vernon Burton," October 5, 2001. *Moultrie v. Charleston County Council*, C.A. No. 9 -01 562 11.

———. *In My Father's House Are Many Mansions: Family and Community in Edgefield, South Carolina*. Chapel Hill: University of North Carolina Press, 1985.

———. "Kester, Howard (1904–1977)." In *Encyclopedia of the Left*, edited by Mari Jo Buhle, Paul Buhle, and Dan Georgakas, 414–15. New York: Garland, 1990.

———. "Ungrateful Servants: Edgefield's Black Reconstruction: Part I of the Total History of Edgefield County, South Carolina." Ph.D. diss., Princeton University, 1976.

———. "Whence Cometh Rural Black Reconstruction Leadership: Edgefield County, South Carolina." *Proceedings of the South Carolina Historical Association, 1988–1989*. Aiken: South Carolina Historical Association, 1989.

Burton, Orville Vernon, Terence R. Finnegan, James W. Loewen, and Peyton McCrary. "South Carolina." In *Quiet Revolution in the South: The Impact of the Voting Rights Act, 1965–1990*, edited by Chandler Davidson and Bernard Grofman, 191–232. Princeton, N.J.: Princeton University Press, 1994.

Butchart, Ronald E. "Laura Towne and Ellen Murray: Northern Expatriates and the Foundation of Black Education in South Carolina, 1862–1908." In *South Carolina Women: Their Lives and Times*, vol. 1, edited by Joan Marie Johnson, Valinda W. Littlefield, and Marjorie Julian Spruill, 12–30. Athens: University of Georgia Press, 2010.

———. *Schooling the Freed People: Teaching, Learning, and the Struggle for Black Freedom, 1861–1876*. Chapel Hill: University of North Carolina Press, 2010.

Butter, Irene H., and Bonnie J. Kay. "State Laws and the Practice of Lay Midwifery." *American Journal of Public Health* 78, no. 9 (September 1988): 1161–69.

Calonius, Erik. *The "Wanderer": The Last American Slave Ship and the Conspiracy That Set Its Sails*. New York: St. Martin's, 2006.

Campbell, Emory S. *Gullah Cultural Legacies: A Synopsis of Gullah Traditions, Customary Beliefs, Art Forms, and Speech on Hilton Head Island and Vicinal Sea Islands in South Carolina and Georgia*. Charleston: BookSurge, 2008.

———. "Revelation of GullahGeechee Mystique: The Role of Effective Scholarly Studies." Paper presented at the Association for the Study of African American Life and History annual meeting, Jacksonville, Florida, October 2013.

———. "A Sense of Self and Place: Unmasking My Gullah Cultural Heritage." In *African*

American Life in the Georgia Lowcountry: The Atlantic World and the Gullah Geechee, edited by Philip Morgan, 281–92. Athens: University of Georgia Press, 2010.

Carney, Judith. *Black Rice: The African Origins of Rice Cultivation in the Americas*. Cambridge, Mass.: Harvard University Press, 2001.

Carney, Mabel. *Country Life and the Country School: A Study of the Agencies of Rural Progress and of the Social Relationship of the School to the Country Community*. Chicago: Row, Peterson, 1912.

Cha-Jua, Sundiata Keita, and Clarence Lang. "The 'Long Movement' as Vampire: Temporal and Spatial Fallacies in Recent Black Freedom Studies." *Journal of African American History* 92, no. 2 (Spring 2007): 265–88.

Charron, Katherine Mellen. *Freedom's Teacher: The Life of Septima Clark*. Chapel Hill: University of North Carolina Press, 2009.

Chesnut, Mary. *Mary Boykin Chesnut: A Diary from Dixie*. Edited by Ben Ames Williams. Boston: Houghton Mifflin, 1949.

———. *The Private Mary Chesnut: The Civil War Diaries*. Edited by C. Vann Woodward and Elisabeth Muhlenfeld. New York: Oxford University Press, 1984.

Clarke, Erskine. *Dwelling Place: A Plantation Epic*. New Haven, Conn.: Yale University Press, 2005.

Colaico, James A. "The American Dream Unfulfilled: Martin Luther King, Jr. and the Letter from Birmingham Jail." *Phylon* 45, no. 1 (1984): 1–18.

Cooley, Rossa B. *Homes of the Freed*. New York: New Republic, 1926.

———. *School Acres: An Adventure in Rural Education*. New Haven, Conn.: Yale University Press, 1930.

Cotton, Dorothy. *If Your Back's Not Bent: The Role of the Citizenship Education Program in the Civil Rights Movement*. New York: Atria, 2012.

Creel, Margaret W. *A Peculiar People: Slave Religion and Community among the Gullah*. New York: New York University Press, 1989.

Cross, Wilbur. *Gullah Culture in America*. Westport, Conn.: Greenwood, 2008.

———. "Penn Center: A History Preserved, a Culture Shared, a Future Changed." Unpublished manuscript in possession of Cross.

Curry, Connie. "An Official Observer." In *Hands on the Freedom Plow: Personal Accounts of Women in SNCC*, edited by Faith S. Holsaert, Martha Prescod, Norman Noonan, Judy Richardson, Betty Garman Robinson, Jean Smith Young, and Dorothy M. Zellner, 45–48. Urbana: University of Illinois Press, 2010.

Dabbs, Edith M. *Sea Island Diary: A History of St. Helena Island*. Spartanburg, S.C.: Reprint Company, 1983.

———. *Walking Tall: A Brief Sketch of Penn School, Forerunner of Penn Community Services, Frogmore, South Carolina*. Frogmore, S.C.: Penn Community Services, 1964.

Dabbs, James McBride. *Haunted by God: The Cultural and Religious Experience of the South*. Richmond, Va.: John Knox, 1972.

———. *The Road Home*. Philadelphia: Christian Education Press, 1960.

———. *The Southern Heritage*. New York: Knopf, 1958.

———. *Who Speaks for the South?* New York: Funk and Wagnalls, 1964.

Daise, Ronald. "Gullah Geechee Cultural Heritage Corridor Vision and Implementation." Paper presented at the Association for the Study of African American Life and History annual meeting, Jacksonville, Florida, October 2013.

———. *Reminiscences of Sea Island Heritage*. Orangeburg, S.C.: Sandlapper, 1986.

Danbom, David. *The Resisted Revolution: Urban America and the Industrialization of Agriculture, 1900–1930*. Ames: Iowa State University Press, 1979.

———. "Rural Education Reform and the Country Life Movement." *Agricultural History* 53, no. 2 (April 1979): 462–74.

Dewey, John. *Democracy and Education*. London: Macmillan, 1916.

Du Bois, W. E. B. *Black Reconstruction in America: An Essay toward a History of the Part Which Black Folk Played in the Attempt to Reconstruct Democracy in America, 1860–1880*. New York: Russell and Russell, 1935.

Dunbar, Anthony P. *Against the Grain: Southern Radicals and Prophets, 1929–1959*. Charlottesville: University Press of Virginia, 1981.

Dusinberre, William. *Them Dark Days: Slavery in the American Rice Swamps*. New York: Oxford University Press, 1996.

Economist. "Gullahs v. Golfers: Preserving the Culture of the Sea Islands." January 31, 2008.

Edgar, Walter, ed. *The South Carolina Encyclopedia*. Colombia: University of South Carolina Press, 2006.

Egerton, John. *Speak Now against the Day: The Generation before the Civil Rights Movement in the South*. New York: Knopf, 1994.

Escott, Paul D., and David R. Goldfield, eds. *The New South: Documents and Essays*. Vol. 2 of *Major Problems in the History of the American South*. Lexington, Mass.: Heath, 1990.

Fairclough, Adam. *Martin Luther King, Jr.* Athens: University of Georgia Press, 1995.

———. *To Redeem the Soul of America: The Southern Christian Leadership Conference and Martin Luther King, Jr.* Athens: University of Georgia Press, 1987.

Ferguson, Leland. *Uncommon Ground: Archaeology and Early African America.* Washington, D.C.: Smithsonian Books, 2004.

Finnegan, Terence. *A Deed So Accursed: Lynching in Mississippi and South Carolina, 1881–1940.* Charlottesville: University of Virginia Press, 2013.

Foner, Eric. *Freedom's Lawmakers: A Directory of Black Officeholders During Reconstruction.* Rev. ed. Baton Rouge: Louisiana State University Press, 1996.

———. *Nothing but Freedom: Emancipation and Its Legacy.* Baton Rouge: Louisiana State University Press, 1983.

———. *Reconstruction: America's Unfinished Revolution, 1863–1877.* New York: Harper and Row, 1988.

Forten Grimké, Charlotte. *The Journal of Charlotte Forten Grimke.* Edited by Brenda Stevenson. New York: Oxford University Press, 1988.

———. *The Journal of Charlotte L. Forten: A Young Black Woman's Reactions to the White World of the Civil War Era.* Edited by Ray Allen Billington. New York: Norton, 1953.

———. "Life on the Sea Islands." *Atlantic Monthly,* May 1864, 582–96.

———. "Personal Recollections of Whittier." *New England Magazine,* June 1893.

Frank, David. "Gullah as a Language." Paper presented at the Association for the Study of African American Life and History annual meeting, Jacksonville, Florida, October 2013.

Fraser, Gertrude J. *African American Midwifery in the South: Dialogues of Birth, Race, and Memory.* Cambridge, Mass.: Harvard University Press, 1998.

Freewoods Foundation. *The African-American Family Farm, Postbellum to 1900: Operation Reachback: The Farmers Speak.* Myrtle Beach, S.C.: Freewoods Foundation, 1991.

Gantt, Jesse Edward, Jr., and Veronica Davis Gerald. *The Ultimate Gullah Cookbook: A Taste of Food, History, and Culture from the Gullah People.* Beaufort, S.C.: Gullah House Foundation, 2003.

Garrow, David. *Bearing the Cross: Martin Luther King Jr. and the Southern Christian Leadership Conference.* New York: Morrow, 2004.

———. "Where Martin Luther King, Jr., Was Going: Where Do We Go from Here and the Traumas of the Post-Selma Movement." *Georgia Historical Quarterly* 75, no. 4 (Winter 1991): 719–36.

Georgia Writer's Project. *Drums and Shadows: Survival Studies among the Georgia Coastal Negroes.* 1940. Reprint, Athens: University of Georgia Press, 1986.

Gerteis, William S. *From Contraband to Freedman: Federal Policy Toward Southern Blacks.* Westport, Conn.: Greenwood, 1973.

Glotzer, Richard. "The Career of Mabel Carney: The Study of Race and Rural Development in the United States and South Africa." *International Journal of African Historical Studies* 29, no. 2 (1996): 309–36.

Goodwine, Queen Quet Marquetta L. "Penn Center." In *South Carolina Encyclopedia,* edited by Walter Edgar, 711. Columbia: University of South Carolina Press, 2006.

Green, Jonathan. *Gullah Images: The Art of Jonathan Green.* Columbia: University of South Carolina Press, 1996.

Grose, Philip G. *South Carolina at the Brink: Robert McNair and the Politics of Civil Rights.* Columbia: University of South Carolina Press, 2006.

Guthrie, Patricia. *Catching Sense: African American Communities in a South Carolina Sea Island.* Westport, Conn.: Bergin and Garvin, 1996.

Hall, Jacquelyn Dowd. "The Long Civil Rights Movement and the Political Uses of the Past." *Journal of American History* 91, no. 4 (March 2005): 1233–63.

Hegstrom, Margaret E. *Penn: A History, 1862–1982.* Columbia: Office of the Governor, 1982.

Hoffer, Peter Charles. *"Cry Liberty": The Great Stono River Slave Rebellion of 1739.* New York: Oxford University Press, 2010.

Hoffman, Paul E. *A New Andalucia and a Way to the Orient: The American Southeast during the Sixteenth Century.* Baton Rouge: Louisiana State University Press, 1990.

Hollings, Ernest F. *The Case against Hunger: A Demand for a National Policy.* New York: Cowles, 1970.

Hollings, Ernest F., and Kirk Victor. *Making Government Work.* Columbia: University of South Carolina Press, 2008.

Holloway, Joseph E., ed. *Africanisms in American Culture: Blacks in the Diaspora.* Bloomington: Indiana University Press, 1991.

Howie, Stephen S. *The Bluffton Charge: One Preacher's Struggle for Civil Rights.* DuBois, Pa.: Mammoth, 2000.

Hurst, Rodney L., Sr. *It Was Never about a Hot Dog and a Coke: A First Person Memoir.* Livermore, Calif.: Wingspan, 2008.

Hutchison, Janet. "Better Homes and Gullah." *Agricultural History* 67, no. 2 (Spring 1993): 102–18.

Jacobson, Paul H. "Hospital Care and the Vanishing Midwife." *Milbank Memorial Fund Quarterly* 34, no. 3 (July 1956): 253–61.

Jacoway, Elizabeth. *Yankee Missionaries in the South: The Penn School Experiment.* Baton Rouge: Louisiana State University Press, 1980.

Johnson, Andrew. *The Papers of Andrew Johnson.* Vol. 8. Edited by Paul H. Bergeron. Knoxville: University of Tennessee Press, 1989.

Johnson, Guion G. *Social History of the Sea Islands.* Chapel Hill: University of North Carolina Press, 1930.

Johnson, Guy Benton. *Folk Culture on St. Helena Island.* New York: Columbia University Press, 1932.

Johnson, Thomas L. "James McBride Dabbs: A Life Story." PhD diss., University of South Carolina, 1980.

Jones, Charles Colcock, Jr. *Gullah Folktales from the Georgia Coast.* 1888. Reprint, Athens: University of Georgia Press, 2000.

Jones, Maxine D., and Joe M. Richardson. *Education for Liberation: The American Missionary Association and Africans Americans, 1890 to the Civil Rights Movement.* Tuscaloosa: University of Alabama Press, 2009.

Jones, Thomas Jesse. *Education in Africa: A Study of East, West, and Equatorial Africa.* New York: Phelps-Stokes Fund, 1922.

———. *Negro Education.* Washington, D.C.: Government Printing Office, 1917.

Jones-Jackson, Patricia. *When Roots Die: Endangered Traditions on the Sea Islands.* Athens: University of Georgia Press, 1987.

Jordan, Vernon E., Jr., and Annette Gordon-Reed. *Vernon Can Read! A Memoir.* New York: Public Affairs, 2001.

Joyner, Charles. *Down by the Riverside: A South Carolina Slave Community.* Urbana: University of Illinois Press, 1984.

———. "'One People': Creating an Integrated Culture in a Segregated Society, 1526–1990." In *The Meaning of South Carolina History: Essays in Honor of George C. Rogers, Jr.,* edited by David R. Chesnutt and Clyde N. Wilson, 214–44. Columbia: University of South Carolina Press, 1991.

———. "San Miguel de Gualdape: The First Lost Colony." Unpublished, undated paper. In the possession of Charles Joyner and Vernon Burton.

———. *Shared Traditions: Southern History and Folk Culture.* Urbana: University of Illinois, 1999.

Kelly, Burnham. *The Prefabrication of Houses: A Study by the Albert Farwell Bemis Foundation of the Prefabrication Industry in the United States.* New York: The Technology Press of the Massachusetts Institute of Technology and John Wiley and Sons, 1951.

Kemble, Fanny. *Fanny Kemble's Journals.* Edited by Catherine Clinton. Cambridge, Mass.: Harvard University Press, 2000.

Keyserling, Harriet. *Against the Tide: One Woman's Political Struggle.* Columbia: University of South Carolina Press, 1998.

Kiser, Clyde Vernon. *Sea Island to City: A Study of St. Helena Islanders in Harlem and Other Urban Centers.* New York: Columbia University Press, 1932.

Krueger, Thomas A. *And Promises to Keep: The Southern Conference for Human Welfare, 1938–1948.* Nashville: Vanderbilt University Press, 1967.

Kyriakoudes, Louis M. "T. J. Woofter, the St. Helena Island Study, and Black Yeomanry: A Reappraisal." Paper presented at the Southern Historical Association, Atlanta, November 2005.

Ladner, Joyce. "What 'Black Power' Means to Negroes in Mississippi." *Trans-action* 5, no. 1 (November 1967): 7–16.

Lang, Clarence. "Locating the Civil Rights Movement: An Essay on the Deep South, Midwest, and Border South in Black Freedom Studies." *Journal of Social History* 47, no. 2 (Winter 2013): 371–400.

Lare, Marvin Ira, ed. *Champions of Civil and Human Rights in South Carolina: An Anthology of Oral History Interviewers and Original Sources.* Columbia: University of South Carolina Press, forthcoming.

Lau, Peter F. *Democracy Rising: South Carolina and the Fight for Black Equality since 1865.* Lexington: University of Kentucky Press, 2006.

Lawson, Stephen F. "Long Origins of the Short Civil Rights Movement, 1954–1968." In *Freedom Rights: New Perspectives on the Civil Rights Movement*, edited by John Dittmer and Danielle L. McGuire, 9–37. Lexington: University of Kentucky Press, 2011.

Lewis, John. *Walking with the Wind: A Memoir of the Movement.* New York: Simon and Schuster, 1998.

Lincoln, Abraham. *The Collected Works of Abraham Lincoln.* Vol. 5. Edited by Roy P. Basler. New Brunswick, N.J.: Rutgers University Press, 1953.

Littlefield, Daniel C. *Rice and Slaves: Ethnicity and the Slave Trade in Colonial South Carolina*. Urbana: University of Illinois Press, 1991.

Martin, Frank, ed. *Moments from the Past: An Exhibition in Celebration of the Penn Center of the Sea Islands*. Orangeburg: I. P. Stanback Museum and South Carolina State University, 1998.

Martin, Jay. *Education of John Dewey: A Biography*. New York: Columbia University Press, 2002.

Martin, Josephine W. "The Educational Efforts of the Major Freedmen's Aid Societies and the Freedmen's Bureau in South Carolina, 1862–1870." PhD diss., University of South Carolina, 1971.

Mathiasen, Karl. "Evaluation," October 1978. PSP.

Mathiasen, Karl, Susan Gross, and Nancy Franco. "Steering Nonprofits: Advice for Boards and Staff." In National Trust for Historic Preservation in the United States, *Preservation Information: One in a Series of Historic Preservation Information Booklets*. Washington, D.C.: National Trust for Historic Preservation, 1998.

Mays, Benjamin Elizah. *Born to Rebel: An Autobiography*. Athens: University of Georgia Press, 1987. Revised, with foreword by Orville Vernon Burton, 2003.

McDonough, Julia Anne. "Men and Women of Good Will: A History of the Commission on Interracial Cooperation and the Southern Regional Council, 1919–1954." PhD diss., University of Virginia, 1993.

McNulty, Blake. "William Henry Brisbane: South Carolina Slaveholder and Abolitionist." In *The Southern Enigma: Essays on Race, Class, and Folk Culture*, edited by Walter J. Fraser Jr. and Winfred B. Moore Jr., 119–29. Westport, Conn.: Greenwood, 1983.

McPherson, James M. *The Abolitionist Legacy: From Reconstruction to the NAACP*. Princeton, N.J.: Princeton University Press, 1975.

———. *Battle Cry of Freedom: The Civil War Era*. New York: Oxford University Press, 1988.

———. "White Liberals and Black Power in Negro Education 1865–1915." *American Historical Review* 75, no. 5 (June 1970): 1357–86.

Miller, Edward A., Jr. *Gullah Statesman: Robert Smalls from Slavery to Congress, 1839–1915*. Columbia: University of South Carolina Press, 1995.

Mizell, M. Hayes. "The Impact of the Civil Rights Movement on a White Activist." Paper presented at the Southern Historical Association Annual Meeting, Fort Worth, Texas, November 4, 1999.

Morris, Aldon D. *The Origins of the Civil Rights Movement: Black Communities Organizing for Change*. New York: Free Press, 1984.

Morris, J. Brent. "'We Are Verily Guilty Concerning Our Brother': The Abolitionist Transformation of Planter William Henry Brisbane." *South Carolina Historical Magazine* 111, nos. 3–4 (July–October 2010): 118–50.

Moore, Winfred B., and Orville Vernon Burton. *Toward the Meeting of the Waters: Currents in the Civil Right Movement of South Carolina during the Twentieth Century.* Columbia: University of South Caroling Press, 2008.

Moutoussamy-Ashe, Jeanne. *Daddy and Me: A Photo Story of Arthur Ashe and His Daughter.* New York: Knopf, 1993.

———. *Daufuskie Island: A Photographic Essay.* Colombia: University of South Carolina Press, 1982.

———. *Viewfinders: Black Women Photographers.* New York: Reed Business Information, 1993.

Nichols, Patricia C. "Creoles of the USA." In *Language in the USA*, edited by Charles A. Ferguson and Shirley Bryce Heath, 69–91. New York: Cambridge University Press, 1981.

———. *Voices of Our Ancestors: Language Contact in Early South Carolina.* Columbia: University of South Carolina Press, 2008.

North Carolina Mutual Life Insurance Co. "Penn Celebrates Centennial: First Negro School in South." In *Whetstone Education Issue*, second quarter, 1962, Durham, North Carolina. In possession of Mr. Thomas Barnwell and Vernon Burton.

Ochiai, Akiko. *Harvesting Freedom: African American Agrarianism in Civil War Era South Carolina.* Westport, Conn.: Praeger, 2004.

Ohles, Frederik, Shirley Ohles, and John Ramsey, eds. *Biographical Dictionary of Modern American Educators.* Westport, Conn.: Greenwood, 1997.

Opala, Joe. *The Gullah: Rice, Slavery, and the Sierra Leone–American Connection.* Freetown, Sierra Leone: U.S. Information Service, 1987.

Parker, Franklin. "The Creation of the Peabody Education Fund." *Peabody Journal of Education* 70, no. 1 (Fall 1994): 149–56.

Peabody, Francis Greenwood. *Education for Life: The Story of Hampton Institute, Told in Connection with the Fiftieth Anniversary of the Foundation of the School.* Garden City, N.Y.: Doubleday, Page, 1926.

Petersen, Charles E. "Early American Prefabrication." *Gazette des Beaux Arts* 53, no. 6 (January 1948): 37–46.

Pollitzer, William S. *The Gullah People and Their African Heritage*. Athens: University of Georgia Press, 1999.

Power, J. Tracy. *I Will Not Be Silent and I Will Be Heard: Martin Luther King Jr. and the Southern Christian Leadership Conference, and Penn Center*. Columbia: South Carolina Department of Archives and History, 1993.

Powers, Bernard E., Jr. *Black Charlestonians: A Social History, 1822–1885*. Fayetteville: University of Arkansas Press, 1994.

Reynolds, John. *The Fight for Freedom: A Memoir of My Years in the Civil Rights Movement*. Bloomington, Ind.: AuthorHouse, 2012.

Richards, Graham. *Race, Racism, and Psychology: Towards a Reflexive History*. New York: Routledge, 1997.

Richardson, Joe M. *Christian Reconstruction: The American Missionary Association and Southern Blacks, 1861–1890*. Athens: University of Georgia Press, 1986.

Riney-Kehrberg, Pamela. "Separation and Sorrow: A Farm Woman's Life, 1935–1941." *Agricultural History* 67, no. 2 (Spring 1993): 185–96.

Rose, Willie Lee. *Rehearsal for Reconstruction: The Port Royal Experiment*. New York: Oxford University Press, 1996.

Rosengarten, Theodore. *Tombee: Portrait of a Cotton Planter*. New York: Morrow, 1986.

Rowland, Lawrence S., Alexander Moore, and George C. Rogers Jr. *The History of Beaufort County, South Carolina*, Vol. 1, *1514–1861*. Columbia: University of South Carolina Press, 1996.

Saville, Julie. *The Work of Reconstruction: From Slave to Wage Labor in South Carolina, 1860–1870*. New York: Cambridge University Press, 1996.

Schwalm, Leslie A. *A Hard Fight for We: Women's Transition from Slavery to Freedom in South Carolina*. Urbana: University of Illinois Press, 1997.

Sellers, Cleveland, and Robert Terrell. *River of No Return: The Autobiography of a Black Militant and the Life and Death of SNCC*. Jackson: University Press of Mississippi, 1990.

Shick, Tom W., and Don H. Doyle. "The South Carolina Phosphate Boom and the Stillbirth of the New South, 1867–1920." *South Carolina Historical Magazine* 86, no. 1 (January 1985): 1–31.

Shuler, Kristina A., Ralph Bailey Jr., and Charles Philips Jr. "A History of the Phosphate Mining Industry in the South Carolina Lowcountry with a focus on Ashley Phosphate Company." *South Carolina Antiquities* 38, nos. 1–2 (2006): 20–52.

Simkins, Francis Butler. *Pitchfork Ben Tillman, South Carolinian*. Baton Rouge: Louisiana State University Press, 1944.

Simkins, Francis Butler, and Robert Henley Woody. *South Carolina during Reconstruction*. Chapel Hill: University of North Carolina Press, 1932.

Smith, Mark M. *Stono: Documenting and Interpreting a Southern Slave Revolt*. Columbia: University of South Carolina Press, 2005.

Span, Christopher M. *From Cotton Field to Schoolhouse: African American Education in Mississippi, 1862–1875*. Chapel Hill: University of North Carolina Press, 2009.

Stack, Sam F., Jr. "John Dewey and the Question of Race: The Fight for Odell Waller." *Education and Culture* 25, no. 1 (April 2009): 17–35.

Swanson, Merwin. "The 'Country Life Movement' and the American Churches." *Church History* 46, no. 3 (September 1977): 358–73.

Synott, Marcia G. "Alice Buck Norwood Spearman Wright: A Civil Rights Activist." In *South Carolina Women: Their Lives and Times*, vol. 3, edited by Joan Marie Johnson, Valinda W. Littlefield, and Marjorie Julian Spruill, 200–20. Athens: University of Georgia Press, 2012.

———. "Moderate White Activists and the Struggle for Racial Equality on South Carolina Campuses." In *Rebellion in Black and White: Southern Student Activism in the 1960s*, edited by Robert Cohen and David J. Snyder, 106–25. Baltimore: Johns Hopkins University Press, 2013.

Thornton, John. "African Dimensions of the Stono Rebellion." *American Historical Review* 96, no. 4 (October 1991): 1101–13.

Tindall, George B. *South Carolina Negroes, 1877–1900*. Columbia: University of South Carolina Press, 1952.

Towne, Laura M. *The Letters and Diary of Laura M. Towne, Written from the Sea Islands of South Carolina, 1862–1884*. Edited by Rupert Sargent Holland. Salem: Higginson, 1912.

———. "Pioneer Work on the Sea Islands." *Southern Workman* 30, no. 7 (July 1901).

Turner, Lorenzo Dow. *Africanisms in the Gullah Dialect*. Columbia: University of South Carolina Press, 1949.

Utsey, Walker Scott, ed. *Who's Who in South Carolina, 1934–35*. Columbia, S.C.: Current Historical Association, 1935.

Uya, Okon Edet. *From Slavery to Public Service: Robert Smalls, 1839–1915*. New York: Oxford University Press, 1971.

Wells, Tom H. *The Slave Ship "Wanderer."* Athens: University of Georgia Press, 1967.

West, Earle H. "The Peabody Education Fund and Negro Education, 1867–1880." *History of Education Quarterly* 6, no. 2 (Summer 1966): 3–21.

Williams, Heather Andrea. *Self-Taught: African American Education in Slavery and Freedom.* Chapel Hill: University of North Carolina Press, 2005.

Williamson, Joel. *After Slavery: The Negro in South Carolina during Reconstruction, 1861–1877.* Chapel Hill: University of North Carolina Press, 1965.

Wolf, Kurt J. "Laura M. Towne and the Freed People of South Carolina, 1862–1901." *South Carolina Historical Magazine* 98, no. 4 (October 1997): 375–405.

Wolfe, Michael C. *The Abundant Life Prevails: Religious Traditions of Saint Helena.* Waco, Tex.: Baylor University Press, 2000.

Wood, Peter. *Black Majority: Negroes in Colonial South Carolina from 1670 through the Stono Rebellion.* New York: Norton, 1974.

Woofter, T. J., Jr. *Black Yeomanry: Life on St. Helena Island.* New York: Holt, 1930.

Young, Andrew. *An Easy Burden: The Civil Rights Movement and the Transformation of America.* New York: Harper Collins, 1996.

Zuczek, Richard. *State of Rebellion: Reconstruction in South Carolina.* Columbia: University of South Carolina Press, 1996.

INDEX